LIGHT BULB M

AND THE POWER OF

CRITICAL THINKING

Insights from Inquiring Minds and Literary Heroes

First Edition

GLORIA MOSS PhD

KATHERINE ARMITAGE

TRUTH UNIVERSITY PRESS

https://truthuniversity.co.uk/
infotruthuniversity@protonmail.com

Truth University Press is a department of the Truth University.
It furthers the university's objective of excellence in research, scholarship and education by publishing worldwide.
Truth University Press is a registered trademark of the Truth University in the UK and certain other countries

First Published in the United Kingdom by Truth University Press 2022

First Printed in the United Kingdom 2022

ISBN 978-1-7391117-1-7

Acknowledgements

The authors would like to warmly thank those who have helped bring this book into the public light. Our gratitude goes to our designer Shannon Rowan of Rowanberry Books for designing the cover and progressing the book to the publication stage. Grateful thanks also go to Peter Andrews who proof read the manuscript. Our gratitude also extends to the contributors, without whom this book would not have been possible. They have given generously of their time to commit their thoughts to paper to share their questioning journeys with readers. Finally our thanks go to Stewart Johnston who's been our boy Friday along the way.

CONTENTS

PART I

Light Bulb Moments and Critical Thinking: Current Knowledge

Light Bulb Moments

Every Friday, Oliver would come from school for his piano lesson. He was an energetic eleven-year-old who liked to play his piano pieces at top speed, often to the detriment of accuracy. Sometimes the same mistake would occur again and again, despite the teacher pointing this out. She then closed the piano lid and talked through the problem that Oliver was making, pointing out the patterns in the music and addressing his mind, rather than his fingers. When he opened the lid, he played the problem passage again and this time played it perfectly. This was a Light Bulb Moment because Oliver had worked things out in his mind.

In this case, the link between Critical Thinking and the Light Bulb Moment was immediate. Sometimes it can happen over a longer period. The mind can take time to develop and sometimes things don't slot into place for a while. Or a key piece of information may take a while to come to your attention and surface and the light bulb will not illuminate until that piece of the jigsaw arrives. This may be because a new discovery is made, whether scientific or historical, and the bigger picture becomes apparent. The new piece in the jigsaw may shake things entirely, which is why, often, that element will not be revealed to the public. So we can have deathbed confessions and governments releasing information and documents years after the event. This will defer the time at which the Light Bulb Moment finally occurs.

What we can say with certainty is that Light Bulb Moments only occur on the back of Critical Thinking: without Critical Thinking, there can be no Light Bulb Moments. As one lady, Deborah has written in a blog about Light Bulb Moments, these occur following a certain process. As she writes:

The first step to finding a solution would be to gather all the information I can find. Examine the problem from every angle. Take note of what works, what doesn't work and what sort of works. I will take the time to read articles or books on the subject or check out YouTube videos. I try to find out as much information as I can about the problem I am trying to solve. Sometimes I actually find the answers I am looking for, other times I just seem to find a direction in which to focus my thoughts. I find it easier to find a solution if I can focus my thoughts in one direction rather than being randomly scattered.

So, according to Deborah, the process begins by examining a problem 'from every angle'. What is this if not Critical Thinking? And this is precisely what the famous inventor Thomas Edison, the inventor of the phonograph, the telegraph and the first functional incandescent lighting system, including a generator, wiring and a carbon-filament bulb (yes, he did not invent the light bulb, Sir Joseph Swan, an English Physicist, chemist and inventor is credited with developing the first incandescent light bulb, but Edison worked out how to make it functional). Now, Edison is also celebrated for describing genius as '1% inspiration and 99% perspiration', and for saying 'I have not failed. I've just found 10,000 ways that won't work.' This is akin to Deborah's description of a Light Bulb Moment following a process that involves looking at a problem from every angle. It is just the final part of that process that produces the Light Bulb (excuse the pun!) Moment.

What is more, science backs up the view that Light Bulb Moments follow a period of Critical Thinking. For the consensus among scholars is that insight (the Light Bulb Moment) is primarily a function of previous experience and acquired knowledge (Sawyer, 2011; Carpenter, 2020) rather than of a sudden restructuring of thoughts; the mind seems to gradually get closer to the correct solution. Indeed, of the studies that underpin this finding, the first, conducted by the celebrated nineteenth-century American psychologist William James, led to the so-called associationist theory according to which new ideas are combinations of existing ideas. In this way of thinking, Light Bulb Moments are merely the result of having a lot of information – all gathered through a process of Critical Thinking – with the person making connections between elements within that.

Significantly, research by Dr Christian Windischberger and his colleagues at the Medical University of Vienna, Austria, used a type of fMRI to scan twenty-nine people's brains while they solved problems designed to elicit a Light Bulb Moment (Thomson, 2018). The scans revealed that the brain region involved was the prefrontal cortex. The significance? Well, the prefrontal cortex, the part of the brain that covers the front part of the frontal lobe, is the brain region involved in planning complex cognitive behaviour, decision-making and personality expression. The first two of these activities are involved in connected thinking processes of the kind found in Critical Thinking. So, Windischberger and his colleagues were essentially showing that Light Bulb moments can arise from connected Critical Thinking. This underscores the importance of Critical Thinking in our lives and justifies the focus on it in this book.

With this in mind, we present the views of people from across the globe - from Britain, Sweden and Poland to Canada, the US and New Zealand - and show how the process thinking critically has impacted their lives and opinions. You will see that in the case of these twenty-four people, Light Bulb Moments can happen in the short, medium or long term, and can have lasting impact. Indeed, some explicitly mention the liberating effect that this has on their lives and thinking, allowing them to envisage fresh possibilities. In some cases, the effects can be momentous.

So, this book takes you on a journey to discover what we already know about Critical Thinking, and the conscious and unconscious obstacles that may lie on its path. All of that is in Part I of this book, with Part II presenting you with the very personal accounts of people's thought journeys. You are not being asked to agree with what all these people think but to consider their thoughts and consider the triggers – whether personal or factors external to the person – that may have triggered their thinking process. We then move in Part III to a consideration of the processes and factors that ignited the Light Bulb Moments in these personal accounts. In doing this, we are sailing in uncharted waters since there has been no research hitherto on this question. So hold on tight as we sail into waters that could be smooth or rough.

We are about to set sail, with the first stage of our journey being a relatively simple one, visiting definitions of Critical Thinking and the advantages put forward for Critical Thinking over the ages and by different organisations. In Part II you can read, as we have mentioned, the accounts of twenty-four people's journeys in Critical Thinking and – putting judgement of their views to one side, decide for yourself what prompted them on their journeys. In Part III, we will present our own views as to the personal factors and external triggers that set our contributors down a path of questioning and then map these factors against those volunteered by respondents to an online survey on this topic.

So, hold on tight while the ship sets sail to the shores of Critical Thinking, with our first port of call being in the relatively steady waters where we explore the term. What exactly is Critical Thinking?

Definitions of Critical Thinking

Our explorations take us back to ancient Greece, where, 2,500 years ago Socrates discovered, by a method of questioning, knowledge that people - including those in authority - could not always rationally justify their beliefs. His method consisted of asking probing questions, seeking evidence and closely examining reasoning and assumptions. All this was neatly summed up in the quote attributed to him by Plato (fifth century bc) that 'A life without investigation is not worth living' (Apology, 28, 1897). A not dissimilar view came from Plato's near-contemporary Aristotle (384–322 bc), who wrote that 'It is the mark of an educated person to search for the same kind of clarity in each topic to the extent that the nature of the matter accepts it' (Nicomachean Ethics, 1 1094a24-1095a).

A hiatus of a few hundred years elapsed before we reached the Middle Ages and here, the US-based Foundation for Critical Thinking could serve as our guide. Here are a portion of the stepping stones that they highlight on their whistle-stop tour of Critical Thinking

> In the Middle Ages, the tradition of systematic critical thinking was embodied in the writings and teachings of such thinkers as Thomas Aquinas (Summa Theologica) who to ensure his thinking met the test of critical thought, always systematically stated, considered, and answered all criticisms of his ideas as a necessary stage in developing them. Aquinas heightened our awareness not only of the potential power of reasoning but also of the need for reasoning to be systematically cultivated and 'cross-examined.' Of course, Aquinas' (1225–1275) thinking also illustrates that those who think critically do not always reject established beliefs, only those beliefs that lack reasonable foundations.

If we fast-forward to the fifteenth century, we learn how

> Sir Thomas Moore (1478-1535) developed a model of a new social order, ***Utopia***, in which every domain of the present world was subject to critique. His implicit thesis was that established social systems are in need of radical analysis and critique.

Remaining with English critical thinkers, we read next of Francis Bacon (1561–1626) who was

> explicitly concerned with the way we misuse our minds in seeking knowledge. He recognized explicitly that the mind cannot safely be left to its natural tendencies. In his book The ***Advancement of Learning*** (1605), he argued for the importance of studying the world empirically. He laid the foundation for modern science with his emphasis on the information-gathering processes. He also called attention to the fact that most people, if left to their own devices, develop bad habits of thought (which he called 'idols') that lead them to believe what is false or misleading. He called attention to 'Idols of the tribe' (the ways our mind naturally tends to trick itself), 'Idols of the market-place' (the ways we misuse words), 'Idols of the theatre' (our tendency to become trapped in conventional systems of thought), and 'Idols of the schools' (the problems in thinking when based on blind rules and poor instruction). His book could be considered one of the earliest texts in critical thinking.

This thinking led Francis Bacon to emphasise the importance of 'grounded conclusions' – a habit of mind not dissimilar to the methods of thinking advocated by Descartes (1596–1650) some twenty or so years later in France. So it was that Descartes began

> what might be called the second text in critical thinking, ***Rules for the Direction of the Mind***. In it, Descartes argued for the need for a special systematic disciplining of the mind to guide it in thinking. He articulated and defended the need in thinking for clarity and precision. He developed a method of critical thought based on the principle of systematic doubt. He emphasized the need to base thinking on well-thought through foundational assumptions. Every part of thinking, he argued, should be questioned, doubted, and tested.

You can read the steps that moved us from there to the current day on the Foundation for Critical Thinking website but we will fast-forward now to modern times where we are awash with definitions of Critical Thinking. Given constraints of space, we will just sample a few here from the English-speaking countries of Britain, the US and Australia. If we take Britain first, then we find this definition from the BBC's Bitesize learning resources pages:

> Critical thinking involves questioning rather than simply accepting information that you hear or read. It enables you to identify different points of view, put together arguments, and evaluate the arguments made by others. [BBC, Bitesize]

Then, from the University of Edinburgh, we read that

> Critical thinking is the art of making clear, reasoned judgements based on interpreting, understanding, applying and synthesising evidence gathered from observation, reading and experimentation.

In actual fact, this last definition is taken from a book by two senior lecturers at London Metropolitan University, Tom Burns and Sandra Sinfield, authors of a book on study skills (2016, p.94). They are also founders of the Association for Learning Development in Higher Education.

Then, from the US, we find Dr Peter Facione writing that

> The ideal critical thinker is habitually inquisitive, well-informed, trustful of reason, open-minded, flexible, fair-minded in evaluation, honest in facing personal biases, prudent in making judgments, willing to reconsider. [1990]

More recently, the Foundation for Critical Thinking defines it as the ability to check for 'clarity, accuracy, precision, relevance, depth, breadth, significance, logic, and fairness', with well-cultivated critical thinkers defined as those who

- Raise vital questions and problems, formulating them clearly and precisely

- Gather and assess relevant information, using abstract ideas to interpret it effectively
- Come to well-reasoned conclusions and solutions, testing them against relevant criteria and standards
- Think open-mindedly within alternative systems of thought, recognising and assessing, as needs be, their assumptions, implications and practical consequences.

Finally, from Australia, the Australian Christian College offers us the following definition of critical thinkers as people who can

- understand the links between ideas
- determine the importance and relevance of arguments and ideas
- recognise, build and appraise arguments
- identify inconsistencies and errors in reasoning
- approach problems consistently and systematically
- reflect on the justification of their own assumptions, beliefs and values

Having travelled a fair bit in pursuit of definitions, what elements if any do these definitions share? Well, the BBC and the US Foundation for Critical Thinking both prioritise questioning skills; these two, as also those definitions used by the University of Edinburgh and the Australian Christian College, refer to the importance of assessing, appraising, interpreting and evaluating information and arguments. These steps are reminiscent of those identified in the well-known 'Thinking Triangle' formulated by Bloom in 1956:

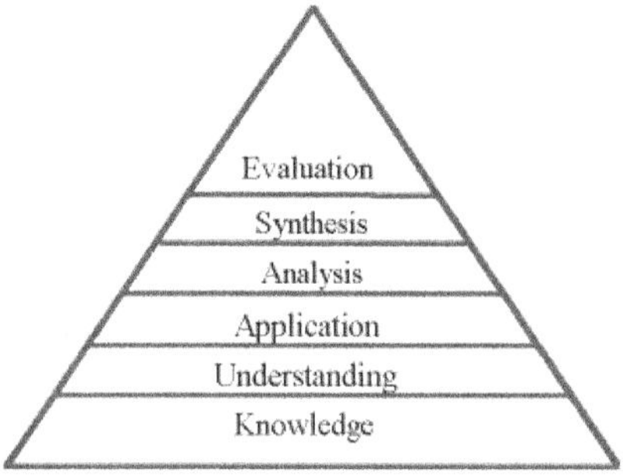

Figure 1: Bloom's Thinking Triangle.

As you can see, this contains six levels of intellectual skill with 'knowledge' (being aware of something and remembering information related to it) at the base of the triangle. The next step is 'Understanding' (comprehension) and beyond that is 'Application' (using the knowledge), followed by 'Analysis' (engaging in a methodical and detailed examination), 'Synthesis' (combining information and ideas into something new) and, finally, 'Evaluation' (judging the value of information). As you can see, with each step up the pyramid, the processes become more intense and sophisticated.

We can then can add to these elements those identified in the US and Australian definitions that call for skills of self-evaluation. In this way, the US Foundation for Critical Thinking refers to the importance of 'thinking open-mindedly' and the Australian College calls for people to reflect on their own assumptions, beliefs and values. We can therefore see that there is much uniting these definitions across time and geographies.

With so many definitions produced in a geography extending from the US to Britain to Australia there must well be advantages to Critical Thinking. We will cast our anchor in a new port and explore these there.

Advantages of Critical Thinking

When we look at the benefits credited to Critical Thinking, we find a broad consensus across a range of geographies as to the high value of this skill.

From Britain, for example, we find benefits emerging from commentators in a variety of sectors, whether education, industry, government or law and the judiciary.

Where **Education** is concerned, the following advantages are put forward by the Australian Christian College:

- Studies indicate that critical thinking skills are among the most highly valued attributes that employers seek in job candidates. They want staff who can solve problems, make decisions and take appropriate action. In an Australian context, a 2015 report indicated that demand for critical thinking skills in new graduates rose 158 percent over three years.

- Research also indicates that critical thinkers experience fewer negative life events, such as racking up credit card debt or getting arrested for drink-driving.

- They need critical thinking skills to discern falsehood and make reasoned arguments for their faith (2 Cor 10:5).

Then Dr Doris Zahner, Chief Academic Officer of the American-based Council for Aid to Education (CAE), states that Critical Thinking skills are associated with better academic and post-academic outcomes (2022).

Moving on to the **World of Work**, we find the ability to think and reason – two elements in Critical Thinking – presented as a priority by the World Economic Forum (WEF), a private organisation that influences political, business, cultural and other leaders of society to shape global, regional and industry agendas. The WEF is a powerful and influential, if controversial, voice. But leaving to one side the problematic nature of a private organisation such as this training up the leaders of democratic nation states (alumnae of their Young Leaders Programme include Boris Johnson, Justin Trudeau, Angela Merkel, Emmanuel Macron and Jacinda Ardern), and also the fact that the WEF is working towards a Great Reset and a Fourth Industrial Revolution (sometimes referred to as society 4.0) whose roots are in AI and net-zero carbon emissions, let us focus on their Future of Jobs Report.

Written in 2020, the WEF's most recent Future of Jobs Report identifies Critical Thinking and problem solving top as the number one set of skills that employers believe will grow in prominence until 2025 (WEF, 2020).

So, following on from this, one could expect to see Critical Thinking and problem solving skills prioritised across all sectors. The question of whether these skills are available in the workplace is one that we will return to a in bit when looking at how Critical Thinking can be put into practice.

Meanwhile, one of those organisations following the WEF's vision for a Fourth Industrial Revolution is Deloitte, an international professional-services network. In 2019 they conducted a survey of 612 technology, media and telecom (TMT) organisations and published their findings in Deloitte's 2019 Industry 4.0 Readiness Report. Of the so-called high-innovator organisations in the sample, defined as those placing a high priority on innovation, embracing experimentation and giving their leaders the leeway to learn from failure, the number-one skill that high innovators are working hardest to develop is not technical but rather Critical Thinking skills (Hupfer, 2019). These 'high innovator' organisations make up 29% of the sample of organisations – almost a third of the complete sample.

To put this into context: of the 'high innovator' group of organisations, 71% strongly believe that autonomous technologies will augment the efforts of human workers, while just 29% consider that the technologies will replace humans (ibid.). So, in 'high innovator' organisations, a premium is placed on human as against non-human skills, and the human skill on which the greatest value is placed is Critical Thinking.

Where individual countries are concerned, Britain's Richard Wainer, former Head of Education and Skills at the Confederation of British Industry (CBI), the main umbrella organisation for British industry, expressed the clear view that 'The ability to think, reason and make sound decisions is a vital skill for the workplace and crucial for employees who want to do well and advance.'

His view is not unusual. In the US, for example, in 2006 a major report by a consortium of more than 400 US employers ranked 'Critical Thinking' as the most desirable skill to look for in new employees. Then, a little over ten years later in 2019, a survey of 2115 executives by the American Management Association (AMA) showed that an overwhelming number of executives consider that to grow their businesses they require employees to show competence in 'the four Cs': critical thinking/problem solving, communication, collaboration and creativity. These are in fact the attributes highlighted by the WEF in 2020 as well as in an earlier report of 2016.

Then, on the website of the US-based National Career Development Association – one providing professional development, publications, standards and advocacy to practitioners and educators – you can find an article (Safi and Burrell, 2007) that states that

> Questions define variables, state factors, outline tasks, clarify issues, and express problems. Complex questioning drives thought beyond what is superficial. . .Asking questions forces public managers . . . to look at their sources of information and consider the validity and quality. . . This kind of in-depth questioning and analysis helps assure that the solution would actually solve the problem, not just be the best of mediocre options. [p.4]

A similar sentiment is expressed by the authors of an article in the Harvard Business Review on the power of questions in sustaining organisations (Brooks and John, 2018):

> Questioning is a uniquely powerful tool for unlocking value for organizations: it spurs learning and the exchange of ideas, it fuels innovation and performance improvement, it builds rapport and trust among team members. And it can mitigate business risk by uncovering unforeseen pitfalls and hazards.

Then, from Australia, we find a 2015 report by the Foundation for Young Australians that claims that demand for Critical Thinking skills in new graduates had risen 158% in three years. This data was drawn from an analysis of 4.2 million online job postings from 6,000 different sources in the period 2012–2015. It is clear from this that Australian employers place a high premium on Critical Thinking skills in their workforce (The Conversation, 2016).

What of other sectors? In the **Legal Sector,** a series of tests have been created to measure Critical Thinking in the law, suggesting that these skills are valued there. Law firms use the Watson-Glaser test while entry to the Bar Professional Training Programme demands success in the Bar Aptitude Test (BAPT). These tests measure people's ability to

- draw inferences
- recognise assumptions
- use deductive reasoning
- make logical interpretations
- employ argument evaluation

Then, where **Health** is concerned, at the time that this book went to press, the world was emerging from a worldwide alleged health crisis – one that prompted mass vaccination with an experimental product. So it was a little concerning to find that there were only a couple of links on the role of Critical Thinking in the health services. The first came from an article from 2014 on the development of Critical Thinking in nursing (Papathanasiou et al.), with the article stating that

> Nursing students in order to learn and apply critical thinking should develop independence of thought, fairness, perspicacity in personal and social level, humility, spiritual courage, integrity, perseverance, self-confidence, interest for research and curiosity. Critical thinking is an essential process for the safe, efficient and skillful nursing practice. The nursing education programs should adopt attitudes that promote critical thinking and mobilize the skills of critical reasoning.

Most people would agree with the thoughts expressed here while questioning perhaps the extent to which these qualities were manifested during the covid crisis.

The second link came from a one-day course on Critical Thinking, for managers and decision-makers in the NHS, and the problematic nature of this leads us to discuss this reference later on when discussing obstacles to the exercise of unfettered Critical Thinking.

Finally, one might expect to find reference to Critical Thinking from **Government** sources? Strangely enough, especially given the powers exercised by governments, there is almost no information on the value placed by governments on Critical Thinking. There is some information from the New South Wales Government in Australia but as we shall see later when investigating obstacles to Critical Thinking, these are problematic for several reasons. In terms of **Citizens,** however, and the benefits of Critical Thinking to this part of the population, we find researchers at Geneva University describing this as a necessary skill 'for citizens to participate in a plural and democratic society' (Lombard et al., 2020). They are not alone in this view since in 2011 the official curriculum for French-Swiss secondary schools (CIIP) wrote that

> In a society deeply modified by scientific and technological progress, it is important that every citizen masters basic skills in order to understand the consequences of choices made by the community, to take part in social debate on such subjects and to grasp the main issues.

Let us now pull this all together and see where the benefits have taken us. It seems that many countries, sectors and powerful non-governmental organisations are agreed on the multiple benefits of Critical Thinking. In a sense, this is nothing new since the philosopher René Descartes stated that

> If you would be a real seeker after truth, it is necessary that at least once in your life you doubt, as far as possible, all things.

Then, Carl Jung (1875-1961), the Swiss psychiatrist and psychoanalyst and founder of analytical psychology, stated that

The ability to ask questions is the greatest resource in learning the truth.

This is similar to the thoughts of Albert Einstein (1879-1955), his contemporary who put the art of asking questions at the very heart of critical inquiry. Here are some of his words as reported by Warren Berger:

> Question everything.
>
> The important thing is not to stop questioning. Never lose a holy curiosity. Don't stop to marvel.
>
> It's not that I'm so smart but I stay with the questions longer.

> I have no special talents. I am only passionately curious.
>
> It is a miracle that curiosity survives formal education.
>
> If I had an hour to solve a problem and my life depended on the solution, I would spend the first 55 minutes determining the proper question to ask for once I know the proper question I could solve the problem in less than 5 minutes.

Indeed, the act of posing questions is a key part of the definitions of Critical Thinking offered by the BBC and the US Foundation for Critical Thinking, and so we can add Descartes, Jung and Einstein to those advocating for the importance of asking questions. With the weight of all these benefits behind us, let us move on now to look a little more deeply at the human factors involved when Critical Thinking and Light Bulb Moments come into play. Following that, we will look at the factors that can help and hinder the use of Critical Thinking.

The role of mind, body and emotion in Critical Thinking

The definitions of Critical Thinking presented to us on a day-to-day basis – for example, those of the BBC, of the University of Edinburgh, of the Foundation for Critical Thinking in the US and of the Australian Christian College – all describe Critical Thinking in language that is rather cerebral, using words such as 'understand', 'recognise', 'identify', 'synthesise', 'think', 'reflect', 'reasoned', 'evidence' and 'determine'. Moreover, we saw earlier on how Dr Christian Windischberger and his colleagues at the Medical University of Vienna, Austria described Light Bulb Moments – something triggered by Critical Thinking – as happening in the prefrontal cortex (Thomson, 2018). Is this then a purely cognitive process?

If we take a step back to the act of thinking then we find that this does not operate purely in the mind. The brain is entwined with the whole body through the nervous system – via the spinal cord, for example – and includes all the systems, organs, musculature, liquids and chemicals constantly influencing the brain. There is no separation between body and mind (Payne, 2014). Brain activity, for example, produces electrical currents due to nearly 100,000 chemical reactions occurring in it per second. These chemical reactions are carried out in our brain by tiny cells (neurons) that process and transmit information through electrical and chemical signals that they pass on to each other at the speed of 420 kilometres per hour – faster than the speed of a racing car! Note that after processing this information, when we arrive at an insight – a Light Bulb Moment – our brain literally lights up.

The link between mind and body can go even further. According to research conducted in the US in 2015, emotions can influence decision-making at various points, but the research does not consider the extent to which emotions may prompt a decision (rather than simply colour it), nor the extent to which emotions may relate to Critical Thinking (Lerner et al., 2015). So this research does not help us understand the way emotion may or may not trigger Critical Thinking.

The closest we get to research examining how emotion may trigger Critical Thinking is from Tracy Bowell 2018, who states that 'emotion and reason work together to form, scrutinise and revise deeply held beliefs' (p.170). She has not, however, discussed how emotions can interact with Critical Thinking, the only person to have done so being David Matsumoto, who views emotions as upsetting the balance of Critical Thinking (2021). Indeed, he writes that 'When emotions run high, thinking critically and strategically is almost impossible.' One of the factors we can test, through the twenty-four first-person accounts gathered in this book, is the extent to which emotion may act in a positive, and not simply a negative way, perhaps by triggering Critical Thinking. We will do this in Part III, where we will draw out the factors that prompted the twenty-four critical thinkers in Part II of this book to embark on their journeys of questioning.

Speaking of this, we do need to move on now to what we currently know concerning factors that can encourage Critical Thinking as well as those that can hold it back. This is the topic of our next section.

Helping and hindering factors

It may sound strange, but more effort has been put into understanding the factors that discourage Critical Thinking than into understanding those that encourage it. In fact, we have come across virtually nothing that isolates the factors that encourage it. And since Descartes and Jung believed that the perception of truth rests on the ability to think critically, the stakes are high. The absence of Critical Thinking will quite simply prevent people from perceiving the truth and so identifying the factors that encourage it – widely neglected up until now - is one of the main reasons for writing this book.

So we will begin by summarising what we do know, namely the factors that hinder Critical Thinking. We will need to wait until Part III and the new research reported there to find out about the factors helping to ignite Critical Thinking.

Hindering factors

Reading the academic and grey literatures, it quickly becomes clear that the main obstacles to Critical Thinking are twofold. These concern firstly the lack of training or education in Critical Thinking skills, leading to skills shortages in the workplace, and secondly the psychological obstacles. We will start off by looking at the first of these two factors namely the absence of education and training.

Education-based obstacles: lack of encouragement given to critical thinking

According to educationalist Barry Mansfield (2022) there is a serious deficit of Critical Thinking skills training in the government-devised national curriculum in Britain. He argues that the national curriculum demands that students 'think critically' in only three subjects, namely history, citizenship and art and design, and reaches the alarming conclusion that the process of learning Critical Thinking skills is 'left entirely to chance' with no framework provided for their development. Despite this deficit in the teaching of Critical Thinking at school level, universities across the world – whether Edinburgh, Leeds, Sussex, Newcastle or Sydney – tend to restrict Critical Thinking skills resources to Learning Resources hub, without integrating the teaching into the academic curriculum. We say this since there is no evidence that these skills are systematically taught as part of an undergraduate or postgraduate degree programme.

So, what are the consequences of this at best patchy teaching of Critical Thinking skills? Some clues come from Michael Peters, Professor in the Faculty of Education at Beijing Normal University, who pulls no punches in asserting (2017) that

> Criticality has been avoided or limited within education and substituted by narrow conceptions of standards, and state-mandated instrumental and utilitarian pedagogies. There have been attacks on the professional autonomy of teachers as arbiters of truth.

This view is echoed, with somewhat greater reserve, by our four academics from the University of Geneva, who write of the need for students to be 'better equipped with reasonable thinking for deciding what to believe or do: critical thinking' Lombard et al., 2020).

These somewhat disturbing views prepare us for the rather shocking findings of a 2022 OECD report, 'Does Higher Education Teach Students to Think Critically?' The study, conducted in August 2022 in the US, Chile, Finland, Italy, Mexico and the UK, and involving 800,000 students at over 1,300 institutions, found that

- only 45% of graduates in six countries demonstrated Critical Thinking skills at the end of their degrees
- the 'learning gain' of students between the start and the end of their courses was small on average
- there were big discrepancies between courses: fields closely aligned to real-world occupations (for example, business, agriculture and health) scored the worst; humanities students achieved higher scores.

What are we to make of these disturbing findings? According to one of the authors of the OECD report, Dr Van Damme, the results reflect a move away from the teaching of Critical Thinking in higher education. Dr Doris Zahner, Chief Academic Officer at the Council for Aid to Education, a nonprofit educational assessment organisation in the US providing thought leadership on assessments of Critical Thinking, stated that

> Critical Thinking is a skill that I think many people just assume is taught. However, it has never been reported in university transcripts, so there has traditionally been no way of knowing if a student has developed these skills (Williams, 2022).

She went on to state that

> Universities, at least the ones that we have talked to, have said 'It is not our job; they should have learned these things in high school' ... everyone feels like it is somebody else's responsibility to teach these things. [ibid.]

So, we have a deficit at university level in the teaching of a skill that is completely central to people's ability to pose questions and evaluate evidence. The absence of Critical Thinking skills is extremely likely to affect graduates' ability to practise these skills and, through that, weigh up information. A cynic might argue that a citizenry with ill-formed thoughts increases a government's power and that it is not in the interests of governments to enhance people's Critical Thinking skills. Indeed, as Frederick the Great of Prussia (1740–82), a great warmonger, said, 'If my soldiers were to begin to think, not one of them would remain in the army.' And a cynical Henry Ford remarked that 'It is well enough that people of the nation do not understand our banking and monetary system, for if they did, I believe there would be a revolution before tomorrow morning.'

Aside from the cynic's view as to the potential advantages to governments of keeping populations in ignorance, a further factor in the neglect of Critical Thinking skills training in both schools and universities may be a growing emphasis on postmodernist and neo-Marxist ways of thinking. We say this since both of these approaches have been said to hijack the liberal arts education in favour of a more dogmatic view of reality in which Critical Thinking has little place. In fact, this dogmatic view of reality may be one of the factors behind the increasing use of testing formats such as multiple choice, true/false, and fill-in-the-blank questions in education. This style of testing is likely to encourage convergent over divergent thinking – a tendency that would be reinforced by a lack of training in Critical Thinking skills. The two independently and conjointly would create a situation where children, and subsequently adults, struggle to think independently.

What of the world of work? Are people with Critical Thinking skills available to employers? We will look at this in the next section.

Work-based obstacles: skills shortages

The only data available on the availability of Critical Thinking skills in the working population comes from a 2019 report by the US's Society for Human Resource Management that identified technical and soft-skills shortages that affect 75% of the 83% of US organisations experiencing difficulties in hiring appropriate staff. Of the soft-skills deficits experienced by these organisations, the major one is given is shortages of personnel with Critical Thinking and problem-solving skills (Society for Human Resource Management, 2019).

In addition to skills gaps in students coming out of education and recruits for organisations, we find obstacles in the approaches to Critical Thinking taken at governmental or National Health Service level as we can see in the following cases from Australia and the UK. So we have used these cases as illustrative of government and public-sector obstacles.

Work-based obstacles: lack of encouragement by public sector and governmental bodies

It is interesting to see a site from the New South Wales (NSW) Government in Australia from 2019, praising the benefits of Critical Thinking. There you can find recommendations for respectful debate, discussion, evaluation and analysis of information alongside a reference to 'extremist messaging' – one that would appear to imply an absence of Critical Thinking. So how much encouragement is really being given to Critical Thinking here?

Any doubts that we might have had from this reference to 'extremist messaging' is increased in the light of a report by Amnesty International stating that the extension of powers under the Public Health Act 2010 in New South Wales 'led to the undue restriction of peaceful protesters' rights to freedom of expression and peaceful assembly'. The reference here to alleged restrictions of freedom of expression cannot easily be reconciled with the statements on the NSW website encouraging Critical Thinking. This suggests that the words on the NSW website are perhaps mere verbiage, not intended for real enactment.

Then staying with the public sector, and returning again to the situation in the UK, it is concerning to find references to the development of Critical Thinking skills for employees in the National Health Service (NHS) as skills that are benchmarked not against any neutral aims of objective thinking but solely against 'organisational aims'. The details of the course can be viewed in the reference section under 'NHS', and from that you will see from that the NHS training course was aimed at managers and individuals 'involved in the decision-making process'. And whist the title of the training course sounds positive enough – this is given as 'Critical Thinking and Decision-Making' – the details of the course objectives are somewhat disturbing since they are described as being to

- Understand how individual and organisational character drive our reasoning and
- Improve 'Judgement & Decision Making' to drive the organisation forward

Why disturbing? Well, both objectives show that the acquisition of Critical Thinking skills is not designed to foster objective thinking, but rather to foster thinking that serves the needs, quite explicitly, of the organisation. This is extremely concerning where health is concerned and it would be reassuring for the public to know, especially in the wake of a medical pandemic policy rolled out by government and the NHS, that the Critical Thinking skills exercised by managers and decision-makers have been honed against an objective benchmark rather than one that merely serves the organisation and its growth objectives.

Having looked at structural obstacles to the development of Critical Thinking in education, government and the health service, it is time now to consider the next major cause of obstacles – those caused by human psychology.

Psychological obstacles

We now reach a major factor that stands in the way of people exercising Critical Thinking skills. This is human psychology. A large volume of research here has focused on the factors that drive conformity; and since this can put a halt to the exercise of Critical Thinking, and stop independent thinking, its importance cannot be overemphasised. In the confines of this book, we will offer a glimpse of the very substantial literature charting people's tendency to conform, and with that, drive out objective Critical Thinking.

A number of major factors have been identified as driving **conformity**. One is **informational conformity** (Deutsch and Gerrard, 1955), a process that describes people's tendency to conform because the issues are complex. This links to **decision fatigue** (Baumeister, 2003) and **cognitive load** (Sweller, 2010), concepts in turn related to Nobel Laureate Kahneman's description of people as **cognitively lazy** (2011). The argument goes that our brains have evolved to conserve energy for 'more important' tasks and so when an intuitive decision can be made that is often good enough, people will **satisfice** (Simon, 1957). Factors in satisficing (having the meaning of making cursory decisions) can include both a surplus of information (Dwyer, 2017) and also **convergent thinking**, in other words, the tendency to move towards a single well-defined answer as against a divergent solution (Guilford, 1950). As we saw above, styles of educational testing can influence people's thinking, with closed forms of questioning (in other words questions that close down options) may encourage convergent thinking. Personality can also be a factor, with some people having differing dispositional tendencies as between convergent and divergent thinking. There may also be a link with tolerance of ambiguity with convergent predispositions less tolerant of ambiguity than divergent thinkers.

We are left with four further factors. One is the tendency to conform **in order to fit in**; another is people's inclination to **follow authority**; the third is the tendency to **group think**; and the fourth concerns the phenomenon known as the **illusory truth effect** in which information is repeated sufficiently often to ensure compliance. These are all important and so we will look at each in turn.

Firstly, there is the tendency to conform **in order to fit in**. This was amply demonstrated by studies by two psychologists, Muzafer Sherif and then, quite separately by Solomon Asch. We will begin by looking at Sherif's studies. In his experiments, participants were asked to estimate how far a dot of light in a dark room had moved and although in reality, the dot remains static, it appears to move due to something known as the autokinetic effect (essentially, tiny movements of the eyes make it appear that a small spot of light is moving in a dark room).

Sherif asked participants how far the dot had moved in two situations. In one, the participants were asked on their own and in the second, as part of a group. In the first situation, participants' answers answers varied considerably. In the second situation however, when participants were then asked to be part of a group, Sherif found that the responses converged toward a central mean. These results, published in 1935, demonstrated that in an ambiguous situation, people will conform to the group, an example of informational influence. Sherif's discoveries did not end there for when subjects were asked if they had been influenced by the opinions of others, most of them denied this. It seems that each person believed that he or she was making an objective decision. What is more, when a third stage was added in which subjects were shown the light a third time, in solitude again, their estimate tended to be the compromise that the group had arrived at, or closer to it than their original evaluation had been.

Two exciting conclusions followed from this. Firstly, that the subjects had conformed to group norms, often without realising it, and secondly that the group norms were established by finding an intermediate position from the extreme positions originally taken by the subjects. This showed the tendency in people to conform to group opinion though it may have more objective reality than someone's individual opinion.

At around the same time, in the 1950s, another psychologist, this time the celebrated Solomon Asch, was keen to ascertain whether the extreme conformity that arose in the uncertain task involved in Sherif's experiment would be reversed if people were engaged on a low-uncertainty task. So he devised a series of studies in which participants were asked to complete what he believed was a simple perceptual task: participants were asked quite simply to choose a line that matched the length of one of three different lines.

When asked individually, participants would choose the correct line 99% of the time, but when asked in the presence of confederates who were instructed, unbeknown to the participants, to select the wrong line, around 75% of participants conformed to the group opinion at least once, and 50% gave the same wrong answer as the others on more than half of the trials. Only 25% of participants refused to be swayed by the majority's blatantly false judgement on all of the twelve trials. Over all the trials, the average conformity rate was 33%, but conformity was dramatically reduced to 5–10% when just one of the confederates – rather than none - gave the correct answer. What were the reasons for the strong conformity, even with a low uncertainty task?

- Asch interviewed participants after the experiment and discovered that
- All participants felt anxious, feared disapproval from others and became self-conscious.
- Most explained they saw the lines differently to the group but then felt the group was correct.
- Some said they went along with the group to avoid standing out (this is **normative conformity**) although they knew that the group was wrong.
- A small number of people actually said they saw the lines in the same way as the group (taking information without question from the group is **informational conformity**).
- When others were viewed as more powerful, influential, or knowledgeable than themselves, they were more likely to go along with the group.

So, fear of disapproval was an important factor in participants' conformity, and Asch went on to discover that if the participant was asked to write down their answer rather than call it out, conformity was reduced to 12.5%. Another study at that time, however, by Deutsch and Gerrard

(1955) found conformity rates of almost double that (23%) even in conditions of high anonymity and high certainty about the answer. Deutsch and Gerrard also found that those who are 'conformers' typically have high levels of anxiety, low status and high need for approval, and often have authoritarian personalities.

Note that cultural differences are important and that people from cultures that view conformity more favourably – typically Eastern societies – are more likely to conform.

As for people's inclination to conform in line with **authority**, an extremely important question, this is starkly demonstrated by the research of Yale psychologist Stanley Milgram. He began his experiments in 1961, shortly after the trial of the World War II criminal Adolf Eichmann had started. Eichmann's defence that he was merely following instructions when he ordered the deaths of Jewish people roused Milgram's interest and prompted the research. The question that he sought answers to concerned how people would behave when told to give an electrical shock to another person. To what extent would people obey the dictates of the situation and ignore their own misgivings about what they were doing?

Milgram devised an extraordinary study to test this question. In the experiment, participants were told that they were involved in a learning experiment, that they were to administer ever increasing levels of electrical shocks and that they should continue to the end of the experiment. Briefed that they would be the 'teacher' and another person the 'learner', they sat in front of a machine with a number of dials labelled with steadily increasing voltages. The third switch from the top was labelled 'Danger: Severe Shock', the last two simply 'XXX'. The results? Fully 65% of the participants administered the maximum shocks, while just 35% stopped before reaching the highest level. All the while, the learner was heard screaming in agony and begging the teacher to stop.

Of course, the participants were not really delivering electrical shocks, and the 'learner' in the Milgram experiment was an actor following a rehearsed script. The 'learner' was kept out of sight of the participants so they came to their own assumptions about the pain they were causing. Moreover, the procedure was that each time the participant baulked at giving the electrical shocks, the experimenter – an authority figure dressed in a white lab coat – ordered them to continue. And note that the participants were not specially selected sadists – they were just ordinary people who had volunteered for the experiment.

According to Milgram, certain situational factors explain the high levels of obedience and low levels of Critical Thinking, witnessed so dramatically:

- The physical presence of an authority figure.
- The fact that Yale, a trusted and authoritative academic institution, sponsored the study (this led many participants to believe that the experiment must be safe).
- The shocks were said to be painful, not dangerous.

Note that when other people refused to go along with the experimenter's orders, 90% of participants refused to deliver the maximum shocks. So, as in the Asch experiment, dissenting voices can break the spell and restore the use of Critical Thinking. However, without those dissenting voices, people's Critical Thinking capabilities can, it seems, be suspended.

Incidentally, as bad as Milgram's findings appear to be, a very recent study by Polish psychologists (Doliński et al., 2017) produced even more dramatic results, with 90% of the eighty participants going all the way to the maximum level of electrocution after being 'ordered' to by the experimenter. This shows, like Milgram's experiment, that people's deference to an authority figure can remove all traces of Critical Thinking.

Then there is the disturbing effect of what has become known as **group think**, one identified by Irving Janis, Yale social psychologist and professor emeritus at the University of California, Berkley in 1972. How did he uncover this effect? He was he analysing major policy-making decisions, such as decisions regarding the Bay of Pigs, the attack on Pearl Harbor, and Appeasement in the 1930s and concluded that a set of small group processes were at work that radically altered people's normal thinking processes in a rather terrifying way. He labelled this process 'groupthink' (1972) and defined it as

> A mode of thinking that people engage in when they are deeply involved in a cohesive group, when the members' strivings for

unanimity override their motivation to realistically appraise alternative courses of action.

Janis identified eight aspects to this. The first two consisted of the illusion of invulnerability and the inability to be wrong. The other six consisted of the collective rationalisation of the group's decisions, an unquestioned belief in the morality of the group and its choices, stereotyping of the relevant opponents or out-group members, the presence of 'mindguards' who act as barriers to alternative or negative information, self-censorship, and an illusion of unanimity. Decision-making affected by groupthink neglects possible alternatives and focuses on a small number of goals, ignoring the risks involved in a particular decision. It fails to seek out alternative information and is biased in its consideration of that which is available. Once rejected, alternatives are forgotten, and little attention is paid to contingency plans in case the preferred solution fails.

The fourth and final psychological phenomenon is known as the **illusory truth effect.** This acts in such a way that the more we are exposed to certain information, the more likely we are to believe it. This is familiar to many of us from the words attributed to Joseph Goebbels (1897–1945), Adolf Hitler's Propaganda Minister in Nazi Germany. He said, 'If you repeat a lie often enough, it becomes truth' to the point 'when those who are being manipulated are confident they are acting on their own free will'. These ideas underpin a great deal of marketing and public relations, so we will look at this in more detail.

Marketing and public relations

Edward Bernays, the father of modern public relations and nephew of Sigmund Freud, referred to the 'engineering of consent' (1947), describing how if a message is repeated across various media, online as well as offline, then the message will be absorbed and will override the effects of Critical Thinking. According to Bernays, messages could be conveyed using graphics (on walls and walking surfaces), or commentaries (using the printed word and audio-visual media) or public announcements (in shops and transport facilities). Of course, a range of verbal effects could be used in this last category in order to strengthen the impact of the message. As marketing and advertising teach us, these could range from punchy brevity ('Think different', Apple, 1997), alliteration ('Fly the friendly skies',

United Airlines, 1966) in thought to the 'rule of three' ('Just do it', 'Vorsprung Durch Technik', 'Beanz Meanz Heinz', 'Diamonds are forever' . . .).

As we know, creating familiarity and what is known as 'top-of-mind awareness' are high priorities for marketeers and giant corporations can employ sophisticated psychological techniques to market their products. Ironically, research shows that repetition may not actually improve comprehension, since there is evidence of a wear-out effect over time (Alpert, Golden and Hoyer, 1983). It seems that eventually Critical Thinking will kick-in again but initially, repetition will lead to its suspension. This is extremely concerning since propaganda uses the same techniques as marketing and public relations, and its purpose can be even more sinister when we understand its purpose to be 'the more or less systematic effort to manipulate other people's beliefs, attitudes, or actions' (Encyclopedia Britannica). It was in fact Edward Bernays who wrote a book on this topic (1928) with his opening paragraph stating that

> The conscious and intelligent manipulation of the organized habits and opinions of the masses is an important element in democratic society. Those who manipulate this unseen mechanism of society constitute an invisible government which is the true ruling power of our country.

He could hardly have been clearer in showing the role that propaganda plays in overturning the exercise of Critical Thinking.

That corporations can use propaganda is concerning enough, but its use by governments and educational bodies is perhaps more disturbing. And lest anyone should doubt that governments engage in propaganda, one need only consider how the lexicon of covid-19 mimics that of commercial advertising. Whether it is the brevity of 'Stop covid' or the rule of three in 'Stay alert, control the virus, save lives', or the alliterative flair of the 'new normal' and 'clap for carers', this is clearly the language of advertising and propaganda. Using Bernays' own definition, this is manipulation of the opinion of the masses.

What is more, people who held views at odds with the government line were not given airspace – remember how the lack of dissenting stooges in Asch's experiments pushed up levels of conformity? – and doctors, scientists and other authority figures from highly ranked universities were used to convey the covid narrative in regard to testing and vaccination. Knowing from Milgram's work how the presence of an 'expert' can produce obedience, you might judge this to have been an unbalanced strategy that encouraged conformity and the absence of Critical Thinking. This is not in any way to present an opinion concerning covid, but merely to point out the negative effects on Critical Thinking that the use of experts is likely to cause. Were there to be debate between experts with opposing views, then this negative effect on Critical Thinking is less likely to occur, but debate tended not to be encouraged during the alleged pandemic.

Another voice that has delved into the use of propaganda was Dr Robert Burrowes, less of a household name than Bernays, but with powerful thoughts nonetheless. In a powerful online essay he writes that propaganda is

> delivered by education systems as 'knowledge', by the corporate media as 'news' and by the entertainment industry as films, television programs, video games, music, literature and in other forms. But all propaganda is designed to instill and reinforce a limited set of fears, approved beliefs and endorsed behaviours so that the 'individual' responds submissively within the carefully managed system of elite political, social and economic control.

He then goes on to state that

> Education is designed to teach the individual a limited range of technical functions intended to help create, maintain but essentially serve the emerging technocratic tyranny (as it supersedes the existing version of industrial capitalism), making the individual a passive consumer and politically submissive. . . . Its purpose is to ensure that an intelligent mind does not develop that is capable of seeking out relevant evidence, critiquing society and responding powerfully.

He follows this by stating that

> The freedom to think for oneself is not a human right in any meaningful sense of the term and, even if it were, it would really only

> mean the freedom to think for oneself within certain clearly defined and narrow parameters.

His dramatic conclusion is that in the course of compulsory education 'The freedom to think for oneself and act accordingly is strangled at a very young age.'

With so many factors potentially undermining people's ability to utilise Critical Thinking skills, whether it is the lack of focus on these skills in school and university curricula, or whether it is the use of propagandistic techniques in the presentation of government policies, we need to ask how individuals can rise above propaganda, and see it for what it is. How people can be encouraged to rise above pressures to conform in societies where the skill of Critical Thinking is neither widely taught in schools or universities nor widely practised is the subject of our next and final section.

Escaping the effects of propaganda and pressures to conform

How should individuals rise above the effects of propaganda and pressures to conform? One commentator, Dr Noam Shpancer, wrote an interesting piece stating that

> The antidote to the process of propaganda is the process of finding factual truth. The best way we have for doing that is through scientific inquiry, which referees competing claims systematically based on evidence. [2017]

He discusses the tension that exists between propaganda and science as a tension between feeling and thinking. He describes these elements as being in competition with each other and how the competition is rigged on the basis that

> Emotional reaction precedes reasoned analysis, like biting must have preceded the evolution of teeth. We are more likely to act on a feeling without much thought than to act on a thought without much feeling.

He then quotes E. O. Wilson as saying that 'People would rather believe than know', and ends with the ominous conclusion that

> The propagandist's appeal to emotion is therefore bound to find a more ready reception than the scientist's appeal to reason. Emotional reactions easily drown out and overtake intellectual analysis and fact-based reasoning. That's the psychological edge exploited by the propagandist.

The question then for us is how the individual can rise above the emotional pressure of propaganda and group pressure. Is following the science the answer as E.O. Wilson appears to imply? It seems that he has not entertained the possibility that science could also lie for he writes that 'For science, factual truth is the agenda; it follows the evidence wherever it might lead'. Left out of his discussion is the notion of scientism, a move to invoke science in order to cloak an ideological agenda. As Erman Sozudogru, a teaching fellow in the philosophy of medicine at UCL, has argued, the mantra 'Follow the Science' has been found to be a somewhat hollow one (Bauer, 2021):

> While scientists are working around the clock to enhance our understanding of this there is no conclusive data that can determine the best method to combat Covid-19. What drives decisions is our value judgements.

Given the fact that there may be no single version of a scientific truth, the question as to how people can rise above the emotional lure of propaganda and scientism is all-important. Unfortunately, it seems that no serious attempts have been made to answer this question which, given the importance of Critical Thinking, and its role in guiding us to the truth, is an extraordinarily serious gap. It is one that has prompted new research, reported for the first time in Part III of this book. Some words about this research follow before we move to Part II and our first sample of Critical Thinkers, from whom we can infer triggers and personal attributes that inform their critical thinking.

Cutting Edge New Research: Methodology

Parts II and III of this book that follow are dedicated to filling the gap in terms of our understanding as to the triggers that prompt people to become Critical Thinkers. We do this firstly, by presenting the hand-picked accounts of people who have embarked on journeys of questioning over a long period. You can find these in the section that follows (Part II) with one of these included in the Afterword. As you will see, they cover a very wide range of topics, and as you read their individual stories, whether you agree with what they say or not, you may want to ponder the elements that ignited their questioning.

In Part III, we move on to providing our conclusions as to the factors that lie behind these people's Critical Thinking journeys. So we also look at responses to an online survey that was directed at people with a questioning mind, asking them to identify the attributes and trigger factors that started them on their questing journeys, and we looking at the responses of the seventy-four people who responded to this.

Following the paths of iconic literary heroes

There is one other aspect to our research. Although academics have neglected to look at the triggers that encourage people to ask questions, novelists have been intrigued by this question for a long while. Famous novels in this genre include *Brave New World* by Aldous Huxley, *Nineteen Eighty-Four* by George Orwell and *Fahrenheit 451* by Ray Bradbury (the story details of these three books can be found in Appendix C).

Many of you will be familiar with the heroes of these novels whose questioning leads them to resist the oppressive constraints of the societies in which they live. The titans in these books will be known to many. The best known is probably Winston Smith (*Nineteen Eighty-Four*), the man who quietly secretly resists the conforming hand of Big Brother by inquiring of the past, whether in his personal life, restoring memories of his mother, or hunting down the truth about Oceania's past. His sexual relationship with Julia, like his acquisition of a diary in which he writes down his thoughts, a crime punishable by death, are valiant attempts to assert his individuality.

He goes to enormous lengths to resist the dehumanising pressures to conform to the society that he lives in. The only safe place to write his diary is in an alcove in his house beside a screen, where he believes that he cannot be seen. It is there that he takes out his diary, which also appears as a precious relic of the past with its 'smooth, creamy paper, a little yellowed by age... of a kind that had not been manufactured for at least forty years past'. In it, he takes pride in writing 'Down with Big Brother' and also 'Freedom is the freedom to say that two plus two equals four. If that is granted, all else follows.' (part 1, chapter 7). His high intelligence is marked by the early responsibilities given to him at the Records Department of the Ministry of Truth, where he is responsible for sanitising the past.

Then there is Bernard Marx of Brave New World, another triumph of British fiction. Bernard feels dislocated from the controlling society of World State, a nightmarish society in the future. Somehow, his programming as an Alpha Plus male has not gone according to plan since he is physically shorter than his counterparts in society, and this triggers him to pose questions concerning the society in which he finds himself. Finally, we have Guy Montag, a fireman whose job it is to burn books and assist the process of shutting down Critical Thinking and erasing knowledge of the past. His questing journey begins when he meets nature-loving teenager Clarisse, and is furthered by Professor Faber, who can fuel his desire for knowledge and answer his many questions. Eventually, he breaks free and escapes the confines of his thinking and of the society in which he lived.

In Part III, we compare the insights about human nature developed by these famous novelists with the findings that emerge from a comparison between the trigger factors for our twenty-four critical thinkers and those of the seventy-four online-survey respondents. Could it be that our literary icons experienced the same triggers as our thoughtful contributors and online-survey respondents? Or could their attributes and triggers have been completely different? We will find out in Part III. From there, we undertake a study of the personality types of critical thinkers, using as our samples the online-survey respondents as also people attending a Questioning Science event. The personality test that these critical thinkers completed is the most widely used personality instrument in the world – the Myers Briggs Type Inventory (MBTI) – and for the first time ever we look at whether or not critical thinkers share similar personality types.

Before we move on to these exciting new pastures, a brief word about the methodology used in selecting the fascinating contributions gathered together in the next part, Part II, of this book.

Accounts of contemporary critical thinkers

Our twenty-four unique voices, some of whom may be known to readers, were gathered through a process known as 'purposeful sampling' – one widely used in qualitative research to identify and select information-rich cases related to the phenomenon of interest (Creswell and Plano Clark, 2011; Palinkas et al., 2015). In this case, the subject matter under investigation is Critical Thinking and the trigger factors as well as personal attributes that prompted this mode of thinking. A further criterion in the selection of contributors was their availability, willingness to participate and ability to communicate their experiences and opinions in an articulate, expressive and reflective manner (Spradley, 1979; Bernard, 2002).

Care was taken by the two authors of this book to ensure, as far as possible, that contributions came from a number of parts of the world, and at the time of writing, contributors were based in Britain, Sweden, Poland, New Zealand, Canada and the US. They all followed the brief that was presented to them – namely to describe how Critical Thinking influenced their journey through life and their questioning of the mainstream reality in which they lived. Their accounts, as you will see, are highly personal and wide-ranging, with each person's journey focused on specific interests, be it finance, law and order, health, media, ancient and modern history, geopolitics, farming, education (both school and university-level), telecommunications, automation, philosophy or spirituality. They all write in a highly articulate and expressive way, with moments of humour and emotion too in their first-person accounts.

While listening to the voices of our twenty-four contributors, you may want to consider the elements that catapulted them into questing journeys. In doing that, you may want to compare these trigger points with those in your own life. Then, you can sit back and relax and compare your own impressions of the triggers to our contributors' journeys with those that we identify ourselves in Part III of this book.

We do hope that you enjoy reading people's journeys and learn, through that, how Critical Thinking can flourish when we take the job of thinking into our own hands. You will see that, like the famous literary heroes of the three novels that we will bring into our discussion in Part III, our contributors and indeed online respondents pose questions despite pressures to conform that are sometimes similar to those affecting the participants in the celebrated experiments of Solomon Asch, Stanley Milgram and Irving Janis. So, the ultimate hero in this book is Critical Thinking, which can guide us to the truth and provide a light in the darkness.

References

Alpert, M., Golden, L., and Hoyer, W. (1983), The Impact of Repetition on Advertisement Miscomprehension and Effectiveness, NA – Advances in Consumer Research, Volume 10, editors, Richard P. Bagozzi and Alice M. Tybout, Ann Abor, MI: Association for Consumer Research, 130–135.

American Management Association (AMA) https://www.amanet.org/articles/ama-critical-skills-survey-workers-need-higher-level-skills-to-succeed-in-the-21st-century/

Amnesty International (2021), 12 April. https://www.amnesty.org.au/protect-the-right-to-protest-in-nsw/.

Aristotle (2014), Nicomachean Ethics, translated by Roger Crisp. Cambridge: Cambridge University Press.

Australian Christian College (2019), Critical Thinking: An Essential Skill for Every Student, 10 November. https://www.acc.edu.au/blog/critical-thinking-essential-skill/.

Bauer, G. (2021), You can't "Follow the Science", Spiked, https://www.spiked-online.com/2021/03/31/you-cant-follow-the-science/

Baumeister, R. F., and Heatherton, T. F. Self-Regulation Failure: An Overview, Psychological Inquiry, copyright, 1996; 7(1): 1–15.

BBC, Critical Thinking and Problem Solving.

https://www.bbc.co.uk/bitesize/guides/zcjhfcw/revision/1

Berger, W. A more beautiful question, https://amorebeautifulquestion.com/einstein-questioning/

Bernard, H. R. (2002), Research Methods in Anthropology: Qualitative and Quantitative Approaches, third edition. Walnut Creek, California: AltaMira Press.

Bernays, E. (1928), Propaganda. New York: Horace Liveright. https://archive.org/details/BernaysPropaganda/page/n3/mode/2up

Bloom, B. (1956), Taxonomy of Educational Objectives: The Classification of Educational Goals: Handbook 1: The Cognitive Domain. New York: David McKay.

Bowell, T. (2018), Changing the World One Premise at a Time: Argument, Imagination and Post-Truth, in M. A. Peters, S. Rider, M. Hyvönen & T. Besley (editors), Post-Truth, Fake News (pp.169–185). Springer, Singapore. https://doi.org/10.1007/978-981-10-8013-5_15.

Bradbury, R. (1953), Fahrenheit 451, New York: Ballantine Books.

Brooks, A. and John, L. (2018). The Surprising Power of Questions, Harvard Business Review, May-June, https://hbr.org/2018/05/the-surprising-power-of-questions

Burns, T., and Sinfield, S. (2016), Essential Study Skills: The Complete Guide to Success at University, fourth edition. London: Sage.

Burrowes, R. J. (2020), Why Do Most People Believe Propaganda and False Flag Attacks?, Ground Report India.

https://groundreportindia.org/monthly/reports/2020/11/why-do-most-people-believe-propaganda-and-false-flag-attacks/

Carpenter, W. (2020), The Aha! Moment: The Science behind Creative Insights, in Toward Super-Creativity: Improving Creativity in Humans, Machines, and Human–Machine Collaborations, edited by Sílvio Manuel Brito. eBook in TechOpen. https://www.intechopen.com/books/6935

Deborah (2021), What Is a Light Bulb Moment?, 11 February, Veterans Affiliate Success (website). https://veteransaffiliatesuccess.com/what-is-a-light-bulb-moment/

Deutsch, M., and Gerard, H. B. (1955), A Study of Normative and Informational Social Influences upon Individual Judgment.

Doliński, D.; Grzyb, T.; Folwarczny, M.; Grzybała, P.; Krzyszycha, K.; Martynowska, K.; and Trojanowski, J., Would You Deliver an Electric Shock in 2015? Obedience in the Experimental Paradigm Developed by Stanley Milgram in the 50 Years Following the Original Studies, Social Psychological and Personality Science, 8 (8), https://doi.org/10.1177/1948550617693060

Dwyer, C. (2017), Critical Thinking: Conceptual Perspectives and Practical Guidelines. Cambridge: Cambridge University Press.

Facione, P. A. (1990), Critical Thinking: A Statement of Expert Consensus for Purposes of Educational Assessment and Instruction, The Delphi Report. Millbrae, CA: California Academic Press.

Foundation for Critical Thinking. https://www.criticalthinking.org/pages/our-conception-of-critical-thinking/411

Free Press, https://freepress.org/article/why-do-most-people-believe-propaganda-and-false-flag-attacks

Guilford, P. (1950), Creativity, American Psychologist, 5, 444–454.

Hupfer, S. (2019), Critical Thinking Rivals Technical Skills for Industry 4.0 Success, Deloitte. https://www2.deloitte.com/us/en/pages/technology-media-and-telecommunications/articles/critical-thinking-skills-required-industry-4-0.html

Huxley, A. (1953), Brave New World. London: Chatto and Windus.

Janis, I. (1972), Victims of Groupthink: A Psychological Study of Foreign-Policy Decisions and Fiascoes. Boston, Mass.: Houghton Mifflin.

Kahneman, D. (2011), Thinking, Fast and Slow. Great Britain: Penguin.

Lombard, F.; Schneider, D. K.; Merminod, M.; and Weiss, L. (2020), Balancing Emotion and Reason to Develop Critical Thinking About Popularized Neurosciences, Science and Education, 29, 1139–1176. https://doi.org/10.1007/s11191-020-00154-2; https://link.springer.com/article/10.1007/s11191-020-00154-2#citeas

Mansfield, B. (2022), Critical Thinking in Schools Needs Critical Thought, School Management Plus, 24 January. https://www.schoolmanagementplus.com/curriculum/critical-thinking-in-schools-needs-critical-thought/

Matsumoto, D. (2021), Emotions and Critical Thinking, Humintell, January. https://www.humintell.com/2021/01/emotions-and-critical-thinking-update-2021/

New South Wales (2019). https://www.steptogether.nsw.gov.au/step-together-home/blog/2019/encouraging-critical-thinking.html

NHS. https://www.nhsprofessionals.nhs.uk/en/partners/academy-courses/personal-development-courses/critical-thinking-and-decision-making.

Orwell, G. (1949), Nineteen Eighty-Four. London: Secker and Warburg.

Palinkas, L.; Horwitz, S.; Green, C.; Wisdom, J.; Duan, N.; and Hoagwood, K. (2015) Purposeful Sampling for Qualitative Data Collection and Analysis in Mixed Method Implementation Research, Administration and Policy in Mental Health and Mental Health Services Research, 42(5), 433-455. https://www.ncbi.nlm.nih.gov/pmc/articles/PMC4012002/

Papathanasiou, I.; Kleisiaris, C.; Fradelos, E.; Kakou, K.; and Kourkouta. L., Critical Thinking: The Development of an Essential Skill for Nursing Students, Acta Informatica Medica, 21 August, 22(4): 283–286.

Payne, H. (2014), Our Body and Mind Are One, Link, 1 (1). https://www.herts.ac.uk/link/volume-1-issue-1/our-body-and-mind-are-one

Plato (1897), The Apology, translated by Henry Carey. http://faculty.sgc.edu/rkelley/The%20Apology%20of%20Socrates.pdf

Safi, A., And Burrell, D. N. (2007), 'Why Government Managers Need to Develop Critical Thinking Skills', 6 January. http://ftp.ncda.org/aws/NCDA/pt/sd/news_article/5332/_PARENT/CC_layout_details/false

Sawyer, K. (2011), 'The Cognitive Neuroscience of Creativity: A Critical Review', Creativity Research Journal, 23 (2): 137–154. DOI: 10.1080/10400419.2011.571191

Shpancer, N. (2017), 'The Con of Propaganda', Psychology Today, 15 February. https://www.psychologytoday.com/us/blog/insight-therapy/201702/the-con-propaganda

Simon, H. (1957), Models of Man: Social and Rational: Mathematical Essays on Rational Human Behavior in a Social Setting. New York: John Wiley and Sons.

Society for Human Resource Management (2019). https://www.shrm.org/about-shrm/Documents/SHRM%20State%20of%20Workplace_Bridging%20the%20Talent%20Gap.pdf

Spradley, J. P. (1979),The Ethnographic Interview. New York: Holt, Rinehart & Winston.

Sweller, J. (2011), 'Cognitive Load Theory', Psychology of Learning and Motivation, 55, 37–76. Academic Press,

Thomson, H. (2018), Aha! What Happens in your Brain When You Have a Lightbulb Moment, New Scientist, 17 May.

https://webcache.googleusercontent.com/search?q=cache:chVhi4GIh30J:https://www.newscientist.com/article/2168976-aha-what-happens-in-your-brain-when-you-have-a-lightbulb-moment/&cd=1&hl=en&ct=clnk&gl=uk,

University of Edinburgh. https://www.ed.ac.uk/institute-academic-development/study-hub/learning-resources/critical

The Conversation (2016), What is Critical Thinking and Do Universities Really Teach It?, 22 November. https://theconversation.com/what-is-critical-thinking-and-do-universities-really-teach-it-69046

Van Damme, D. (2022), Does Higher Education Teach Students to Think Critically?, 30 August. https://blog.oecd-berlin.de/wp-content/uploads/2022/09/Dirk-Van-Damme-Does-higher-education-teach-students-to-think-critically-Hamburg-30-August-2022.pdf

Wainer, R. (2010), https://www.cambridgeassessment.org.uk/insights/role-value-and-impact%20of-critical-thinking-on-attainment/

WEF (2016), Ten 21st-Century Skills Every Student Needs, 10 March. https://www.weforum.org/agenda2016/03/21st-century-skills-future-jobs-students/

WEF (2020), These Are the Top Ten Job Skills of Tomorrow, 21 October. https://www.weforum.org/agenda/2020/10/top-10-work-skills-of-tomorrow-how-long-it-takes-to-learn-them/

WEF (2022), Carbon Neutral and Net Zero – What Do They Mean?, 23 August. https://www.weforum.org/agenda/2022/08/carbon-neutral-net-zero-sustainability-climate-change/

Williams, T. (2022), Do Universities Teach Students to Think Critically?, Times Higher Education Supplement, 6 September.

Zahner, D. (2022), Does Higher Education Teach Students to Think Critically? https://blog.oecd-berlin.de/wp-content/uploads/2022/09/Doris-Zahner-CAE-CLA-Does-higher-education-teach-students-to-think-critically-Hamburg-30-August-2022-.pdf

PART II

Critical Thinking Journeys

HOW WE ACQUIRE KNOWLEDGE

Opening Up New Vistas: The Power of Asking Questions

GLORIA MOSS

Following a career as a Training and Development Manager, creating human systems that worked for the employees, Gloria Moss moved into academia, becoming a professor and publishing her strong evidence for cognitive sex differences (as applied to design) in books such as Gender, Design and Marketing *(Routledge) and* Why Men like Straight Lines and Women Like Polka Dots, *as well as articles in her eighty-plus peer-reviewed journals. She also led projects on Best Practice Leadership, researching the benefits of inclusive leadership – a style that far surpasses top-down autocratic control in terms of the levels of productivity, motivation and well-being that it brings about. It is the subject of a book on the topic published by Routledge. She has also published extensively on historical topics and runs two conferences a year: Questioning History and Questioning Science.*

My personal journey

My journey began with a degree in French language and literature, then one in medieval studies and then degrees in the social sciences, including a PhD. Over an extended period of time, starting from the 1990s, the process of removing myself from the status quo gradually evolved with the realisation that it no longer provided solutions or accounts of events or phenomena that matched reality. This process was kick-started by the process of applying critical thinking to a number of topics that came my way. The first case concerned some snippets of information about the

Great Fire of London, and the anomalies that came to light caused me in the fullness of time to question the official account that this great fire was the product of negligence on the part of Thomas Farriner, the baker in Pudding Lane.

And so it was with the second topic – that of the Dead Sea Scrolls site of Qumran. Anomalies in the evidence led me towards an interpretation that was at odds with the mainstream. Likewise, it was a chance event at an art gallery in London that drew me into the sex-difference debate and to research over a twenty-year period that produced powerful evidence for cognitive sex differences. My findings cut against the mainstream view that there were no differences between males and females.

Finally, it was my own professional interest in organisations, and how best to fashion these so that they can support productive and creative work by people with high levels of positive mental well-being, that led me to undertake cutting-edge work on Best Practice Leadership. This work highlighted the importance of a humane style of leadership that again was not widely supported by the mainstream – indeed, just as with the work on gender and design, there were forces keen to suppress the work.

So, the process of asking questions opened up new vistas and made it apparent that society was not always welcoming of these insights. This produced determined efforts to map the new territories and restore critical thinking to areas of interest and to learning institutions. Hence participation in the development of the Truth University (www.truthuniversity.co.uk) and its publishing arm, Truth University Press. My travels along this path began with questions concerning the Great Fire of London before moving to sex differences and finally leadership. The staging posts on these journeys are set down below.

(I) Great Fire of London, 2–7 September 1666

In my thirties I was struck by the fact that Sir Christopher Wren sought to replace the tower of St Paul's Cathedral with a dome; he went on his only trip abroad to Paris – a long ten-month fact-finding trip concerning architecture – very shortly before the fire broke out, allegedly as the result of negligence by the baker Thomas Farriner in Pudding Lane, in September 1666; and he was then the person selected to oversee the redevelopment of the cathedral and other churches. All this when he was an astronomer and mathematician, but no architect. I sensed that something was not quite right.

Many years later I looked into the facts and found strong evidence to justify these suspicions. Eventually, I wrote an article on the Great Fire of London that was published in *OffGuardian* in 2019. Here are some key facts – just a small selection of the facts that I cited in the article and elsewhere.

- In 1661, Wren had begun advising on the repair of the *Old St Paul's.* He planned to replace the dilapidated tower with a **dome.**
- Between June 1665 and March 1666, Wren spent ten months in Paris – his only journey abroad in the course of his whole life (he lived into his nineties). In one long letter written by Wren himself, the two people that he expressly wished to meet (and undoubtedly met) were the architect François Mansart and the Italian sculptor and architect G. L. Bernini. He also viewed Jacques Lemercier's church of the Sorbonne (1635–1643) and the Val-de-Grâce by François Mansart (1645–62), both domed-buildings, and fulfilled his aim of returning with 'almost all France on paper'. Back in England, in fact, he spoke of 'daily conference with the best Artists', French and Italian, and first-hand study of modern design and construction (*Oxford National Dictionary of Biography*: Wren).
- In August 1666, wooden scaffolding had been erected for some building work to be carried out, and tar (an inflammable material) had been applied to the leaking roof.
- On September 1, John Gaunt, a newly appointed trustee of the New River Company (it had created a canal that diverted river water into a reservoir in Islington) turned off the water supply, locked the door and disappeared, taking the keys with him (Tinniswood, 2004). So, when the fire broke out, it had to be put out with water taken from the Thames by buckets – far less effective than had the water from the reservoir been available.

The effects of the four-day fire were severe. Around eighty per cent of London was destroyed by the Great Fire, which ravaged 13,200 houses, eighty-seven parish churches, the Royal Exchange, the Guildhall and St Paul's Cathedral, with the value of the destroyed property being put at around £1.5 billion in today's values. In terms of the human costs, it is estimated that around 100,000 people (one-third of London's population) were rendered homeless; and under the law at the time, tenants, not landlords, were held liable for the damage.

The official story has much to arouse suspicion, with just a select few details mentioned here:

- The fire began on 2 September, and spread down Pudding Lane and Fish Lane to the Thames, helped, it is said, by a strong wind from the east. A contemporary, Thomas Vincent, noted that the fire was spreading in the opposite direction to the wind, so how can the eastward, northward (up to Cannon St) and southward (to the Thames) directions of the fire be explained? The spread of the fire was unusual. Pepys, informed of the fire at 3 a.m. on 2 September, and seeing it from his window, thought it 'far enough off' to justify going to bed. He later wrote that he was 'unused to such fires as followed'.
- Thomas Farriner (1615–1670), the baker blamed for the fire in his bakery at Pudding Lane, claimed that at midnight, a few hours before the fire broke out, only one grate had any smouldering embers and these had all been raked over; that he had gone through every room in the bakery after midnight; and that he had closed all the doors and windows to prevent draughts. Note that he died just four years later in 1670, in his mid-fifties, so did not remain long on the scene to protest his innocence.

- Melted pieces of pottery found in a shop near Pudding Lane were found to have been affected by temperatures as high as 1,700 degrees Celsius. Great know-how must have gone into the creation of these temperatures.

- Thomas Bloodworth, Lord Mayor of London, declared that the fire was so small 'a woman might piss it out' (so the normal process of forcible demolition of buildings was not used until the third day of the fire, when it had already spread extensively), and he refused to supply additional soldiers on the first day of the fire. Pepys noticed on the first day 'nobody to my sight endeavouring to quench it'.

- On the second day, Thomas Vincent noted that the wood removed from houses had been placed in the spacious and fashionable shopping area of Cornhill (towards the north of the city), but had not been removed from there, and the wood had caught fire. The diarist John Evelyn noted that it was not until the fourth day that the gentlemen 'began to bestir themselves, and not till now, who had stood as men interdict, with their hands a cross'. On the fifth day of the fire, the Earl of Oxford noted that many of the constables who should have been at fire posts were absent.

- People who published and sold unlicensed books and broadsheets were arrested. This resulted in the suppression of all unauthorised accounts alongside rumours that the fire had been started by conspirators. In 1667, the Privy Council ordered the public burning of a pamphlet that could have provided evidence presented to the Commons' inquiry into the causes of the fire (Dolan, 2001).
- The authorities and King were quick to speak of an inquiry into the fire and a committee to oversee the reconstruction of London. The committee members were appointed by 25 September, just two weeks following the fire, and they included Wren, who according to some accounts was a Master Freemason. According to a page on 'St Paul's draughtsmen', now removed from the St Paul's Cathedral website, he produced only ten per cent of the drawings for St Paul's Cathedral. Why has this page been removed from the cathedral's website? I wondered.

The notion that the fire was the outcome of a plot does not appear in any official accounts of the fire, even to this day. One academic dismissed discussion of a plot as evidence of a 'plot mentality' (Marshall, 2016). But why? To dismiss the possibility is without justification for three reasons:

i. The original inscription on the Monument built to commemorate the fire referred to a conspiracy by the 'popish faction'. The words were 'In perpetual remembrance of the most dreadful burning of this protestant city, begun and carried on by the treachery and malice of the popish faction.' These words were erased in 1830.

ii. At least three contemporaries suspected foul play. Farriner concluded that *'It **was absolutely set fire on purpose**'* (October Sessions of the Old Bailey, London, 1666); Pepys wrote *'that there is plot in it and that the French had done it'* (a Frenchman, Robert Hubert, was executed for the crime in October 1666);
iii. Thomas Vincent, a witness and Nonconformist minister, spoke of rumours that fire balls were thrown to provoke the furious flames. He expressed surprise at the way St Paul's Cathedral, then the largest church in Britain and the third largest in Europe, had caught fire. He singled out the fact that the building was made of stone and that great beams and stones fell and *'Great flakes of stone scale[d] and peel[ed] off **strangely** from the sides of the walls.' He mentioned the fact that St Paul's Cathedral was 'naked of houses about it'* (this is corroborated by contemporary engravings) and also stood high above all buildings in the City (it was atop Ludlow Hill). He noted that *'strangely the cathedral t[ook] the fire at the top'*, a phenomenon clearly illustrated in Hollar's engraving of 1666 showing the fire coming from, *inside* the roof of the building. Is this because of the wooden scaffolding erected in August 1666?

It is tempting to ask who would benefit from the Great Fire of London, and four possibilities came to mind:

1. Landowners. The landowners and Crown benefited from the fire and the financing of new stone and brick buildings. A note on landowners: most Londoners lived as leaseholders, renting their homes from the owners, and their leases required them to cover the full costs of any damage (and also to pay the rent for the full term of the lease, even if the property no longer existed). The trial and execution of Robert Hubert in October 1666, in making the fire an act of war, put the responsibility back on to the property owners, but a parliamentary report issued in January 1667 concluded that the fire was not a malicious act and so responsibility once again fell on tenants. Their obvious inability to cover the costs of rebuilding London led to the setting up of the Fire Courts, to better distribute the burden (*Oxford National Dictionary of Biography*: Farriner), but the burden of the rebuilding still fell on the mass of people rather than just landowners, through new taxation introduced. For, in 1667, King

Charles II ordered a new tax on coal arriving in London – a tax that was doubled in 1670.

2. The King. The King stood to have a new capital city built with funding coming from taxation; landowners could rely on tenants to foot the bill for rebuilding. He had spent nine years in exile and would have acquired a taste for continental design and architecture. He used a Parisian tailor, Sourceau, for example, who had worked for him while he was in exile in France in the late 1640s.

3. Finance/insurance. Insurance active arose in 1680 when the first insurance company, the Fire Office, was established by Nicholas Barbon. The creation of other insurance companies followed, until by 1690 one in ten houses in London was insured.

Concluding comments: My study of the Great Fire of London highlighted serious anomalies that call into question the official version of its history – that it was started by accident in Pudding Lane. No official history of the Great Fire has highlighted these anomalies; and in the face of the many that exist, one has to ask why not? Could the official history be there to conceal the fact that the Great Fire was not just allowed to happen, but planned? I wrote up my findings much later in an article for *OffGuardian* (2019) and the comments that appeared below my article added to my sense that what I had found was just the tip of an iceberg. My questions about the Great Fire of London led me to ask questions concerning the Gunpowder Plot, and this triggered a further article for *OffGuardian* (2020). This attracted just under four hundred comments, showing that other people experienced similar concerns.

Three other areas of study fuelled my determination to question. The next concerned a study of the ancient site of Qumran, close to which the Dead Sea Scrolls were discovered.

(II) The Dead Sea Scrolls site of Qumran

It was near the site of Qumran, by the Dead Sea, that the famous scrolls were discovered in 1946–1947. They were found in eleven caves near Qumran, and are thought to have been written by the Essenes – one of the three main groups of Jews at the time. The standard interpretation is that this was a small community of pious Jews who prayed and ritually abluted themselves in the many baths that constitute the Qumran site.

Over time, a succession of anomalies led me to question this interpretation. Why would a small community need four cemeteries, with one containing 1,100 grave plots? Why would it need a greater concentration of baths (ten in total) than is found in other sites in the land? Why would it need a fortress at its entrance with no externally facing windows – a genre found at Ein Gedi, south of Qumran, where precious aromatics, used for healing and perfumes, were cultivated? Why would only fifteen per cent of the exhumed bodies have been over the age of forty, when Josephus wrote of the Essenes that 'They live long . . . most of them reach the age of more than a hundred years' (JW, II, viii, 10, 151)?

Other anomalies became apparent. Whereas in the main cemetery all the bodies were male, elsewhere nine of the skeletons were those of women (with earrings found), and there were six of children. Scholars wondered how this could be when Pliny had described the Essenes as celibate. Then a report indicated that the corpses were associated with horsemen, labourers and scribes as well as people of diverse ethnic origin (Steckoll, 1963 and 1966) and the bodies had been buried immediately after death, thus preventing the normal Jewish practice of a second burial. Moreover, the bone marrow, teeth and base of the cranium in seventy-five per cent of the disinterred corpses were impregnated with madder dye; and perfume bottles and stoppers with tubular orifices used for aerating or testing a substance at regular intervals were found (but excluded from the official inventory); and a juglet was found in cave three, and analysis showed the contents had the same composition as date stone liquid a liquid used in the modern pharmaceutical industry. Speaking of caves, the so-called scroll jars found there were twice the height of the scrolls, most of which were not found in the scroll jars. How could this all be explained? I wondered.

These anomalies kick-started a long period of research in which I visited the site and libraries in Jerusalem as well as in London. The findings took me in a different direction from the mainstream story, suggesting that the site of Qumran was being run as a medical centre using precious and extraordinary herbal medicines. One could only be in awe of the wisdom of the Essenes in constructing such a positive system of health care at a time when there was no other organised system. I submitted an article to one of the main journals of Dead Sea Scrolls study, only to have it roundly rejected. Fortunately, it was accepted by journals in other fields, but the experience, coupled with the strong evidence that I had submitted, caused me to ask what other information was being blocked.

How strong was the evidence? Well, it included and went beyond the following points; and readers can read the full articles referenced at the end of this piece.

1. Cemeteries. The madder dye found in the corpses at Qumran, and also in the associated site of En el Ghuweir, comes from the plant *Rubia tinctorum,* a herb that according to the ancient author Pliny has diuretic and anti-paralytic effects and is also effective against jaundice and sciatica. Would you believe it, Pliny even recommended that the madder be taken alongside daily baths! So here was a health reason for the many baths at Qumran. Modern analysis has shown that madder contains quinine – a substance thought to cure malaria, leg cramps, internal hemorrhoids and varicose veins.

2. Perfume bottles. Many scholars have thought it necessary to disassociate the site from the Essenes on account of the find of perfume bottles. However, Christian monks have long been associated with healing, so why not the Essenes – a name that some think derives from the word *assaya*, meaning healer. The perfume bottles could have stored precious aromatics – balsam and frankincense, for example – that had immense healing qualities and that may have grown at Qumran. What is more, the precious nature of these healing substances – increased by their scarcity in the ancient world since they only grew in certain parts of the ancient world, the Dead Sea area being one of them – helps explain the vast and otherwise incomprehensible treasure detailed in the so-called Copper Scroll – one of the scrolls found in the caves near Qumran.

3. The jug from the cave. Although chemical analysis revealed that the liquid in the jug was from pulverised date stones, the scholars reporting this denied that this had been used in ancient times. In fact, I looked up the ancient author Pliny, who described it as an ingredient in eye salves. Dioscorides, the first-century-AD herbalist (and 'father of herbal medicine'), moreover, described it as able to halt haemorrhaging and help with certain female conditions when used with raw liver. So this reinforced the notion of healing at Qumran.

All in all, the evidence argues strongly in favour of Qumran being a healing centre, and yet nowhere is this reflected in the writings of other academics. This drove me to explore further in this and other areas, and follow where the evidence took me.

The next opportunity happened by accident – or perhaps with the guiding hand of Fate.

(III) Cognitive sex differences

In the 1990s. I wandered into a water colour exhibition in the Mall Gallery in Central London. I jotted down the numbers of the paintings that appealed to me most and, when I searched in the catalogue, found that eighty per cent of the paintings on my shortlist were by women. Could it be that most of the water colourists were female? In fact, most were men and I realised that my personal selection was statistically significant.

At the time, returning to look at the paintings in the gallery, I thought that I could discern differences in the paintings of the men and the women. His had distinct shapes and contours, a limited range of colours and a realistic look; hers were more whimsical, with more colour and distance from reality. This was a mere impression, and I was sure that there would be academic literature charting such differences as there might be between men's and women's graphic expression, and their preferences too. In fact, searches revealed that the only research that had been conducted concerned children and young people's drawings and paintings, and these certainly highlighted a picture of differences where creations were concerned. No studies had at that time been conducted concerning preferences. What is more, an academic writing at around that time, Firat, took the view that 'gender is an unproductive dichotomy rooted in cultural understandings of what it means to be masculine and feminine' (Moss, 2016, p.5). This seemed strange based on my impressions then and also subsequently.

The absence of any academic literature on the topic of differences in the visual creations and preferences of males and females kick-started twenty years of research since it was vital to fill the gap. My findings are recorded in a large number of peer-reviewed articles as well as books and chapters that I wrote from the mid-1990s until around 2017. The findings give the lie to the notion that gender is an unproductive dichotomy since the research (my own research on design as well as earlier research on children's drawings and paintings) shows that there are consistent and systematic differences in the features (colour, shape and theme) that inform men's and women's graphic expression. These differences span graphic, product and web design, and point to a greater use of colour, curvilinear shapes and animate themes on the part of women as compared with men, and all at an extremely high level of significance. They occur across cultures and are apparent in graphic expression from a very young age.

The $64,000 question concerned preferences. Would men and women show the tendency that I did in the Mall Gallery to prefer graphic expression created by their own gender? There had never been any research on this topic, so it was with a mixture of excitement and trepidation that I embarked on academically robust studies. I showed samples of male- and female-created designs – whether web designs, graphic designs or Christmas images – to unsuspecting males and females in the UK and beyond. The results came back as clear as day. Each gender has an extremely marked tendency, statistically speaking, to prefer designs created by their own gender. In fact, the statistics were off the charts (Moss, 2016).

The implications are absolutely massive. In the world of **consumer products,** women make eighty-three per cent of all purchases, and yet most product and web designers as well as senior graphic designers and designers of cars are male. So women are unlikely to be served the kinds of design that would have most appeal to them and merchandisers and retailers of **grocery products, furniture, over the counter medicine, books, cars** and **retail interiors and exteriors and websites** are failing to maximise sales.

That is not all. In the world of **Fine Art**, women's work is sidelined because it has less appeal to the largely male art dealers historically involved in the world of art, and so we have a situation where just half of one per cent of all the paintings in the National Gallery in Britain are the work of women. Yes, only 14 paintings in the National Gallery are the work of women. Even in the Museum of Modern Art in New York, a mere five per cent of the art on display is created by women. All this when it seemed to me that the features and themes of early cave art marked this out as the work of females, and not the males that so many leading art historians assume to be the case (Moss, 2014). Could the absence of female art in national galleries be because art collectors and art historians had historically been men and their preferences were based, quite naturally, on their male-typical aesthetic preferences, imagined and presented as universal preferences? Could it be presumption, rather than evidence-based inquiry, that led them to assume that the original cave artists were male, the then Leonardos of the world (ibid)?

Then there were the implications for **Education.** At school level, most teachers and assessors are female, and girls achieve higher grades than boys. At tertiary level, most teachers and assessors are male and boys achieve higher grades than girls. So we could be seeing the effects of a 'like attracts like' phenomenon here – something that I noted in an article in the Journal of Art and Design Education, a peer-reviewed journal, back in 1996 (1996).

Of course, quite apart from the serious effects of the indirect discrimination that results from men and women holding broadly different aesthetics – women's work is rejected by male decision-makers since it does not match the standards of good design or art that they have modeled on their own preferences - there is the wider question as to why these differences in creations and preferences exist. The answer, I would suggest, is a mixture of nature and nurture, with a substantial contribution from nature.

Mention of nature is to speak of so-called 'essential' differences between men and women and this is by no means a popular view in today's world. However, it is supported by a weight of substantial evidence. In terms of visuo-spatial skills, this is the largest of the sex differences after height, and the psychology literature is definitive on differences in targeting accuracy, colour perception and, to a lesser extent, field independence (the ability to perceive a stimulus independent of its environment) in males and females. This results in documented physiological differences between the way that men and women perceive. For example, men's eyes are spaced on average up to 5 millimeters further apart than women's, giving them better stereoscopic vision; a higher proportion of men are colour-blind (8–14%) compared to women (0.8–1%); and up to fifty per cent of women may have a fourth colour pigment (one up on men's three), giving them access to hundreds of millions more colours (Moss, 2016).

The further question then arises as to the reasons for these well-documented physiological differences. Evolutionary psychology suggest that these differences evolved over the ninety-nine per cent of human history in which men and women served as hunter-gatherers, with men's superior targeting skills and colour-blindness assisting the job of hunting since colour blindness allows the hunter to see through animals' camouflaging (this is why the army often selects colour-blind recruits); conversely, women's superior colour vision would have assisted in detecting changes of mood and temperature in the adults and children that they were responsible for (for indeed it was the women who were in charge of base camp, not only designing and building it but also managing those who lived there while the men were absent hunting) and would have assisted also in detecting ripe as against unripe berries. Women's fondness for curvilinear shapes, moreover, would have triggered ready perception of rounded berries and helped bond women to demanding and often recalcitrant babies and children whose round-shaped heads have been documented across all mammals.

So, this research carried out over a span of some twenty years prompts the question as to why Western society persists in claiming that there are no differences between men and women when the evidence shows overwhelming differences in the visuo-spatial field, one that as we said, after height, shows the largest and most robust findings of sex difference. There is currently fierce opposition to presenting data concerning cognitive sex difference, even in the visuo-spatial field where the differences are clearly documented, and this makes it a battle royal to get findings through peer review and into the public consciousness.

Indeed, when presenting information on my findings (1996b) at a sociology conference early on in my research, I discussed the findings from a large dataset showing how boys and girls coloured in cooker outlines in different ways (the boys typically drew the four sides of the oven door in a single colour and likewise the hobs, while girls used an assortment of colours) and pointed out that these differences were statistically extremely significant. Although I explained that these differences were part of a wider pattern of differences emerging from other studies that I had conducted by that point, the questions at the end of my talk were hostile and I even overheard someone in the break asking, 'Who allowed her here?'. In fact, I was arguing for the effects of sociology in the long term – over the span of human hunter-gatherer activity that spans 99% of human history– while sociologists focus on short term effects.

So, persisting in maintaining that gender is an irrelevant variable is not simply perverse, but flies in the face of hard evidence. How can this status-quo view continue to be supported when there is copious evidence against it, certainly where height and visuo-spatial differences are concerned?

Similar questions arose once I added the subject of leadership to my professional areas of research. This was a natural thing to do since my professional background had been in Human Resources and Organisational Psychology, with many years spent in industry improving the culture and quality of management. The first job was as site training manager at Britain's largest manufacturing site outside Derby (you could smell it from miles away!), and the second was as UK training manager at Eurotunnel, the precursor to Eurostar, the cross-Channel train operator. Once I had moved from industry to academia to research design creations and preferences, the decision to undertake research on Best Practice Leadership was a natural one and vital at a time when styles of management were increasingly toxic.

So welcome, finally, to the study of leadership in industry and in higher education.

(IV) Leadership

I was privileged to lead a funded research project examining the concept of inclusive leadership and its effects on organisations. We defined a style of leadership that was underpinned by two well-known models – servant leadership and transformational leadership – and tested the perceived effects through a questionnaire administered to employees in eleven organisations spanning the public and private sectors and including the NHS, Santander, Sodexo, EY, PageGroup and Network Rail. The survey asked respondents to identify which of several leadership attributes were present in their managers' repertoire of behaviours, and they were then asked to indicate how productive and motivated they felt, and how high their mental well-being.

The responses from over 1,000 employees showed a clear and high correlation between the presence of inclusive leadership attributes and self-perceptions of high productivity, motivation and mental well-being. The correlation was at the 0.86 level, so showed an almost perfect correlation. The top-down leadership attributes on the other hand were not correlated with these positive elements. It was clear that what we were calling an 'inclusive' style of leadership was transformative in its impacts.

So, from this first industry study, I went on to conduct research in two universities – one in the UK and one in Norway – and also conducted research in a leading independent school in the UK, Sevenoaks School. This time, our focus was on the attitudes of students; and using an adapted version of the survey, we found remarkably similar levels of correlation between the perceived presence of leadership styles in management and/or teaching personnel and students' self-perceptions of their own productivity, motivation and well-being. It was clear that inclusive leadership would have the same miraculous impact in the world of learning as it would have in industry. Conversely, sticking with the top-down autocratic leadership style that was prevalent in much of education – certainly prevalent according to a 2006 study in the university sector – would not reap the same benefits as a more facilitative, humane style of leadership.

The inclusive leadership competencies that we identified totaled fifteen, and these included the attributes of listening, confidence giving, 'individualised consideration' (and attribute from so-called 'Transformational' leadership) and empathy. The study in Sevenoaks School revealed a high average correlation of 0.82 between perceiving inclusive leadership attributes in teachers and self-reporting positive effects, but an even higher correlation of 0.87 amongst junior-school pupils and a correlation of 0.89 amongst Black and minority ethnic (BME) students. This latter point is of particular interest since an earlier study that I led, commissioned by the then Leadership Foundation for Higher Education in Britain (now part of Advance HE), the main body advising on leadership behaviours in universities, had found that the fortunes of BME students in universities would improve were leadership to be more inclusive, and less transactional (ie less autocratic and remote) across the hierarchy in universities.

This is an important point since BME students – a little over a quarter of all students in the British system – underperform relative to white students in universities in Britain, and our study identified a move to more inclusive leadership as a factor that could enhance their academic performance. For some reason, the Leadership Foundation chose not to publish the full report, publishing only a short summary that appeared briefly on their website. And I recall going through the comments of the academic who reviewed the report and wondering why he/she chose to question the inclusion of senior academics in our study and recommendations (the reviewer questioned why we had not limited the category of those who should demonstrate inclusive leadership behaviours to lecturing staff). From an organizational perspective, this did not make sense since it is well known that the culture of an organization and its style of leadership is mirrored from the top (Moss, 2019). Could it be that the findings were unwelcome and that asking senior academics in universities to become less authoritarian and more humane was not deemed desirable?

I sensed that there might be resistance to the findings, and so was not surprised to experience difficulties in getting them through peer review. One of the educational journals to whom I submitted the report objected to the size of the BME interview sample, even though a study that I cited in my paper and that was published in a 'top journal' had used an even smaller interview sample. Then two other factors led me to assume that there was strong resistance to the publication of these findings.

The first concerned the view of an editor of a journal of Change Management, initially welcoming of the proposition that I edit a special issue on leadership in universities, who subsequently insisted that this could only go ahead if references to the leadership styles of senior people within the university system were absent. This is rather like asking someone to describe a bird without any reference to its colours, so I had to turn away from this 'opportunity' to edit a special issue on leadership styles in universities.

This was happening in around 2019 and gave grounds for concern because of the earlier unwillingness by the Leadership Foundation for Higher Education (as it was then – it is now part of Advance HE). There were two other factors that prompted cause for concern. The first was the published view advanced in peer review journal articles that the subject of leadership in universities should be divorced from discussions concerning mainstream leadership and should not be subject to the same criteria as applied in other sectors. A cynic might see this as an attempt to protect university leadership from the standards of scrutiny that apply elsewhere and maybe this is a factor in the absence of peer review journal articles on university leadership style since 2006 when an article described the style as autocratic with negative effects on staff. Certainly, my own experience highlighted the near-impossibility of reporting on the often worst-practice leadership present at senior levels in many parts the system.

Fortunately, I was able to publish the full report on leadership and BME students in a book on inclusive leadership published by Routledge in 2019. So readers interested in reading the compelling findings in favour of inclusive leadership and a move from the ubiquitous top-down control found in the higher education sector today, can find them there.

Conclusions

The process of questioning followed from noticing anomalies between official accounts of events and phenomena and underlying facts. It continued in the face of evidence of the determination of vested interests to keep a lid on certain truths. Ultimately, we are led to the realisation that the mainstream system cannot be relied upon to present us with unvarnished truth. The best way to rectify this situation is to create systems that are beyond the mainstream, be they publishing houses, academic journals or universities.

References

Dolan, F. (2001), Ashes and the Archive: The London Fire of 1666, Partisanship, and Proof, Journal of Medieval and Early Modern Studies, 31 (2), 391-93

Marshall, A. (2016), The Great Fire, 1666, and the conspiracy mentalitie in Restoration England, in: The Great Fire reconsidered, 3 September 2016, St Paul's Cathedral, London UK

Moss, G. (2020), Remember, Remember, the 5th of November, OffGuardian, 4 November, https://off-guardian.org/2020/11/04/the-gunpowder-plot-and-second-lockdown-on-5-november/

Moss, G. (2019), The Great Fire of London: Cui Bono?, OffGuardian, 1 September, https://off-guardian.org/2019/09/01/the-great-fire-of-london-cui-bono/

Moss, G. (2019), Inclusive Leadership, Basingstoke: Routledge

Moss, G. (2016), Gender, Design and Marketing, Basingstoke, Routledge

Moss, G. (2014), Why Men like Straight Lines and Women like Polka Dots, Psyche Press

Moss, G. (2010), Water and Health: a forgotten connection?, Perspectives in Public Health, 130 (5), 227-232

Moss G. Medicine 2000 years ago (2000), The case of Qumran and other biblical sites. Journal of the royal Society for the Promotion of Health, 120(4): 255–261

Moss G. (1999), Religion and medicine: The case of Qumran, Faith and Freedom, 51(146 Pt1): 44–61

Moss, G (1999), Gender and consumer behaviour: further explorations, Journal of Brand Management, 7

(2), 88-100

Moss, G. (1996), Do males and females make judgements in a self-selecting fashion? Journal of Art and Design Education, 15 (2), 161-170

Tinniswood, A. (2004), By permission of heaven: the story of the Great Fire of London, London: Pimlico

Questions on the Path of Life

SIR JULIAN ROSE

Julian is one of the pioneers of UK organic farming. He went on to develop his farm as a mixed organic enterprise selling all its main produce locally, while refusing to sell to supermarkets. He developed a theory of local production and consumption which he named 'The Proximity Principle.' His advice on regeneration of rural economies has been sought by local authorities, development agencies and government. He is currently President of The International Coalition to Protect the Polish Countryside, ICPPC, and with his wife (Co-founder ICPPC) Jadwiga Lopata, led the campaign that successfully ended with Poland banning the import and planting of genetically modified seeds in 2006. He is co-founder of The Hardwick Alliance for Real Ecology (HARE).

It all started for me in our local church, St Mary's, Whitchurch-on-Thames, South Oxfordshire. The date: 1953.

On Sundays, my mother would take my elder sister Penelope and me to the 10-a.m. Anglican service. There were usually around thirty local residents occupying the old oak pews, most fairly aged and rather pale.

The place was always cold and distinctly damp.

I was seven years old and curious about the service, the vicar, the bell puller and the organist, but somewhat more curious about the sad-looking figure of a man called Jesus whose torso appeared to be nailed to a wooden cross.

One Sunday the vicar read the following from a prayerbook and asked the congregation to repeat it: 'Forgive me, Lord, for I am a poor and miserable sinner.'

We were on our knees and I remember looking up and seeing the passive, expressionless face of my mother and other members of the congregation as they solemnly repeated this prayer.

Some message came to me at that moment, and I refused to repeat this phrase.

'I'm not old enough to sin' was my indignant thought. 'Why should I repeat this phrase?'

So I didn't, and felt rather proud of it. Some sort of special energy passed through me, providing the strength necessary to stick to my rejection of this profoundly depressing statement of self-inflicted guilt.

This 'admission of guilt' was, as I was to find out later in life, based upon a life-repressing socio-religious theory called 'original sin' – a mythical proclamation so thoroughly enforced that even today the subconscious mind of many millions of Christian worshippers falls prey to its dark power.

My awakening had begun. I had identified original sin to be a scam. I was already a conspiracy theorist at the age of seven!

I came into (back to) this world on March 3rd 1947. On the chosen day there was a dramatic snowstorm which blocked the roads and prevented the doctor from getting through to Hardwick House, the family home. However, the midwife, having come the day before, was on hand to help with my birth.

My mother, with some sense of premonition, had her bed moved down to the old Elizabethan drawing room, requesting that it be placed under the plaster-cast head of Julius Caesar which gazed down from the ornately decorated ceiling alongside other historical figureheads.

At around 1.30 p.m., while serving lunch to the family in the downstairs dining room, my mother announced that she needed to go upstairs to lie down. Not long after she had left the room: 'You just popped out' – according to my late mother's account – 'and I went back downstairs to serve the desert.'

I was the fifth child – and the midwife wasn't even needed. I wonder what impression that stately old ceiling left on my newly landed soul and freshly opened eyes, while an historic blizzard was raging outside the window.

For the first eight years of my life I absorbed the world around me. I loved to watch the haystacks being built, the farmers cultivating the fields and the dairy cows slowly roaming the meadows. My mother educated Penelope and me at home, which was quite common in those days.

At the age of eight, I underwent my first shock confrontation with 'the system'. I was sent to a boy's private school where each term involved being away from home for around three months, and boys were only allowed to see their parents for two Sundays during each term.

I had my second 'awakening' at this boys' prison camp. It involved learning to keep my sensitive soul in my pocket and developing the necessary skills for surviving the daily torture of what is known as 'education'. The school, called Hawtreys, occupied a vast old Georgian pile complete with deer park, in the Savernake Forest, near Marlborough.

With just one or two exceptions, the masters were a mixture of pervert, sadist and narcissistic eccentric.

The Latin master invariably put his hand up one's shorts while correcting one's homework. The sergeant major who led physical training had similar licentious traits, while the headmaster took pride in thrashing the life out of those unfortunate enough to fall fowl of his venom. He kept four canes in his study cupboard, each possessing a different degree of elasticity – let's call it 'whackability'.

My heart bled each time a new term started. However, forming some close friendships with other boys and excelling in sport enabled me to survive this training camp for future 'leaders of the empire'.

At my secondary school, based in a Jacobean manor house near the New Forest, the staff were contrastingly human and imaginative and seemed genuinely interested in applying the true principle of *e-ducare* (to lead out from) as the way to encourage the innate creativity which, if not crushed, ferments in all young people.

My initiation into drama happened here. At fifteen I was given the unlikely role of Lady Macbeth in the school play (*Macbeth*), and a year later that of Henry V in Shakespeare's heroic drama of the same name.

The latter experience, in particular, changed my life. I didn't believe I could do it, but the English master, one David Pierce, convinced me I could – and he turned out to be right!

A wave of self-confidence warmed my body and soul after this challenging episode; and although no academic, I went on to have satisfactory passes in exams, as well as representing the school in rugby and cricket first teams.

I didn't try for university. The idea of having to endure any further trials at an academic institution appalled me. I chose instead, at the age of eighteen, to head for Australia. In those days – circa 1965 – one could go down under for just sixty quid on a Greek Chandris Line ship; and that's what I did, sailing from Southampton to Melbourne in five weeks.

Probably the nearest I came to a significant life experience during my one year in Australia was as a cowboy in the Queensland outback, on the 1,600-square-mile Canobie Ranch, situated 110 miles from the nearest town. Working with native aboriginals opened my eyes to the beauty, grace and dignity of this indigenous tribe and opened up in me a profound sense of respect for native peoples in general.

Fast forward some six years. I have studied acting and stage management at the Royal Academy of Dramatic Art in London and had my first experience as a professional actor with two repertory theatre companies in the South of England. The experiences didn't satisfy my creative needs; I wanted something more dynamic.

Then, through the auspices of a friend, I heard about an experimental theatre company operating out of Boston, USA. As it happened, I was headed for the States after the break-up of my first proper romance. My objective was to travel that land so as to clear my mind and mend my heart.

With a Greyhound bus ticket offering '100 days for $100' I set off on my travels and – to cut a long story short – landed up in San Francisco just at the end of the hippy era (1971).

It was here that I had my first profound mind-expanding experience. After finding a job as a waiter in a restaurant styled according to an Elizabethan mansion (the irony!) I befriended a waitress who invited me to come and live in a commune in the hilly and leafy suburbs of San Francisco.

A bunch of young people resided in the small house, and various stimulants were liberally shared around as the contemporary music of the era wafted through the house pretty much 24/7.

For a 'well-bred' English gentleman to land up in such a scene was clearly an unusual happening. But my hair was growing longer and my heart was young; the intoxicating scene offered a moment of true liberation from all that had come before in my not-easy life.

One night, while a party was in full swing, I was asked by a resident to bring him a glass of wine.

Where were the glasses? I enquired.

'On the table between the door and the fireplace,' he replied.

To which I answered, 'There's no such thing as in between.'

I never forgot this. What I had experienced was a quantum truth; at that moment I could see only one fully interconnected passage of time and place. To suggest that something as mundane as a wine glass could interrupt this continuity seemed impossible. Trying to explain what I meant to those completely oblivious to such a reality was quite a joke.

A few months later, after hitch-hiking over to the east coast, I reached Boston. There I met the director of the experimental theatre company my English actor friend had told me about. It was to be a critically important meeting, as a few months after returning to England I got a phone call in the middle of the night inviting me to join the theatre company. I duly returned to Boston and joined 'The Players Theatre of New England'.

The first experimental work I was involved in was entitled *The Universe to Come*. While it never came to performance, it opened up a world of deeply challenging spiritual exploration in me. At the same time I decided to go on a vegetarian diet and found an opening to participate in classes at the Shivananda Yoga Centre in the Boston suburbs.

During this period of time I experienced a profound awakening, acquiring and reading a number of valuable texts on psychology and spirituality. Outstanding among them was Dr Erich Fromm's *You Shall Be as Gods* – a book of great wisdom which spotlights self-recognition of our innate godliness as the key to the full realisation of our human potential.

Fromm also wrote *Escape from Freedom* – a masterful analysis of the human weakness that allowed Nazism to sweep Hitler into power before the Second World War. Strikingly, the very same weakness is allowing what some describe as a global Nazi-based programme of repression to be manifest today.

It was during this time period that I sought the advice of the *I Ching* (*Book of Changes*) concerning my condition and direction of travel. When I threw the three coins six times, according to the Chinese tradition, they fell in exactly the same formation six times in a row, which the *I Ching* translated as 'The Receptive' and the discourse spoke of 'Complete receptivity to Universal cosmic energies'.

In the few months in which these events took place, the sense of burden I carried on my shoulders as the inheritor of the Hardwick Estate lifted. The estate had come to me at the age of nineteen, after the untimely deaths of my brother and father within a few years of each other. I felt the existence of some emerging spirit power opening the way forward to overcoming all challenges that might follow. An extraordinary time.

It's 1972: the theatre company had moved to Antwerp, Belgium, the childhood home of the director's playwright wife. We were soon engaged in the process of establishing a training centre, the Institute for Creative Development, which encompassed a radical academic and arts-based educational centre for children and young adults.

One day, walking in the old medieval town's port area, I noticed a poster announcing a talk to be given by a Dr Devin, a biologist from a British organisation called the Soil Association. It was entitled 'The Laws of the Land'. Intrigued, I signed up.

Dr Devin explained that 'the laws of the land' demand a particular approach to farming which respects the vital role played by the top six inches of the soil. He elucidated the inviolable interconnection between soil, plant, animal and man, and referred to this as a dynamic wheel of health. The method responsible for maintaining the integrity of this dynamic, he said, is called 'organic farming'.

That was it!

I instantly knew what it was I was supposed to do with the Hardwick Estate. It was like a benign electric shock!

Our experimental theatre work was exploring the relationship between movement, music, text and word.

I was in ecstasy. Some fundamental law of physics revealed that these two worlds were actually ONE. The new art of the theatre and the responsible art of agriculture were not worlds apart, as would superficially seem to be the case, but were dynamically complementary.

My transition from drama to farming, which followed, was seamless. Hungry to gain insights into the secrets of of the organic approach to life, I hit upon E. F. Schumacher's iconic work, *Small Is Beautiful*.

This book played a major part in my understanding of 'holistic thinking': what it is and how it must become the basis of all responsible decision-making.

Schumacher's particular speciality was 'intermediate technology' – 'tools as though people mattered'. He established the Intermediate Technology Development Group in 1966, promoting human-scale technologies as key to the proper management of the top six inches of the soil and all areas of work that demand a subtle and creative approach to development of the energy and agricultural sectors of modern society.

At the time of my 'organic awakening' he was president of the Soil Association, an organisation established in 1946 by Lady Eve Balfour, a renowned soil scientist and organic-farming practitioner.

Eve Balfour bravely warned the world of the disastrous effect that the rapidly rising agrichemical and monocultural farming techniques would have on the nutritional value of foods and the fertility of the soils that grow them. She was ignored by all but a few.

In this propitious year of 1975 I started the conversion of the Hardwick farm to an organic system of agriculture. I became the fourth Soil Association certified organic farmer. Swimming against the tide has been the hallmark of my life, and the establishment of an organic regime back in the 1970s was to go exactly in the opposite direction from mainstream farming. Just the kind of friction I thrive on!

Milking cows, washing bottles and the every-other-day delivery round were the start of my career as a full-time farmer, and I threw myself into it with gusto!

This process was rudely interrupted in 1989 when the government chose to ban the sale of certified unpasteurised milk. Shocked, I instantly launched the Campaign to Save Real Milk. Garnering the support of around 120 raw-milk-producing dairy farmers and their customers, and helped by many appearances on mainstream TV and radio, we were able to defeat the imposition of the proposed ban – and 'real milk' thus survives and even thrives to this day.

In 1999 I passed the organic-farming torch on to a fellow traveller and started another huge chapter as co-director of the International Coalition to Protect the Polish Countryside, alongside Jadwiga Lopata, its founder. Fulfilling the needs of this challenge has required me to spend much time in Poland, a country I have come to love. The Polish people carry within a deep sense of spiritual gravity. The nation is heart-led – a rare thing in this day and age – and has a plethora of natural healers as well as those with a strong native knowledge concerning the application of herbal remedies.

I consider myself to be the beneficiary of this knowledge. Jadwiga, growing up on the land in a family steeped in the peasant farming tradition, has frequently come to my rescue with her native knowledge of the natural apothecary of the Polish countryside. She and I have combined our agricultural experiences to become eighty-per-cent self-sufficient in fruit and vegetables on our Eco Centre smallholding near Krakow.

One of my most recent awakenings occurred in Poland while leading a major campaign to prevent GMO seeds and plants being imported into the country. That particular awakening came down to this: two people (Jadwiga and I) were able to confront the global agribusiness behemoth – and win![1] We would never have been able to do this without the consistent unstinting support of higher spiritual powers and a deep belief that doing the impossible is possible!

All the while, simmering steadily on its way to a type of socio-agricultural metamorphosis, the Hardwick Estate builds on its organic-farming reputation. Diverse ecologically complementary enterprises have sprung up wherever a space can be found for them. New blood and new initiatives abound – and the whole estate is heading for a shift into a cooperative

[1] In 2006, Poland's President Lech Kaczyński, banned the import and planting of GMO seeds and plants after ICPP's campaign inspired all sixteen Polish provinces to declare themselves 'GMO Free Zones' and then embrace ICPP's instruction to write to Kaczyński demanding a national ban.

venture to include the participation of existing cottage tenants. My daughter Miriam and son Lawrence are playing an instrumental role in the realisation of this highly significant change.

I am a firm believer in 'practice what you preach'. In my books and essays I lay the ground for what I see as the fundamental way forward for humanity. I base this vision on practical experience and a rational confrontation with reality. However, for all the good that ordinary individuals do in the context of daily life, our world is held in the grip of dark forces. They vampire energy from those who fall into fear or suffer from stress and depression, and they encourage the spread of pain and delusion.

Many demons come with human bodies and are physically indistinguishable from true sentient humans. I have run into all kind of degradations of the true human in the course of my life adventures. At the top end of most religious, banking, political and corporate institutions one will find worshippers and manipulators of Masonic and satanic practices, or those suffering various forms of psychotic and psychopathic sickness. Only rarely does a true human occupy a seat of high authority within the present status quo.

What can we do about this? Here's my suggestion.

Take the view that all these manipulators of mankind are uninvited imposters and have no place in our lives or on our planet. Set your sights on realising your innate potential 'To Be As Gods' – and open yourself to being an emissary of higher powers. Dedicate your actions to giving pleasure to the source from which you come. Similarly, use your talents to give service to humanity.

Soon you will carry such a power of positivity and determination within you that no demon or demonic force can strike you down. Nothing or no one that you feel moved to take on or confront will present an impossible challenge. On the contrary, the more you challenge the source of evil, the stronger becomes your confidence and ability to win the battle which stands in front of you.

'We the people', collectively raising this form of spirit power within each one of us, can and will defeat the perpetrators of our current demise on Planet Earth.

Perhaps you will feel that my life story, here recounted, bears testimony to such a renaissance of the true human condition. I hope so!

Everybody has a role to play in turning around the state of play on our beloved planet. Everyone! There are so many things waiting to be put right and there are so many of us wondering if there is anything we can do!

So, you can see immediately that it is a mindset that is holding us back – not our lack of abilities. Consider these few suggestions for immediate curative change:

- Just after waking up, and before you start worrying about the tasks of the day, give your mind a beautiful vision to dwell upon. Hold this vision for just three minutes. As thought is vibration, you are performing a healing operation both for yourself and for the world around you when you start each morning this way.

- Clear a space beside your sitting-room window and place a window box there. Sow a few seeds of mustard and cress, rocket salad, radish or parsley, and water them every evening so the soil remains damp. Use a compost soil if possible, but any soil will do. Now watch each day until you see a beautiful little green sprout emerging. Then transpose this experience into your vision of a little garden plot – it could be nothing more than a few square metres. Take a piece of paper and sketch out a plan for your very own vegetable patch! Yes, sweet smelling flowers are also allowed – and of course medicinal herbs.

Suddenly you are a gardener! You are teaching yourself the most important primary skill of all: how to grow food. And then the big moment comes: you harvest your mustard and cress and make a fresh green salad or tasty sandwich with it. Yes, all the actions we need to take to change the course of our lives start with a small creative moment of simple pleasure. All real change takes place when you clear your mind and – *just do it!*

MONEY

My Long Journey to Make Sense of Things . . . and I'm Still Travelling!

JUSTIN WALKER

For over forty years, Justin has been on his journey trying to make sense of the seeming madness that now affects the world. Due to family connections, he was allowed to see, albeit briefly, behind the mask to identify the real perpetrators of this contrived state of affairs. Armed with this knowledge, Justin has since co-founded the increasingly influential Hardwick Alliance for Real Ecology (HARE) with Sir Julian Rose.

On 13 December 1955, I apparently popped out in the town of Bolton – at least that's what my parents told me and what is on my birth certificate (or 'legal fiction', as some would now say). I still view Bolton as the centre of my own personal universe and, being a glutton for punishment, I still support Bolton Wanderers.

I was fortunate enough to have a very happy childhood in a loving and typically middle-class family who had made their money from tanning leather and selling hops to the Lancashire breweries. At the tender age of eight, I was sent off to boarding school and then on to Charterhouse, which I left in 1974. Academic I was not! Indeed, my mother kept telling her friends that I was a 'late developer' and that one day I would eventually get there!

I did, however, enjoy my sport along with a penchant for all things military. This meant that I was eventually commissioned into our family Territorial Army regiment (the Duke of Lancaster's Own Yeomanry), whilst for a career I joined my father at the tannery. So far, so good!

However, as I progressed in the TA, whilst learning the intricacies of tanning leather and then selling it on at a handsome profit, I started to get involved with something much more important; and it has now completely taken over my life.

The call of nature

My late uncle by marriage was Sir Harry Pilkington, chairman of Pilkington Brothers Ltd, the glass makers. He was passionate about gardening, beekeeping and wildlife. He also happened to own some beautiful pinewoods behind the sand dunes off Ainsdale Beach, just outside Southport. There, you could stay in his remote 'log cabin' holiday home called Windy Gap, which in those days wasn't on mains electricity. Instead, there was an elderly and grumpy diesel generator which received more than a few curses from my father and grandfather as it spent its time spluttering, deciding whether or not to come to life to provide us all with some lighting.

In this natural paradise, there were red squirrels (and still are) as well as natterjack toads, foxes, badgers and an incredible array of birds and butterflies. From a very early age I had become captivated by wildlife and the need for effective conservation. When I was nineteen I became a volunteer warden at Martin Mere, a Wildfowl Trust sanctuary in West Lancashire. During this time, I met Sir Peter Scott and the writer Gerald Durrell, who both really inspired me – even today, I still like to read Gerald's brilliantly funny books on conservation, and I strongly recommend them to anyone who's feeling a bit down.

It was in the seventies that a popular TV programme grabbed the attention of a very large number of people. *The Undersea World of Jacques Cousteau* inspired many to look at the natural world with completely new eyes, especially the oceans of the world. So when this living legend, Captain Cousteau, told the world in 1977 that the living planet was suffering and that it needed good people to stand for election in order to put things right, I decided that this was my moment to step up to the plate! My journey into green politics had begun!

In August 1978 I bumped into someone who had just joined the fledgling Ecology Party. She told me that their annual conference was about to take place in Birmingham and asked me if I would like to go. Two weeks later I was sitting in a small lecture room at a local college with around eighty other people, including the likes of Jonathon Porritt, Sarah Parkin and Teddy Goldsmith, the founder of *The Ecologist* magazine. There I signed up, and my first 'mission' was given to me.

One of the attendees of this conference was Lord Tim Beaumont of the then Liberal Party. He was a member of the Liberal Ecology Group and was just starting the Green Alliance, which was designed to achieve some sort of inter-party cooperation on green issues. He was also attending the Liberal Party's Autumn Conference at Southport, where I now lived. I suddenly found myself officially representing the Ecology Party as I met the 'great and good' of the Liberal Party. My initiation into mainstream British politics had begun – and, if I'm honest, I was somewhat underwhelmed by the calibre of the people that I was meeting.

Realising very quickly that 'conventional' politicians just could not be trusted, I teamed up with some local fellow members of the Ecology Party and we agreed to put up a candidate in the forthcoming 1979 general election (the one that saw Margaret Thatcher come to power). A still good friend, Peter Hussey, agreed to be the candidate in the Crosby constituency, and I was asked to be the required election agent who planned the actual campaign whilst ensuring that all of the legal paperwork was done properly. Whilst the result obviously did not see Peter elected as an MP (he secured a credible 1,489 votes or 2.4% of the vote), we all came away believing that this had been a worthwhile exercise since mainstream politicians were now hearing about the wisdom of ecology for the first time. We also felt sure that it wouldn't be too long before they would be doing the right things for the planet. How naive and ignorant we were back then!

My unpaid 'career' in the Ecology Party now went from strength to strength. In 1982 I became the National Election Agent, where I bullied and cajoled over one hundred people to become parliamentary candidates for the 1983 general election. Then I was elected on to Party Council to represent the North West of England for eight years, during which time I was responsible for organising some of the national conferences. Due to the electoral success of Die Grünen in West Germany, the party had now changed its name to the Green Party. We achieved a smattering of green councillors (I had stood five times in local elections, but all to no avail). And Party Council had also endorsed the recommendation by the Press and Media Committee to take on Caroline Lucas as our first full-time press officer (not my finest decision, I have to say!).

In 1987 we fast-tracked a new member on to Party Council. His name was David Icke. With our mutual love of steam railways, we soon became friends. And we also found ourselves on the same side as we tried to stop all of the silly infighting that had broken out between competing factions in the Green Party when it achieved an electoral breakthrough at the European elections of 1988 with almost fifteen per cent of the vote.

The truth now emerges

Two years later, David took us all by surprise with his revelatory book *The Truth Vibrations.* Unlike the bulk of the party, I immediately accepted it and realised that there was a whole lot more to life than what was being told to us by mainstream science and politics. After standing in the 1992 general election, I bowed out of the Green Party. I was now starting to realise that we were all being used in some way, and that everything was actually a 'big lie'. The evidence for this had actually been told to me some years before, but I was too ignorant and trusting to understand.

Back in 1972, my uncle, who had been made a life peer in 1968, was sharing a breakfast with me on the Liverpool Pullman. I was going back to school to do my O levels. He was going to London to attend one of his last meetings as a director of the Bank of England – a position he had held since 1955. He suddenly asked me what I was planning to do for a career. When I told him, he responded by saying, 'Always remember these two things: never ever believe anything you read in the press, because we control it, and never ever believe a politician when they say they can do something – they can't unless we say they can!' At the tender age of sixteen this all went completely over my head, but I do remember that strange conversation very clearly.

In 1954 my uncle had attended the first ever Bilderberg Group meeting, held at the Hotel de Bilderberg in the Netherlands, representing British industry. This so-called think tank is a meeting of extremely powerful and influential people which is held annually in sealed-off top-level hotels in Europe and America. Always taking place in absolute secrecy, with no accountability whatsoever, these meetings are where top-level bankers, industrialists, media moguls and politicians – not to mention a smattering of royals – meet to make global decisions that will affect all us all. Whilst there are other very influential and secretive transatlantic 'think tanks', such as the Royal Institute of International Affairs (Chatham House), the Council on Foreign Relations, the Trilateral Commission and the Pilgrims Society, the Bilderberg Group is widely considered by researchers to be the 'flagship' organisation that secretly influences and steers the world.

In 1982 my uncle had arranged for me to have lunch with his fellow Bilderberger friend Aurelio Peccei at a United Nations Environment Programme (UNEP) meeting in London. Aurelio was the co-founder of the Club of Rome, the environmental wing of this elitist, unelected and unaccountable tier of hidden governance that clearly pulls the strings of our elected politicians from behind the scenes. After lunch, Aurelio took me to one side and offered me a job to become one of his political researchers working for him in Rome. But it was what he said next that resonates so strongly with me today.

He said, 'You will be joining us at a very exciting time. We are *creating* a huge environmental problem that will frighten people into wanting a world government run by us!'

At the time, I thought this was brilliant, believing, as Cousteau had told us, that we all needed to come together quickly to see the world protected from the greed and stupidity of humanity. But, as we know today, this 'huge environmental problem' (he was clearly referring to man-made global warming) is now a keystone for the planned 'lockdown' of humanity to give us all a dystopian and Orwellian future that uses bad science and cutting-edge invasive and surveillance technologies to enslave us. And I stumbled unwittingly across this hidden strategy way back in 1981! Fortunately, for personal reasons, I declined Aurelio's kind offer and so did not become a useful idiot for the globalists who currently infest the world today with their planned Great Reset and completely fake Green New Deal.

It's all about the money

Moving on to 2012, I was made aware of yet another 'big secret'. Some-one claiming to be the son of a retired and very elderly director of the Bank of England, who had actually served alongside my uncle, rang me. He told me that his father was not long for this world and that he wanted me to research the word 'Bradbury'. If I did, I would find 'a solution to all of Britain's economic woes'! Having been alerted in this very John Buchan way, I eventually discovered the deliberately suppressed 1914 Bradbury Pound, which was created by HM Treasury at the outbreak of World War One.

In August 1914, Britain was on the gold standard and, with the uncertainty of war, people naturally wanted to exchange their Bank of England 'IOU' debt notes for tangible gold sovereigns. As the private Bank of England had fraudulently created many times more notes than it had physical gold in its vaults to back them up, this meant that there was going to be a run on the banks thus triggering a complete collapse of the British economy just as the nation was mobilising for war. The government acted quickly and decisively. Within four days, the Bradbury Pound Treasury notes (so named after Sir John Bradbury, who, as Permanent Secretary to the Treasury, had his signature emblazoned upon them) were waiting to be given to people as the high-street banks reopened their doors for business. And they were immediately and gratefully received by the people instead of gold sovereigns.

Why? Because this was real or sovereign money that was completely debt-free and interest-free, based as it was exclusively on the credit and creativity of the nation. The sudden emergence of this common-sense fiscal arrangement (which is still used by the Treasury today to create the coins in circulation) completely prevented a sudden collapse of the British economy. However, it was then decided by the politicians to phase out these Treasury notes because the bankers couldn't make a killing out of the killing! The government inexplicably went back to selling bonds (IOUs) in exchange for debt-laden fresh-air money from the City of London financiers in order to win the war. This, of course, ratcheted up our (quite unlawful) national debt to eye-watering proportions.

Returning to this unexpected and anonymous telephone call, I then found myself having meetings with two incredibly wise and well-connected money reformers – the late Ken Palmerton and the late David Pidcock. They both took me under their wing and tutored me about the Bradbury Pound and money creation in general. What they both told me appalled me.

When it comes to global finance, the truth is startlingly simple! The entire financial world – the high-street banks, the money markets, the bond market, the bullion and commodity markets – are all in private, unelected and unaccountable hands where secrecy and hidden manipulation reign supreme. The central banking system, including the Bank of England, the Federal Reserve and the European Central Bank, is completely controlled by a private body that virtually no one has ever heard of or knows anything about. The Bank for International Settlements (BIS) oversees well over ninety-five per cent of the world's money creation, yet it operates in complete secrecy and is not required to experience any sort of public scrutiny or accountability. Indeed, the BIS has actually given itself diplomatic immunity to protect itself from any sort of serious investigation into what it actually does.

The reality is that these unelected and unaccountable globalists are able to create money completely out of thin air as debt. Those who control the money, control the world! And the last thing that these psychopaths want is for good people to know that any sovereign nation can create, issue and control its own debt-free and interest-free money that's based solely on that nation's credit and creativity. As Britain enters a completely contrived and hugely damaging recession to beckon in the Great Reset (as promulgated by the World Economic Forum – those billionaire megalomaniacs who meet in Davos every year), the Bradbury Pound must be immediately restored to save everyone's livelihoods, pensions, life savings and homes from these globalist fraudsters!

A bright future ahead

To close and to bring everything right up to date, three years ago I joined forces with Sir Julian Rose to co-found the Hardwick Alliance for Real Ecology (HARE). Both Julian and I hope that we can help restore the true values and wisdom of ecology where human-scale economics and a real love for our green and beautiful planet can prevail over the dark forces which seek only outright fascism. You can read about Julian's journey elsewhere in this book.

As a postscript, my uncle died in 1983. He may have been a globalist, but to the family he was a lovely, generous and quite eccentric individual who really cared for people and the environment. On one occasion, when he was talking to my father he said that when you are investing millions (billions in today's money) in a country you don't want your investment being damaged by short-term 'here today, gone tomorrow' politicians. He said it was vital that the business world controlled the political narrative so that its investments were properly protected. There's certainly a crude logic here, but the evil mindset today that's currently creating a technocracy of global enslavement cannot be so easily absolved.

The journey continues . . . and there is good news! We need to continue to fight the planned technocracy with truth, just as Václav Havel, former President of Czechoslovakia, suggested in the 1970s and put into effect so extremely successfully in overthrowing the post-totalitarian world that so many were experiencing. As Havel said in his remarkable essay 'The Power of the Powerless' (1978):

> If the main pillar of the system is living a lie, then it is not surprising that the fundamental threat to it is living the truth. This is why it must be suppressed more severely than anything else.

A society based on the power and direction of the truth – what we might call a 'veritocracy' – can harness the collective wisdom and spirituality needed to generate real and lasting peace, happiness and prosperity for all. We stand on the shoulders of giants, so let us learn from their wisdom whilst living in a diverse, balanced and healthy natural world. In other words, Real Ecology!

LAW AND ORDER

From Service to Force: The Shift in Policing

RAY SAVAGE

I'm a gong master and involved with various groups and teams as a speaker and organiser – for example, A Band of Brothers, a mentoring rites-of-passage programme for young men caught in the crime cycle. I help people with Heart Math training and Heart iQ. I am working to create centres locally, regionally and globally which will elevate consciousness in a more cohesive community-based structure, including OneMindCan. For this purpose I've been involved in the planning and development of a wellness/mindfulness retreat centre high in the Ox Mountains of County Sligo, Ireland (see *www.cabraghlodge.ie)*.

Natural health has always been of great interest to me, as it was to my father. Growing good fresh produce on the farm and eating healthily in the interest of prevention was key. I worked with a natural-health company, Herbalife International, and I learnt about Hoxsey therapy, a herbal remedy for cancer which was developed around the time that claims for natural cures for cancer became illegal. A course correction is now needed for humanity's liberation and well-being. There are plenty of visionaries able to restore this planet in accord with its divine plan, taking responsibility for ourselves and our realities, to fulfil our greatest expression in harmony with the Earth. We can create an environment of unconditional love and unity for all sentient life.

I was born in Cape Town, South Africa, where my father was engaged as an engineer implementing electrification of South African Railways. He met my mother at the end of the war and convinced her to join him in Cape Town, where they were married. After a number of years, both sets of my grandparents were becoming older and less well. We returned to the UK in the 1950s as my parents were unhappy living in apartheid South

Africa. We purchased twenty acres of land and lived in a caravan and shed before until we built a house on the land.

Being my father's son has had an amazing impact on me. My father found himself in South Africa feeling dispirited after the war. Born in 1916, he grew up in the 1929 slump which had a major impact on his life. He watched his parents lose businesses in this period, with their lives ending in near poverty. He became a self-qualified engineer, entered the war as an officer and becoming a Normandy veteran, part of the First Tactical Air Force which provided cover to the bridgehead from Normandy to Berlin.

Before putting a foot on French soil, my father felt that he needed to be a spokesperson, so he learnt to speak French. This initial period shaped the way that the rest of his life unfolded. He became very jaded when he met servicemen from other countries and discovered that in Berlin they were all questioning the war. He personally witnessed many deaths and he visited Normandy every year to pay his respects at the gravesides of many who had died there. I must say that walking up the Normandy beaches with him in his nineties was a very humbling experience. In later years he felt there was a hidden hand directing world events that he did not fully comprehend and had a strong dislike of those who he felt seemed to be the grand architects of 'hidden hand' events.

Police experience

My career within the police started in 1966 in Seaford and that is where I witnessed the benefits of so-called 'cooperative policing', a system where the police and public have a strong relationship. In Seaford, the crime rate was low and burglaries were almost unheard of.

I remember my oath 'to protect life and property, *to prevent and detect crime* (my emphasis) and to prevent breaches of the peace'. We were definitely a social service – a support to the people. I worked as a cadet in Hailsham, a rural market town, at the Lewes divisional office and being involved in administration so was able to clearly see how the whole division worked. It was an efficient, cohesive, decentralised, well-oiled machine. We worked happily, with everyone playing their part. At the divisional HQ the personnel were headed up by a chief superintendent and two superintendents, and there was a considerable staff of the lower ranks stationed throughout the division. It is extraordinary for me to observe now the structure of the current police force in that area of Sussex, an area that I know so intimately, and see how few police actually now cover the same area. It's not what it used to be.

After my time in administration, I spent a period training police cadets and equipping them for police service. I served as a constable in Brighton, then Crawley, and as an acting sergeant and latterly as a uniformed sergeant in Crawley. I then served for a period as a Regional Crime Squad detective, covering the whole of the South East of England. I was an intelligence officer for that squad, which led to my promotion to detective sergeant, forming and running a counterterrorist squad based at Gatwick Airport. I was then asked to be involved in policing the miners' strike and since I felt at the time this was a disingenuous use of police resources, I turned down the offer. To a certain extent, my stance blotted my career since I was left to run Crawley Police Station when much of the force was engaged in the miners' debacle. I then requested a transfer to the south coast to be closer to my ailing parents who still had the farm, but this was refused even though there were many positions I could easily have filled with the experience that I had. This, together with disillusionment about the shift of policing from service to force, caused me to leave the service.

Secret societies

During my time in the police, I became aware of a not talked-about element, particularly in the higher ranks of the police service that was loosely spoken of as being connected with the Masons. No precise details were available so my knowledge is pretty vague really.

I can remember the fuss made when a local Masonic lodge was broken into and the standard procedure of the bobbies, including myself, changed. Our duty was to check the premises but the patrol inspector ushered us all from the building before a full search had been made. What did they not want us to see? The idea and existence of a secret society within the police is one which has been widely discussed and some say that the black and white checkerboard design on police uniform is a sign of this. Exactly how it might work was beyond my pay grade so who knows what was at play here.

Immunity from investigation and prosecution

I also noticed during and after my police career that certain well-connected individuals seemed to be immune from investigation and prosecution. A number of incidents of child sexual abuse and serial ritual abuse were reported to me and in all of these, in spite of compelling first-hand evidence (not hearsay), much of which I saw, no proper investigations took place. I called this out on one occasion but I was unknowingly being filmed and the film was posted to YouTube. It attracted over 80,000 views in four days and I was visited by two police officers who warned me not to say anything more about this situation. As for the mothers of the children involved, they have frequently been attacked by the social services and police system and labelled 'psychiatric cases', often being sectioned. I have met some of these mothers and they have told me how bogus narratives have been built against them.

Structural Changes in the Police

The police structure when I first joined was overseen by the Police Authority which was made up of local elected representatives. The Police Authority had a hand in appointing the Chief Constable, and met regularly with him or her to decide on policy for the locality. Whilst there was a central link with the Home Office, it was not the top-down centralised control that we see today.

In 1968 a series of amalgamations started which brought about a centralisation of the provincial constabularies. The name 'constabulary' was dropped, and the word 'force' was introduced instead. The word 'constabulary' indicated service; 'force' needs no explanation! When I joined East Sussex Constabulary there were five independent constabularies covering Sussex – East and West Sussex and the boroughs of Brighton, Eastbourne and Hastings and the service provided by these independent organisations was far superior in the sense of being more efficient and more locally accountable than that is the current Sussex Police. This change was introduced under the guise of affordability and efficiency and was mirrored around the country. Now, it can be clearly seen what a retrogressive step this was.

Centralisation

Amalgamations diminished the service, but created an easier form of centralised control. The number of police personnel involved in front-line services was considerably reduced and policing methods such as Unit Beat Policing (UBP) were abandoned, even though they had been the most effective ever used. Indeed, crime rates with UBP were at an all-time low, and the detection rate had never been bettered. Under this system, the number of bobbies on the beat and active support staff was directly in proportion to the number of people in the community.

In some areas, virtually no crimes remained but now, despite the claims of greater efficiency, crime rates soared and we saw the early stages of civil unrest. Cooperation between the police and the public diminished substantially.

It was during that period that local accountability appeared to disappear, with centralisation enabling the few to exert greater control, and facilitating the manipulation of money.

When one is aware of how money is created and how shortages of funding can be contrived, then it is clear that centralisation and restricted funding may have been planned all along. This whole question of funding, to my mind, needs greater exploration with the key question being where money comes from. One answer was offered in the film by Bill Still, *The Secret of Oz,* which puts forth the view that a private cartel of wealthy people has controlled the printing and supply of money in the Western world, using war, subterfuge, murder and deceit. The film explains that the methods employed included the assassination of four US presidents who had retained their grip on the issuing and withdrawal of money. The 1929 slump that my grandparents were victims of, and the inflation that accompanied that, causing devaluation in real terms, were engineered by this private Western centralised banking cartel. Who knows if this is true but it certainly got me thinking.

I attended a ground-breaking conference as a speaker and participant at Findhorn, the oldest intentional spiritual/eco community in Scotland. I was sharing a platform with Robert David Steele who spoke of the need for the open sourcing of all our societies' structures for a transparent accountability. He said that secrets are convoluted and that their purpose is to keep us in the dark. Here I am reminded of JFK's statement prior to his assassination that secret societies are repugnant, and he referred to the cult that controls the Western world's finance. Also attending were 400 thought leaders from all over the planet, including seventy indigenous leaders, Polly Higgins and Jonathan Porritt. This could be the people's government of the future, rooted in local not central representation.

Successful policing in the future

I referred earlier to the previous system called 'Unit Beat Policing (UBP) in which the strength of a constabulary was determined by the number of people living in an area. In positive, people-centric, service policing; a *per-capita* number of cops is necessary and the figures for the *per capita* ratio of active police on the beat were decided upon in the 1960s. Unfortunately, they were only adhered to for a short while. Why do I say 'unfortunately'? Well, the remit of the old-fashioned beat bobby was perfectly in line with the original oath of the bobby which was really based on prevention of crime, support and service, protection of life and property, and prevention of breaches of the peace. This sits with the common-law ethos of 'cause no harm', 'cause no loss' and 'cause no injury'.

The local bobby as the friend of the local community, performing a service backed by sufficient mobile units, detectives and collators of intelligence, formed the basis of that successful UBP system.

My Journey in Questioning What Is Really Going On

DAVID ADELMAN

David Adelman is the author of the book School: No Place for Children *and founder of The People's Lawyer website. He runs courses teaching people to know their rights and stand in their power!*

My first taste of the system

From an early age I was aware that something was wrong with the system. At the age of about seven I was transferred from one school to another because I wanted things to move more quickly than the first school was prepared to allow. At the second school I made friends with a boy called Brian. This changed my life. Instead of studying hard and getting myself a reputation for being unteachable, I entered a whole new exciting phase of clowning about and being outrageously non-compliant. Brian was funny and crazy – just what the doctor ordered to make life fun and exciting. Together we had such a good time in year 4 that we both ended up bottom of our class by the end of that school year.

In my first taste of sinister top-down tyranny, it was decided behind closed doors that we would be separated, and we were put in different classes for the start of the next academic year. This was a devastatingly low blow. The bubble of excitement was well and truly burst. My strategy to get back at the system was to put my head down and excel. I succeeded in my objective, but this success came at quite a cost: no more clowning around, inordinate amounts of homework when I reached secondary school, and a gradual descent into the black hole of conformity.

My second taste of the system

Toeing the line did have some rewards. It got me to a top university to study law and, ultimately, a job in a law firm in London. I was – or so I thought – now on an upwards trajectory towards a glittering prize. What kind of prize no one ever spoke about. It was an unwritten social norm that you just put your head down and made worldly progress. About three months into the job as a trainee lawyer (or solicitor, as we call them in the UK) I found myself in trouble again with 'authority'. I was contracted to start work at 9.30 a.m., but one day came in at 9.35 a.m. This led to my boss writing to me accusing me of all kinds of things, including a warning that such lateness would not be tolerated. Personally, I struggled to comprehend how being five minutes late could be seen as such a subversive act. I was actually being paid a pittance, which further fuelled my bemusement and resentment. Once again, for the sake of harmony, and as I was a long way from home, I put my head down and made sure that my time of arrival at work complied with the terms of my contract. But a voice inside my head was telling me that the journey ahead was going to be a bumpy one.

My third taste of system

After several more months at the law firm in London, too much compliance was now taking its toll. I had developed symptoms (chronic pain) that led me to a doctor's surgery. After listening for several minutes (or was it seconds?) to my story, the doctor offered me a prescription to 'alleviate the pain'. No investigation was carried out into my stress levels, and I was given no advice about how to manage those levels of stress, or indeed what lifestyle choices needed looking at in order for me to take back control of my health. He simply offered me a prescription for a drug to ease the pain of colitis from irritable bowel syndrome. His attitude was dogmatic and uncompromising. When I asked him how long I should take the medication for, he muttered something about taking it indefinitely. I was twenty-three years old! In otherwise perfect health! What did I need medication for – especially long-term medication? I smelt a rat immediately and resolved to do two things: (a) make radical changes to my diet and (b) never go back to see a medical doctor. I achieved both.

My fourth taste of the system

Fast-forward twenty years. Having quit the law in my twenties and gone to Spain to teach English as a foreign language, I had returned to the UK when I felt that I could go no further or higher as a foreigner. I was now teaching a simplified card game based on bridge, known as minibridge. I was funded to go around English schools teaching mainly eight-to-eleven-year-olds the fundamental skills required to play the game coherently. I received funding to use the game as a tool to assist with the delivery of maths and counting skills. But, prompted by a perplexed teacher, I soon realised that there is only enough counting in minibridge to justify two lessons at most.

Meanwhile, a school in Leeds has started using minibridge sessions for its Social and Emotional Aspects of Learning (SEAL) curriculum. This is genius! The game is a team game (played two against two) and in the course of the game children necessarily, without even realising it, acquire all kinds of both thinking and social skills. Without these skills the game cannot be played effectively. Minibridge provides a micro-environment in which children can be themselves and grow in personal and social confidence. I proposed to my funding association that we should adopt this model, adapting the process of introducing the game and how it was promoted. I was excited about offering to boys and girls something that could clearly benefit them as individuals. My initial request was ignored. I then went on to write a detailed report on how much minibridge could benefit pupils. Again, this was ignored. It was not long before I found myself defunded and out of work.

It was not all bad news. Being made redundant and harbouring a serious grudge against decision-makers for their obvious lack of humanity, I now had time to write a book based on my schooling experiences. That book was published first as an e-book in 2015, then as a paperback in 2018. The title says it all: *School: No Place for Children*.

My fifth taste of the system

Having been defunded, I was now faced with the dilemma of how to survive in an urban environment without an income stream. This led me, apart from writing and publishing the book, to reignite my interest in law. This time, instead of being led by systemic, conventional approaches to law, I followed a trail of dynamic resources, documents and videos, and found that the law is not what we have been led to believe it is. In fact, taking my research further, I soon found that *nothing* is how we have been told it is. This seed was first planted in 2001, when the Twin Towers plus Building 7 (in other words, three buildings) were allegedly brought down by two aeroplanes – a physical impossibility. In addition, we were told that jet fuel, which burns at about 800 degrees, can melt reinforced steel designed to withstand temperatures of over 2000 degrees – another impossibility. I therefore have a healthy distrust of mainstream narrative upon which to build.

In my research, I discovered that we are only obliged by either a contract or our consent. This means that utility bills, for example, are not meant to be paid other than by voluntary contribution. I therefore stopped paying for gas and electricity because I needed to road-test my knowledge and could not afford to pay the bills anyway. Sure enough, the utility companies went through their paces and started threatening me with disconnection and the instalment of prepayment meters for both gas and electricity. After months of study I discovered that there is no such thing as disconnecting a property used as an abode by living men and women. That could have serious consequences, so that the utility companies do not even attempt it. But they use the threat of it as part of their fearmongering. I also found out that putting in prepayment meters requires the written consent of the consumer, customer or account holder. I witnessed first-hand how they pretend that they will obtain a summons under the Gas Acts. Upon digging deeper, I found that the Gas Acts only allow for entry in a gas-leak emergency. I could see a way to stop them by just using paperwork and/or attending their fake hearing in a privately hired room at a magistrates' court.

What I in fact decided to do was let the process unfold and wait for them to attend. Sure enough, the gas agents came with a locksmith and two police officers. By now I had done even more research and learnt that police have no business attending a debt enforcement visit. They cannot do so without risking up to fourteen years in prison under the Criminal Justice and Courts Act 2015. I asked the police, from behind a closed and locked front door, whether they were aware of the law in the form of the Criminal Justice and Courts Act 2015, section 26, regarding abuse of position by constables. When they said that they were not, I read it out to them and within seconds they were gone, muttering that this was a civil matter anyway. Without the police to intimidate the poor householder, the gas agents soon lose heart and withdraw.

My sixth taste of the system

I was now feverishly starting to join the dots across the full spectrum of education, law and health. My book was gaining notoriety and in July 2019 I was invited to be the keynote speaker at the Glastonbury Symposium – a forum for researchers, authors and speakers with an alternative view. The success of that talk potentially made me a putative 'People's Educator', blowing the whistle, just like John Taylor Gatto did before me in the US, on a chronically and dangerously dysfunctional schooling system. I therefore considered a nationwide tour in the following year (2020) to help boost book sales and get an increasingly urgent message out there.

Then along came an alleged pandemic of an alleged contagious disease and we went into an alleged lockdown. I use the word *alleged* simply because I have never seen evidence of a real pandemic with the kind of excess mortality one would expect. Nor, it now transpires, has *anyone* ever seen real-world evidence of an isolated pathogenic virus that transmits from one human to another. This is the gift of covid: it is waking up the already awake to whole new levels. So, if there is no pandemic and no virus, what on earth is going on? The answer: fear porn and mass virtue signalling fuelled by a globalist agenda. Virtue signalling on a scale never before seen made the lockdown more of a neighbourhood-watch scheme on steroids than an authentic incarceration enforced by state agents. Covid is turning out to be the gift that keeps on giving. Some of us were now out on the streets, sounding a rallying call for others to join us as we spread some truth and common sense. I was mainly on the streets in Manchester in the second quarter of 2020. Then, as 2020 progressed, I found myself travelling further afield to spread the gospel wider.

Most people in the streets were not exactly supportive. The least troublesome responses were pulling strange faces, making rude gestures and walking away. Other responses were far more confrontational and potentially violent. The people whose minds had been captured by their culture, education and the media reacted negatively to any opinion or posture that contravened accepted dogma.

On November 20 of this same year, I found myself on the promenade at Morecambe in Lancashire, addressing a crowd of about 150 who had assembled to hear speakers like me update them on actual events and their probable explanations. No one knew that I would be there, and the invitation to speak was a surprise to me.

As I took the microphone, I heard myself say, 'Hi, everyone. Some of you may know me; some may not. But my name is ...'

And I hesitated. There were police in attendance, and I did not want to give them a free lunch. We were in 'tier-4 lockdown', and gatherings of over thirty were banned by the regulations in force at the time.

I found myself continuing: 'I am the People's Lawyer.'

I do not know where that came from, but it felt right and has stuck. As soon as we finished our speeches, the three main speakers were all arrested in differing ways with different outcomes. I was merely detained without formal paperwork, put in the back of a van and transported to the local police station in Morecambe. I was released as soon as I gave them what they wanted: a name and address. I knew enough to know that I did not have to give them that information, but I was keen to re-join the battle and get back out on the promenade.

My response to the system

Circumstances are now such that I am combining the two worlds of law and education. I go around the country upgrading people's notion of who they really are at law, how government is simply mind control by another name, and how we can change everything by awakening to the lies that have been visited upon us and the damage that this has caused.

I emphasise that statutory law is not law. Real law is natural or divine, universal law. A man or woman, subject to natural law as creations of the Divine, are only subject to man-made legislation with their consent or via a contract. I use live in-person talks, live videos and pre-recorded presentations via my website (www.thepeopleslawyeruk.com) to consolidate the educational aspects. These events and resources are offered free of charge to all those interested. For those wishing to take their lawful knowledge and competence to another level, I also run an online privacy and universal-rights course, for which there is a fee, and which sustains me through the current crisis.

The most startling information I divulge (and I hasten to add that I am by no means the only one doing this) is that taxation is voluntary. Income tax, council tax and utility bills, for example, are only paid by the sleeping masses who genuinely believe that it is the right thing to do and that they are obliged to do it anyway. But for those who dare to accept another way of looking at things, all the corporations that make demands and threats are in fact committing fraud upon the people by not disclosing that they require our consent or a contract with us.

The matrix is imploding. The safest exit strategy is to turn blind, fearful and ignorant compliance into a knowing, peaceful and confident non-compliance. When we withdraw our time and energy from the narcissistic system, which has no life force of its own, it collapses, and we regain our beloved freedoms. The war on humanity continues with threats of catastrophic weather patterns, global power outages and mass food shortages. Information alone will not save us, but it is an essential starting point and helps bring us together with unity and a common purpose. This is what will save us from a 'smart' life in 'smart' cities with our young ones captured inside the metaverse.

Freeing families from the threat of criminalising home education is my latest emergency remit. This also represents the fusion of education and law. One of our most pressing needs is to ensure that children are removed from school and kept away from danger. This is all about the future, therefore all about the children. Hyper-sexualisation of children aged four and over, gender confusion and re-identification in the classroom, or indeed toxic injections and school lockdowns, will not be allowed on my watch. I have come too far to let this happen.

Journey of an Academic Turned Activist

CHAD MANIAN

Chad Manian is an author, human-rights activist, interdisciplinary research scholar and lecturer specialising in sovereignty, alternate social justice based on common law & equity, community assembly and behavioural futurism. A former trader and finance strategist, he was among the first to predict the financial collapse of 2008.

In 2019 I was working as a lecturer, teaching strategic operations on an economic management programme to health-care students at a university in Berlin. At that point I had devoted myself to academic work following the fast-paced life of a market commentator in financial markets. Prior to that I had worked on the trading floors and at an analyst desk, and had a short spell researching trends for fund managers.

When the pandemic began I was watching with shock and disbelief as the world took a breath before deciding on what looked like a carefully organised response. Having worked closely with lawyers, medical professionals and leading-edge policy-level decision makers, I was no stranger to broad strategic decisions that would have wide consequences.

I had after all been one of the few that predicted the collapse of 2008 a year before it happened. Watching the news about the pandemic from my Berlin campus surrounded by students, I felt that something did not seem right – the decision-making process which ordered the lockdown seemed on one hand to be too knee-jerk reactive while on the other hand seeming carefully orchestrated.

Pandemic

I left my office and after a final drink with my colleagues took the first flight back to London, which turned out to be the last flight back before quarantine.

I returned to London and thus began my journey. As an academic I still had responsibilities, which would now include online teaching and remote dissertation supervision. My medical health-care students had been deployed to work in front-line covid wards and were voicing their concerns with the ground-level management.

I thought this might be unique to the German medical system, but I found an identical approach back in the UK. My friends who were doctors, nurses and consultants expressed the same discontent with what can only be described as overreaction and excessive overreach in both policy and ground-level operations.

Whether in respect of the utterly ill-considered mask mandates or the notably tyrannical vaccine mandates, there was a widespread outcry among health professionals.

I worked with some of the finest epidemiologists, health-care policy researchers and medical statisticians who were out on the streets protesting against government policies. I found that I could not stay silent when my friends were making a stand.

An exercise in defiance

The first protest I ever went to was in Hyde Park – Speakers' Corner – where qualified medical experts were speaking. Several were my friends that I came to support, and several were arrested for what seemed to be spurious reasons. Surely arresting protesters for speaking at Speakers' Corner defies a thousand years of English history and a long-standing tradition of democracy and free speech.

If there were medical reasons for not gathering in large numbers, how was it that no policeman or politician was arrested? Why was no other person arrested for gathering in a crowd?

This seemed really odd to me – almost like a deliberate attempt to silence any voice of dissent. My shock at witnessing this unlawful and borderline-tyrannical behaviour by the police led me to raise complaints along with a handful of activists – including a future candidate for London mayor, who agreed with me that this was totally unjustified and unreasonable.

We wrote to the government and the police, outlining and evidencing our concerns, and requesting a public enquiry to clarify the law and the reason for such actions. Our communication was met with a ridiculous political rebuff that dismissed our concerns using a tone that was both acerbic and condescending.

Tiananmen Square of Britain

Not content, we continued to engage with authorities such as the Mayor's Office as well as chief constables, and we continued to call for greater accountability from the authorities. This led me to attend a peaceful rally of at least 50,000 people in Trafalgar Square on 26 September 2020, protesting against the extension of the Coronavirus Act in the UK. It followed the tradition of other peaceful protests, such as the historic one against the Iraq War on 15 February 2003, which, according to the BBC, was attended by over one million people.

The 2020 protest was attended by people of all ages – children, young adults and older people – and the entire square was filled with people. An array of speakers spoke out clearly against what was beginning to fester into a tyranny, but the mainstream media put out a completely incoherent narrative which sounded more like a government echo chamber. There was little evidence of independent or fair reporting. Worse even than that is the fact that there was a completely uncalled-for and unnecessarily violent attack by the police against those who were peacefully gathering together. Several vulnerable women were brutally attacked by the Territorial Support Group, a special unit of the London Metropolitan Police.

I watched in disbelief as the police moved in and brutally charged into the peaceful crowd and as Trafalgar Square turned into Tiananmen Square. Never before had I seen such horror and violence in a civilised Western democracy. That day presented me with a choice: go home and conform, or defy and rise.

Activism and the hidden law

I had been a human-rights activist my whole life. I did not know how to comply with any system that was corrupt and was never one to back down from a fight. Old habits die hard. After attending the protest in Trafalgar Square, I had to give a voice to my defiance; and having worked in an intellectual role in academia, I found that I could fall back on my background to start fighting back.

I began to look into the legal and political system since I had done a lot of work on corporate governance in the past. What is more, I had also worked as a paralegal in my younger days, so I had that to draw on as well.

Having worked with lawyers, I was able to look into the source of law and was able also to have many deep discussions with some of the most astute legal minds in the land. From this I discovered many interesting facts and problems concerning the legal framework; and in fact, the more meetings, rallies and gatherings I went to, the more information I found on common law.

My investigations led me to discover a great disparity between the idea of law and constitution and the harsh reality of the legal process. I found very little consistency between the philosophy of historical common law and the practical application of statutory law.

Common law, Magna Carta: myths and reality

In the two years since the outset of the pandemic I had encountered numerous individuals advocating many forms of resistance and protest using the common law. While many of these arguments were compelling and based in truth, there were numerous logical errors and problems in terms of modern-day practicalities that made them flawed. Moreover, there was an emotionally driven almost religious fervour to people's ideas that led me to take a critical view of the ideas people in the protest movement were suggesting. At this point no one had arrived at a tried-and-tested method.

Many were advocating using the Magna Carta to avoid arrests as well as modern challenges such as bills, fines, fees and council tax. I found these views to be dangerously absurd and lacking in realism and started to battle-test some of my own interpretations in the modern-day Colosseum of the courts.

I attended many court cases to assist friends and acquaintances in their legal challenges and discovered that my research, reasoning and oral skills were equal to those of any legal professional. Soon I found a way to win cases in court – or at least assist others by representing them. I won case after case.

I found a new pastime that had the benefit of helping innocent victims find their voice and free themselves from unlawful prosecution. This gave me a way to fight against injustice and tyranny. It also helped me gain valuable insights into the workings of the court system, which has an intricate and fascinating side to it.

Courts, tribunals and justice for sale

The courts, like all large corporate institutions, suffer from a range of challenges – from lack of funding and inadequate staffing to lack of accountability.

I came across many excellent and learned judges as well as honourable legal professionals who inspired both respect and my admiration. At the same time, however, I came across many who had very little knowledge of the law and were comfortable simply reading a script or following a computer algorithm with information on what to do. This saddens me as I was witness to numerous miscarriages of justice as well as unlawful abuses of power by robed bigots in wigs.

My experiences in the courts also highlighted the dangers of an opaque, unaccountable legal system that was intoxicated by power and control. This led me to examine the history of the law, which in turn led me down a further rabbit hole.

Every single case I helped or participated in held valuable insights into the judicial process. I found that in some cases judges relied heavily on legal precedent and obscure statutory principles that would mean the difference between freedom and a sentence.

In time I came to realise that cases that had no need or basis ended up in court because of one single factor: profit. The financial interests involved in the court system have gone unnoticed by the public even though they constitute a massive commercial industry.

Following the money and the science

The legal system today is a multimillion-pound sector with colossal financial interests. Where once it was built to serve justice, it is now a commercially driven industry which like all economic ventures exists to make a profit. There is very little care or humanity and no trace of compassion in this profit-oriented, cold, mechanical conveyor-belt system of law courts.

I now consider that the modern court system is focused on churning out verdicts rather than on seeking the truth or questing for justice. The singular outcome in a vast number of covid-related cases appeared to be fines and legal-cost recovery, often achieved through unjust means. The outcomes appeared to be commercially driven, with profit driving criminal elements to proceedings.

This is one of the most heartbreaking facets of the modern legal system. What I witnessed led me to believe that when law stops serving justice it turns into a system of legal entrapment in which people's actions are criminalised and monetised. Follow the money and you will find the link that completes the chain.

Reflections

Important lessons that I learned from this pandemic through my activism both in and out of courts can be summed up in the following conclusions:

Think calmly and critically about what you are being told, regardless of the source of information.

Never make a decision in haste without considering all possible options and explanation of alternatives.

Never yield to pressure of any sort, no matter what the personal cost.

Do not believe and follow anything or anyone blindly without doing your own due diligence.

They who seek truth must be prepared to confront the bodyguard of lies.

Simple solutions

Upon reflection it became clear that the way forward would entail a complete rethinking of the paradigm of modern justice. We will need to rebuild the system from the grass-root level. The old paradigm of law is based on an adversarial model which is drawn from a medieval right of contest in which the two sides would nominate knights to fight to the death to establish a right of claim. This approach evolved into the modern court system of two lawyers representing their sides.

As we progress and evolve as a human society, our justice system must also evolve and facilitate our progress. My reflections led me to consider the following solutions:

- We need to transition from the adversarial towards a more enlightened approach based on an open reconciliatory system. A true justice system must seek to restore and give remedy, rather than try and punish.
- The justice system will also need to be led by the people rather than by corporate officials. A simple solution would be to de-corporatise the law and make it accessible to the common man.
- We must simplify the procedure and the language. Trials should be held in simple plain English that is spoken in everyday parlance.
- Complex rules that are obsolete and outdated should be removed. Procedures that do not aid efficiency or clarity should be dropped.
- We must bring back trial by jury. In a true democracy the people have the power, and the people should make the law through a trial including twelve men/women of conscience and reason.
- All rules, acts and statutes that cause infringement of our rights should be thrown out. 'Legislation harmful to living man, be no law at all' – as quoted by Lord Denning, one of the greatest judges in our history.

A more honourable legal system would return the duty of dispensing justice back to the public. Upstanding members of the community would take back this duty and hold public hearings which would be convened to determine the truth rather than a system in which verdicts are swayed by the most persuasive performer. A functioning equitable justice system would be built on trial by jury, where twelve men/women of reasonable mind, drawn from the community, would decide a matter upon considering all sides.

In closing, it is worth considering the words of Lord Denning, who once said, 'The law is a shield, not a sword.' The great tragedy of our present legal system lies in it being used as a weapon of oppression rather than as a protection against injustice. Perhaps the time has come to restore our rights and rebuild the system from the ground up.

The Final Triggers in the Revelation of Masterful Deception

JAMES HUNT

Now aged sixty-four, James Hunt has been a business lawyer for forty years. He trained in the City of London, founded two law firms and now specialises in helping business owners sell their companies.

Background

I had the great good fortune to be trained by a brilliant and very honest lawyer in the City of London. His name was Jeremy Brownlow. He loved enterprise and entrepreneurs and he was a gifted teacher and rose to the top of his profession.

On jobs on which we worked, Jeremy would say that we needed to 'get to the nub of the problem' – the crux or the central point of any issue. So what do I now see as the nub of the problem in our dysfunctional society?

Moral responsibility

I have always felt that moral decisions are the most difficult and most important for each of us individually and collectively.

My business, Everyman Advisory Limited, takes its name from the *Everyman* fourteenth-century morality play, which tells the story of the journey of an Everyman through his life. When the time comes for him to meet his Maker there is only one person who will speak for him: the Good Deeds

Messenger. This is a profound thought for all of us as we try, day by day, to do what we think is right.

Over the last two years I have come to realise that most of us, most of the time, do not want to have to worry about the morality of what we do. We choose to abdicate difficult moral decisions to others – 'those who know better' or 'the powers that be', as we hear people call the decision-makers.

But presumably we have responsibility to carefully choose those to whom we are going to place the burden of decision-making of the most difficult moral kind. Here is where we see masterful self-deception at play.

Masterful moral self-deception

As I write this article we have just witnessed ten days of mourning for the death of Queen Elizabeth II. I would argue that all critical-thinking men and women, whether royalist or republican, capitalist or socialist, should find our worship of the Queen (following her death) deeply troubling. This worship reveals the most masterful moral self-deception at play.

The media and our political and spiritual leaders have told us for ten days that the Queen was a deeply moral person. Her morality, we are told, is evident from her devotion to duty. We are told that for seventy years she selflessly served the nation and the Commonwealth and was a beacon of virtue because of that service, which, we are told, was down to her faith.

By worshiping the Queen, who is proclaimed by the Establishment to be deeply virtuous, we evidently proclaim our own virtue reflected in her glory.

If it is true that the Queen was deeply moral, we might think there would have been some very profound questions with which she had to grapple during her reign – questions of which we might be aware – particularly as she is the head of the Church of England. This is not so, it transpires, if those issues may be thought of as political: the monarch by convention is supposed to stay silent on such matters.

This means perhaps (but see below regarding the invocation of Magna Carta) that those who are against the monarchy are left to criticise only personal decisions and family morality. Those who are anti-royalist have decried the adultery of the man now King and his friendship with a sexual predator and the actions of the son accused of sexual misconduct towards a minor. But that is not down to the Queen, we are told. She was simply a loving mother. Indeed, standing by her family (no matter that they have sinned) is but part of her morality.

Vacuous circularity in the moral maze

We see then in this structure of the constitutional monarchy how deceit is perfected.

The monarch is worshipped because of her morality, which is assumed from her service and her silent rectitude. But the delivery of the service of the state is down to the politicians who by common account have no virtue and work in a system where psychopaths rise to the top.

We the nation, working through the media and our political and spiritual leaders, were Queen Elizabeth's Good Deeds Messenger in September 2022. It seems we found her to have served us in exemplary fashion over the last seventy years.

As we see a country in deep trouble health-wise, economically, socially and spiritually, is that really our decision regarding ourselves? No, of course not. It is our verdict on Her Late Majesty. It would indeed be an outrage to expect one person, however noble and wise, to accept responsibility for the tragic situation in which the country and the world now finds itself.

So the monarch is purely symbolic, we must conclude. But if so, why the ten days of pomp and circumstance? Here we get to the nub of the matter.

The nub of the problem: undue deference to authority

It is now evident to me that from the day we are born to the day we die we are socially conditioned to be unduly deferential to those in authority. To show deference sounds very gentle and almost inconsequential. But as we have learned over the past two years, when there are profound moral and ethical decisions that must be made there cannot be deference to others.

Why did the police on duty at Number 10 stand idly by as drink for parties was taken through the security gates in flagrant breach of lockdown regulations solemnly made? For a very simply reason: it would not have been deferential to question what was happening.

The penny-dropping moment: the breaking of my deference spell

As I now reflect on the question of what really woke me I can say the penny-dropping moment came at 10.45 a.m. on Friday 10 June 2022. I was in the car driving to see a new friend who lives in the Peak District, and it was the end of a BBC Radio 4 programme that had been broadcast across eight radio channels in the country.

Prince William and his wife, Kate, now the Prince and Princess of Wales, were taking to the radio waves. It was Mental Health Awareness Week and this most virtuous and moral couple were 'doing their duty to the nation'. We were encouraged to go out and meet those who might be suffering because of lockdown. As the fifteen-minute double act finished, the unctuous BBC reporter cooed how wonderful it was that the Royal Family were 'now giving us permission' to reach out and help others.

Where was the moral leadership as we went into lockdown? I asked myself. The week before I had been at an event in the company of a friend by the name of Gary. He had told us that two of his friends committed suicide within three months of lockdown.

The profound mental-health crisis cannot have come as a surprise to anyone who cared to exercise their moral-thinking capacity. A decision had been deliberately made to kill thousands of people in the belief that overall (let us be charitable) other lives would be saved. Where were the moral crusaders back in March 2020? Where were those now occupying the highest role in the Principality of Wales?

Not for them to question the decisions or the moral judgement of the UK Government around lockdown, the apologists would say. At that moment I saw the confected divide between William and Kate and 'money-and status-obsessed' Harry and Meghan – all part of the masterful deception of the soap opera that is the royal family. Our future King and Queen are just a 'classier' part of the same game of masterful deception.

I later recalled the Queen telling everyone it was our 'duty' to take the dangerous experimental drugs. Just an old woman in her nineties being told what to say, one might think if one was being generous to the memory of the late Queen of the World. If one was being an honest constitutionalist, one might have asked why she was interfering in political matters and not remaining neutral.

What though of William and Kate? Just an ignorant young man and young woman belatedly coming to the conclusion (like Rishi Sunak, the then failed prime-ministerial candidate) that there were moral judgements that needed to be made and should have been made differently back in March 2020? Perhaps. But is no one then to be accountable for the morality of our decision-making?

The journey to realisation

But that was when the final penny-dropping moment came.

It had not occurred to me back in early 2021, when I queued up to take the jab, that I needed to be wary of the motives and the honesty of the government, the NHS and the medical profession.

By June 2021 my son, Ben, who had been a zealot for lockdown, unlike his libertarian father, began to have suspicions about the experimental drugs deceitfully promoted as vaccines by the middle of 2021. He alerted me to his concerns.

As a lover of the poetry of the Bard of Avon, he had become convinced that the sublime plays could not have been written by Shakespeare. The De Vere Society, of which he is a member, is dedicated to the belief that the plays were written by Edward de Vere, the Earl of Oxford, Queen Elizabeth I's favourite courtier. If that fact could be so cleverly hidden, what else might the Establishment be capable of? was his thinking.

After six weeks of research I was convinced that the PCR tests were a fraudulent WHO-engineered deceit and that the experimental drugs were very much neither safe nor effective. As I began to suffer from a heavy cold I decided to take a visit to my GP's surgery to get a prescription for the drug ivermectin. If my immune system was compromised, it sounded like this would be a good thing to have in stock.

My deference to the authority of the medical profession made the challenge a very uncomfortable one for me. I was soon, though, amazed at the profound ignorance of my GP's surgery in Chipping Campden. I went to see them just as the vaccines were being promoted in the schools, and at that time I was assured that the experimental drugs were fully approved and not emergency-use authorised.

After pressing my case for ivermectin, the GP's surgery sent a mental-health team to my home. If I would not defer I must be mentally unbalanced was their (convenient) conclusion. It was a shocking betrayal of their duty as doctors. The ignorance and bullying of the doctors was the subject of a complaint by me to the General Medical Council (GMC). The astonishing conclusion of the GMC was that a GP could not be expected to know the regulatory status of the drugs they administer.

Deference to authority (that of the government) evidently meant that this regulator was blind to their very purpose: that the doctors they regulate should first do no harm and then should follow the requirements of the Nuremberg Code, 1947, as to the informed consent of patients to medical procedures.

The coming mortal moral danger

The moral authority of our monarchy has been proclaimed throughout the world during September 2022. Those who have seen the way King Charles (as the Prince of Wales) promoted the Great Reset proposed by the World Economic Forum (WEF) will sense the danger that lies ahead.

The conflating by the WEF of the terrible ecological crisis with the phony climate-change crisis is now our individual moral test. That we are despoiling Mother Earth is not in doubt. That the Earth is not heating up is also not in doubt for those who care to apply critical questioning. It may also be noted that if the regeneration of our soil becomes the priority we would sequester an enormous quantity of carbon – so why the bonkers net-carbon-zero policy? the innocent may ask.

We see the ground being prepared for King Charles III to be anointed World Climate King and the Eco-King of Planet Earth. Charles, we may assume, will quickly lose popularity. As the world descends into dystopia due to net-zero-carbon madness, the real danger (we may then expect) will be the enthronement of the future King William – a very virtuous eco-warrior.

Deferring to that first son of the troubled marriage of Charles and Diana will assuredly put Western civilisation in mortal danger. It is time for us to wake up to our self-delusion that we can delegate moral authority and agency to others. Could it be that the answer lies in Magna Carta?

In 1215 England faced the tyranny of King John. His deceit and corruption was challenged by the barons, and the Magna Carta, one of the most famous documents in the world, was signed.

That document included at Article 61 a procedure under which the barons could declare a lawful rebellion against a sovereign who was behaving improperly. In March 2001 that procedure was invoked as the Blair government put forward legislation whose purpose was to give sovereign power away to the EU – see Barons Invoke Article 61 – Using Article 61 Today (article61pld.com). The Queen, acting through her Privy Council, failed to answer the charge of treason.

Time soon for the people to reject the masterful deception of King Charles III on climate change as he seeks to give away lawful authority to the WEF. A monarch who would promote that unelected organisation, which cares nothing for democracy and believes in transhumanism (man above God), must be challenged under Magna Carta. With no scientific consensus on climate change, how can it not be political, and therefore a breach of convention, for Charles to support the WEF's net-zero-carbon Great Reset?

With a future William V also a committed believer in the net-zero-carbon agenda, a terrible constitutional crisis may soon be upon us. Back in 1688 another William was ushered on to the throne from overseas in what the history books tell us was a Glorious Revolution. What is clear is that we are currently subject to a *glorious deception*, with our unaccountable monarchy able to exert enormous influence on behalf of the globalists.

The barons made the deceptive John answerable to his peers under the common law of England. For those wanting to know how the common law could serve the people, the reader is advised to look at this link: New Chartist Movement, 'The Occulted Powers of the British Constitution'. Perhaps this will inspire their own journey in freeing themselves from the shackles imposed by undue deference and becoming autonomous self-determining beings.

The Solution

If undue deference to authority is the nub of the problem, the solution is amazingly simple: each of us must become critical thinkers with moral decision-making at the very heart of our identities.

Undue deference is driven by fear. We fear, at the subconscious level, being excluded from the tribe. In the past that would have meant almost certain death. It is that terrible fear of exclusion that results in the atrocities of which mankind is capable. We strive to conform, and the greatest conformity is being part of a community that defers to the hierarchy.

We must become more personally resilient, prepared to take moral personal stands and be loving in all that we do. The starting place for this must be a profound reconnection with nature and a love of Mother Earth. At the core of this New World must be communities of sovereign men and women who have the self-confidence to do what they feel is right.

By accepting the unfathomable mysteries of nature, we connect with the deepest sense of ourselves.

Food, farming and education must be re-imagined on a small local scale. 'Small is beautiful' needs to be our mantra at the same time as we embrace collaboration with others on a regional, national and international basis.

Growing sovereign is the answer for each of us as we chuckle and giggle at the current silly world of kings and queens, princes and princesses beloved of Republicans and Democrats. The 'powers that be' must be each of us. It is up to us, not *them*, to take responsibility for all the important decision-making.

HEALTH

A Health Journey

KATHERINE ARMITAGE

I practice homeopathy and I ran an alternative yoga/detox retreat centre, Cranleigh House Wellness Centre, for ten years in Combe Martin, Devon. Before that I trained and worked as an artist and textile designer. I like to think deeply about the problems we face in our world and find spiritual, mental, emotional and physical solutions that we can implement on a small and large scale.

Early encounters with ill health

The journey that brought me to working with health and well-being was mainly to do with my own health problems and the effect of watching my mother die slowly of cancer over forty years ago. This triggered me to question the traditional approaches to cancer involving radiotherapy and chemotherapy. In terms of my own health issues, these began when, a small child, I suffered from excruciatingly painful earache. It would have me screaming, and I would seek the comfort of my parents in the night although they could not help me and neither could our family doctor, Dr Peter. He would prescribe me countless antibiotics but none of them brought me any relief. Looking back, I remember being a lover of milk and this persisted right up into my teenage years. I was frequently sick with colds and suffered with a lot of mucus but it wasn't until much later that I discovered I was intolerant to dairy products. I no longer suffered with mucus after I finally gave them up.

At boarding school, I was allowed to order an extra fruit ration of an orange a day so even at that time, I was looking for natural solutions. I was also foraging, especially for mushrooms and chestnuts in the autumn.

When I was fifteen my mother was diagnosed with cancer. I adored my mother and I can still feel the pain now of her suffering. What followed subsequently was both strange and tragic since our lives went from being that of a happy family to a nightmare of Mum gradually dying over three years. My father was a very good-hearted man who never suffered big health problems and had no real understanding of how the body worked. He enjoyed good health to the very end of his life, playing regular tennis and loving his garden; so when my mother became ill he was entering into unknown territory; and our 'go to' person was one of my mother's cousins, who was a queen's physician.

My mother, who hadn't suffered bad health before, was as naive as my father and chose the chemo/radiotherapy route. She became weaker and weaker and eventually spent a lot of time at the Royal Free Hospital in London. My father would faithfully visit her every day after work in the City, and every weekend our family would drive up from Kent to visit her.

I remember that the first time I ever wore a mask and a protective suit was when we all visited her in the last stages of her illness. She was in an isolation tent and we were told to protect her from germs by not getting close to her. To me, this seemed bizarre to the point of being surreal and it filled me with horror. Years later, when we were told to wear masks for covid, I remembered this day and I did not wear a mask a single time during the alleged pandemic.

I knew Mum was going to die and I really could not contain my grief. I remember crying for an entire day almost without stopping as I was so incredibly sad to say goodbye to her. When she was young, my Mum was an actress in repertory, and she remained a performer and singer, influencing us as kids to have our own little theatre in our attic. Mum played Chopin pieces at night and sang songs as we were going to sleep.

Our house was full of fun, animals and friends. We had wonderful parties and games in a boat on our millpond and our childhood was filled with happy times. Our family holidays were spent bodyboarding on beautiful Devon beaches and we didn't really experience any real suffering until Mum died.

Suddenly, with other deaths in our family, the focus went from life to death, from fun to funerals. I was shaken and traumatised and I'm still now recovering. Even writing this account has brought back a lot of the pain. I had a 'nervous breakdown' at the age of twenty-one and spent three months in the Priory Hospital, Roehampton. I was given ECT treatments (electric-shock therapy), and I was told that I would need to take lithium, a mood stabiliser, for the rest of my life.

I recovered, staying with my great-aunt and -uncle, a naval surgeon. At this point, I was offered a job screen-printing textiles in the Caribbean and within six months was off the drugs. My therapy was determination, tennis and swimming. I have never been to see a psychiatrist since I knew, from my Mum's experience, that the drug route was not the one for me.

My health problems continue

Years went by and although my own health was still not that great it deteriorated rapidly when I got divorced and returned from France with my young son, aged three. I got a job at a nursery school in Fulham and I kept getting flu-like illnesses. I went to see a homeopath and a nutritionist, and I was diagnosed with IBS (irritable bowel syndrome) and ME (myalgic encephalomyelitis). At times I thought I was going to die but I was determined I was not going to share my mother's fate. I followed all sorts of self-prescribed exclusion diets and remember one that started with a strange combination of just lamb and pears and then added in other foods so that I could work out which ones I had a reaction to.

I became my own diagnostician, keeping food diaries and working out that I had a strong intolerance to sugar and mould. If I didn't wash nuts or seeds before eating them, I would, almost immediately, suffer from flu-like symptoms, which later I found to be called fibromyalgia – painful aching through all the muscles. Pain became my teacher. I was perplexed and depressed but I continued experimenting with my diet and also started to study homeopathy. This helped me a lot and I tried different remedies for different symptoms with some success. However, I was still sick.

Before I gave birth to my son in France in 1987, I had read an article in a magazine on homeopathy and allopathy. I decided that I would like to find a homeopathic doctor so I looked through the phone book, in the town of St-Raphaël, where we lived, and I found one – Dr Delmas. She had studied both homeopathy and acupuncture and she recommended that I should not vaccinate my newborn son. She was a wise mentor to me and I listened to her and allowed her to give him a dose of homeopathic

Tuberculinum before and after his BCG, and from then on he didn't have any vaccines since I listened to her reasoning.

Like me, my son also suffered with earache; so she helped him with potentised homeopathic remedies like Sulphur and Bryonia and he didn't have to endure the pain that I had as a child. She told me that if he had a fever, I should put him in a tepid bath if he had sickness or diarrhoea, I should put him on a short fast with just water and some homeopathic Arsenicum. What she suggested worked, and I built up some knowledge and a good collection of the Boiron homeopathic remedies, which were readily available in the French pharmacies. I was even provided with them on prescription, under the health-care system.

Studying homeopathy, on my return to England, was a natural progression; I was exposed to lots of new ideas, fascinating tutors and other people who were on their own healing journeys. We shared our strategies and successes and learnt from each other. Most of these people had abandoned allopathic/orthodox medicine, and many, like me, had had their health messed up by antibiotics. Their digestive systems no longer worked properly which led to numerous complaints such as irritable bowel syndrome, food intolerances, allergies or leaky-gut syndrome. Often these were accompanied by anxiety, depression and low energy, or all three.

Finding solutions, finally

My health improved with a better diet which in my case was a vegetarian one with no dairy and mainly vegan. I was always someone who took a lot of exercise and this helped my morale. When I met my partner, Stewart, in 2005, he introduced me to other health approaches. He'd cured himself of prostate problems with high-potency antioxidants and said that I needed a colloidal plant-derived mineral supplement. He gave me a large capful and I threw it up immediately. I tried again the next day and was sick again and from that point tried much smaller amounts. At that point I was fine and later learnt when we both studied naturopathy with our Body Electronics teacher, Peter Hinde, PhD, that I was sick because, like a dehydrated person who cannot take a full glass of water and has to sip from a sponge, I was so deficient in minerals that my body had to reject them. They were too much for me to assimilate – too rich. This is called a 'healing crisis' and I learnt that I was astonishingly deficient in minerals. We are electrical beings and actually need a full complement in our bodies and if we are deficient in minerals we cannot resonate energetically in the way that we should. A living person is like a great big battery full of water and minerals and we reflect this in our language when we say that we feel 'energised', 'charged up' or 'burnt out'.

A healing crisis is simply the body's way of balancing and throwing off toxins – for example, in the form of mucus. Orthodox medicine tries to suppress the healing crisis – for example, stopping diarrhoea with aptly named products like Arret and Imodium. Homeopathy and naturopathy work with the body's energy so that it can heal itself.

I have realised, in the course of doing research, that the NHS includes very powerful misinformation. For, they inform people that *'Diarrhoea* and vomiting are common in adults, children and babies. They're often caused by a stomach bug and should stop in a few days' going on to state that 'Diarrhoea and vomiting can spread easily.' In fact, most simple diarrhoea and vomiting are caused by poor internal gut health and are not contagious.

The NHS doctors are not taught about internal hygiene. There is no information on how to cleanse the gut on the NHS site and I have come to understand that this is omitted on purpose since those who've set up the medical training – for example, the Rockefeller Institute – don't want the common man to know about these things. Why? Well, a healthy man has far more energy and mental capacity than a sick one and is less easy to make money from. Call me a cynic, but I see that doctors and drug companies make millions from 'contagious' diseases, pandemics and the products and vaccines that they sell to counteract these. They would not make nearly as much if people took more responsibility and received accurate information at school about diet and internal hygiene. Some investigative doctors, such as Dr Tom Cowan and Dr Andrew Kauffman, question the premise of contagion but most people take better care of the drains on their house than they do of their digestive system or their own health. They ignore it at their own peril.

When we did our first naturopathic detox week with our teacher, Peter, things radically changed for the better and my health went from strength to strength. The coffee enemas and small liver flushes are two of my favourite therapies. Beware as these are much maligned on the Internet! I was almost put off, but I changed my mind.

This programme was designed in line with Rich Anderson's recovery programme that he put into practice following a diagnosis of terminal cancer. He wrote a couple of books: *Cleanse and Purify Thyself*, book one and book two. These were our bibles, amongst others.

I've been practising homeopathy now for over twenty years. When I ran my practice and served behind the till at the health-food shop in Fulham Road, I saw hundreds of clients and customers and gave free advice to people. I found the kind of symptoms that I had suffered from were some of the most common amongst our customers and I was able to help them as I was helping myself – through nutrition as well as spiritual and yoga practices. I followed and practised the teachings of the English Master of Yoga George King which were based on selfless service to humanity. Sadly, I also worked with many people who have been damaged by orthodox medicine and by vaccines, and whose children have become autistic, very probably as a result of childhood vaccines.

Questions start to build up on health and climate change

All of this built up a picture in my mind that something was amiss with the NHS. At the same time, I was noticing the effects of the global *Codex Alimentarius* (Food Law or Code) initiative, a massive multi-Nation agreement concerning food and ingredient labelling organised by the United Nations and a central part of a programme by the Food and Agriculture organisation (FAO) and the World Health organisation (WHO). We knew the impact that the new laws were having since when we saw these companies' reps on a monthly basis, they told us of the expensive regulatory hoops that they were having to jump through to get their products on the health food shop shelves. Indeed, we saw the output of small supplement producers disappearing off the shelves. This forced me to question why useful handmade herbal remedies, and those made by smaller companies, were being regulated so harshly and why high-potency vitamin-C supplements a very important part of people's recovery from major illness, were being restricted.

My questioning did not stop there. As I questioned conventional health, I also came to question the views that we were receiving from the mainstream media on climate change. I could see similar patterns in many other sectors such as the law and education to those I'd experienced in the health arena. Everywhere we seemed to be led to hold certain views that supported a particular agenda. Where climate change was concerned for example, there was a tendency to present the notion of anthropogenic climate change as one rooted in a scientific consensus where there was actually no evidence of this. In the same way that doctors who have views that run counter to the party line are muffled, so too are climate scientists.

Below is a piece from the book *The Dark Side of Academia* (Secret Professor, 2022) which sums this up (p.205):

> .....in an article published in 2013 (Cook *et al.*), evidence was presented for the presence of a scientific consensus on man-made climate change (*ibid.*) A withering riposte however (Legates *et al.* 2015) argued that only 41 out of the 11,944 published climate papers examined by Cook explicitly stated man to be the cause of most of the post-1950 warming. The authors of the second article, Legates *et al.*, stated that Cook *et al.* had excluded around 8,000 papers in their sample on the unacceptable ground that the papers had expressed no opinion on the climate consensus.
>
> What is more, Legates *et al.* went on to point out that the sixty-four papers identified by Cook *et al.* as explicitly supporting anthropogenic climate change could be narrowed down to only forty-one on the basis that twenty-three of the sixty-four had not in fact supported anthropogenic climate change.

Does this lack of any scientific consensus explain the relaxed attitude to high carbon-producing travel by certain leading members of society? I read of two examples. One was Michael Bloomberg, Mayor of New York from 2002-2013 and the U.N. Secretary-General's Special Envoy on Climate Ambition and Solutions. He was also Global Advisor to the Winners of The Earthshot Prize, one launched by Prince William and The Royal Foundation in October 2020, It was said that the Earthshot Prize was the most prestigious global environment prize in history but he possessed an expensive jet aircraft (a Dassault Falcon 900) that produces thirty seven times more carbon emissions than an equivalent trip on a commercial flight; his helicopter, likewise, was a gas guzzler (an AgustaWestland AW109) that burns seventy two gallons of fuel every hour (Binder, 2019).

I wondered if he was aware that the science on Climate Change is not a done deal?

The same question might be asked of John Kerry, the man who on January 20, 2021 was sworn in as the US' first Special Presidential Envoy for Climate and the first-ever principal to sit on the National Security Council entirely dedicated to climate change. He had a long history of being associated with the alleged battle against climate change since, in a speech he gave in 2014, he asserted that climate change was 'the world's most fearsome weapon of mass destruction.' I wondered whether he had really looked at the detail of the science.

One reason that I asked myself was because I'd read in several publications that he was suspected of using private jets like the one owned by his family that emit around forty times as much carbon per passenger as commercial flights. After he was criticized for taking the jet to receive a climate award in Iceland in 2019, I read that he had said that 'If you offset your carbon, it's the only choice for somebody like me who is travelling the world to win this battle.' He had added, at the time that he didn't have time to sail the seas (his words were 'I believe the time it takes to get me somewhere, I can't sail across the ocean. I have to fly to meet with people and get things done') but he did not address the fact he had the option of flying commercial airlines that transport hundreds of passengers at a time.

So my reading as well as my experience have led me to doubt the opinions of so-called 'experts' and authority figures in the fields of medicine, science and politics. This is especially the case when they are repeatedly rolled out on mainstream media to speak on a certain subject. This is something that happened on a regular basis during the covid lockdowns.

How experience has fuelled my quest

My journey, informed by my search for solutions to my personal health problems as well as by my prolonged and successful experiences in homeopathy practice, have led me to distrust the advice and treatments suggested by many of the medical profession. I am not, for example, in favour of childhood or baby vaccines since all that tiny babies need is love and breast milk, as nature designed. My own son, after a very promising start, was given DPT and MMR vaccines (one in each arm) when he went to live with his father in France at the age of twelve. He was sick for a whole year after this. To a degree, this has been beneficial since he realised why he was sick and has chosen not to be vaccinated from that point on. He received none of the covid vaccines and has his own homeopathy and flower-essence kits, and messages me for advice. He has also discovered remedies used by the indigenous people where he lives in Mexico and these include one recommended especially for Montezuma's revenge, and there are many others besides.

I have always been surprised, given the choice of energy medicine or orthodox medicine, that so many people don't at least try the former; but there is a huge conditioning to consult a doctor. These subjects are difficult and challenging to discuss for those of us who think that the WHO or the NHS do not have our health and best interests at heart. There are in fact thousands of doctors who disagree with the current medical model and the vaccine programmes funded by Big Pharma, but you won't hear their views since they are silenced by the mainstream media. They don't appear on television except as the subject of a documentary with an ending skewed against alternative medicine.

By way of example, we are told that homeopathy has nothing in it but that at the same time it is dangerous. Then, Dr Andrew Wakefield, a brilliant doctor who conducted research at the Royal Free Hospital into autism and its correlation with gut health was hounded out of the medical profession. Jacques Benveniste, a brilliant French scientist who discovered that water has memory suffered a similar fate. David Noakes and Lynda Thyer were imprisoned for developing GcMAF, a product that appeared to provide a very successful and alternative cancer treatment. The Cancer Act 1939 states that it is illegal in the UK to claim to be able to treat cancer or to advertise the treatment of cancer and I do often wonder why since this stops treatments that I have seen deliver excellent solutions, and treatments with excellent audit trails, kept from the public because of the effects of this legislation. The Act was passed over eighty years ago and with advances in health care, is it not time now to review it?

A young woman came up to me after a talk at Rawfest, a raw-food festival where we were both speaking, to thank me for recommending a book, *Comparing Natural Immunity with Vaccination* by Trevor Gunn, which had helped her, years before, when she was making a decision whether or not to vaccinate her first baby. Juliette Bryant is now a teacher herself, helping many people – you can find her at Juliette's Kitchen. We've both found that the way to good health is holistic, through healthy physical, mental, emotional and spiritual habits. Our understanding of the immune system is changing as we learn more about it, good food and fresh air are vital parts of developing the body's natural immune responses.

If we love and care for each other, we can ask the unpalatable questions and share the answers to help shine a light where there is confusion and darkness. If we keep our minds open and explore the road less travelled, we may find all sorts of solutions to our health problems that are not on offer from our doctor's surgery. We can become self-reliant and self-responsible and reach the point where we can cancel our health-insurance policies since we now know how to look after ourselves, our families and our friends. This can build a community of healthy and resilient men, women and children who are equipped to create a better future.

References

https://www.nhs.uk/conditions/diarrhoea-and-vomiting/

Binder, John (2019), Self-declared climate change 'global leader' Mike Bloomberg enjoys his own fleet of private jets, helicopters, https://www.breitbart.com/politics/2019/12/04/self-declared-climate-change-global-leader-mike-bloomberg-enjoys-his-own-fleet-of-private-jets-helicopters/

The Secret Professor (2022), *The Dark Side of Academia*, UK: Truth University Press

Liberating Myself from the Tribe

EVE GILMORE

A writer and speaker on health, Eve Gilmore is a retired naturopath, homeopath, clinical nutritionist and physiokey practitioner, and has an MsC in natural medicine. She is the author of Go Paleo? - Feeding the Urban Caveman *and* The Urban Caveman Recipe Book.

My own journey of awakening began in childhood. I remember spending time with loving and familiar beings who were not embodied, but who were real – an awareness that I lost around the age of three. When I was six or seven I was awoken by a loving energy emanating from a white hand above my bed. I used to wake my brother and he would snuggle up beside me to stare at this hand until the energy withdrew and it faded away.2

Early encounters with the medical system showed it to be uncaring and illogical, with treatments often worse than the presenting problem. Debilitating stomach pain, inexplicable to doctors, who accused me of fabricating it to gain attention, made me realise they didn't understand the body. I couldn't work out why doctors were at a loss to explain causation and why illness was often perceived as random.

The death of a beloved pet prompted me to ask a deaconess at school if animals had souls, to which she replied that they did not. She then launched into a monologue about how humans have dominion over all of nature. Everything inside me told me this was wrong. I had never been able to muster respect for a God so insecure He needed to be worshipped,

---

[2] I later read of a priest who had had the same experience and that it was understood to be a sign of protection.

or comprehended how the sacrificial death of His Son could save the world. And failing to understand what I had done to make myself a sinner, I concluded religion didn't have the answers either.

Having always been the only person in the cinema who never stood for the national anthem despite my mother's embarrassment, I strongly resisted accompanying her to wave at the Queen Mother when visiting a nearby town. I remember being shocked that my mother would participate in such a humiliating ritual, and felt that to do so myself would be an act of betrayal. I now realise that marching round the playground waving a flag on Empire Day, and thanking God for being born British, had instilled a lifelong acquiescence to institutions in a generation being groomed for the Second World War.

Conditioning eventually prevailed over me too, and at the age of twenty I embarked on student nurse training at St Bartholomew's Hospital in the City of London. Having been founded in 1123, the hospital was steeped in tradition. I was there when it was celebrating its 850th anniversary, which warranted an article in *Reader's Digest*, of which I still have a copy. I was in awe of the traditions, the antiquated uniforms and the old buildings. What I was not prepared for was the hierarchical structure, at the top of which presided the consultant. He would appear on the ward surrounded by an entourage of doctors in descending order of importance, the medical students sometimes acting as stooges to his displays of knowledge and wit.

Below the lowly medical students were the senior nurses. If a junior nurse had an observation about a patient it went, Chinese-whispers style, up the ranks of the nursing staff, who conveyed it to a junior doctor and somewhere along the way it got translated into Latin. Bottom of the heap, I realised, were the patients, who were sometimes ignored altogether during these visitations, information about their condition having being obtained from the ward sister, who had heard it from ... well, you get the picture.

I saw how medical mystique, combined with the assumption that the patient knew less about his body than the doctors, excluded the patient from any meaningful participation in decision-making. The signing of a preoperative consent form was in reality another ritual designed to protect the surgeon, particularly since the phrase 'and whatever is considered necessary' gave carte blanche to remove bits the patient didn't realise he had. I realised that much of it was unnecessary and detrimental to health and that all of it was traumatic to the body. No consideration was given to the quality of life after such procedures. Some were experimental or educational and even, on occasions, fatal. Examples? In the seventies, stomach ulcers were believed to be caused by excess stomach acid triggered by stress. Vagotomies – cutting of the vagus nerve in the belief it would inhibit the production of stomach acid (a vital secretion needed for digestion), though the procedure resulted in severing the most important connection between the brain and the rest of the body – were all the rage.[3]

I have since learned that many medical protocols are founded on myth rather than science, and that they come and go according to fashion. Tonsillectomies in the fifties and sixties meant few survived childhood with their immune system intact, and this gave way in the eighties to the insertion of grommets. We are all familiar with the proliferation of hysterectomies over the last few decades (the biggest risk factor being private medical insurance). As a practitioner in the nineties, I had first-hand experience of a cartel run by doctors (via the local golf club) that ensured no one spoke out about the unnecessary surgery that took place or the practice of anaesthetising and pretending to operate on private patients. One of my patients was the wife of an orthopaedic surgeon who refused to go along with this, and as a result he was bullied, ostracised and reported to the GMC for misconduct.

In the 1970s, ninety per cent of the patients at Barts suffered from cancer – a rare disease that warranted transferral to a specialist centre. Patients destined for radiotherapy were marked up with purple marker pens, but as vomiting, diarrhoea and weight loss took hold, they soon resembled tattooed concentration-camp victims. Young leukaemic girls arrived from all over the country with full heads of hair and eyes full of hope, and it broke my heart knowing the inevitable suffering that would follow.[4] Unaware then of how totalitarian methodologies were used to instil a fear of disease so strong that it overrode all other considerations, I struggled to

---

[3] This theory was eventually disproved in the 1980s with the discovery of the bacterium *Helicobacter pylori*.

[4] One per cent of tumour cells are destructive. Ninety-nine per cent are benign daughter cells. Cytotoxic drugs or chemotherapy destroys only the daughter cells, which has the effect of activating the most malignant cells. It also damages the liver, brain and immune systems.

understand how people would submit to treatments that were so obviously destructive.

My experience at Barts also woke me up to the power of institutions. Medical students were still sometimes admitted for their expertise at rugby. Misogynistic and with a tradition of drinking clubs, medical training ensured that students absorbed by osmosis a sense of superiority towards anyone outside the profession. I had seen that the training of doctors involved techniques used by the military. It was strongly hierarchical and was designed to prevent questioning. It was an abusive system that relied upon long hours and mental and physical stress, including sleep deprivation and constant examination. It tended to turn out doctors who had lost touch with their humanity.

This period was also a catalyst for my spiritual awakening. Theatres used to give free tickets to nurses, so we often benefited from good seats at West End productions. Sitting near the front of the stalls, I can still recall the shift in consciousness prompted by the entrance of an actor whom I had never met, but whom I recognised immediately. The words 'Oh, it's you' formed in my mind, and I was propelled into a *knowing* that I had existed before I was born. I felt too big to be confined by a small body and entered, at this point, into a state of heightened awareness and oneness.

For until that moment I had not questioned the 3D reality in which I lived. However, I knew this actor so well that he felt like part of me. How did I know he had a pathological hatred of all things medical? I was so connected to him that one day I went to Oxford Street and just knew he was going to be there, which, of course, he was. After about three days, I plunged into a state of despair. I had been unable to recall how I knew him. I couldn't carry on nursing and had no explanation for what had happened to me. I was placed on sick leave and referred to a psychiatric social worker, who introduced me to the concept of reincarnation. My 'treatment' consisted of a reading list of research into all matters spiritual.

In parallel with this, my time at Barts was becoming one of disillusionment – a word that simply means 'waking up from an illusion'. I enrolled on a drama and theatre arts course and went on to work at Thames Television in both current affairs and light entertainment. I have fond memories of shows such as *The Kenny Everett Video Show* and *The Morecambe and Wise Show.* I relocated to Granada TV in Manchester, where I trained in production and helped edit a sitcom which launched the careers of

Stephen Fry, Hugh Lawrie, Ben Elton and Emma Thompson. I also worked with U2 – a shy young band over from Ireland for the day, overwhelmed and awe-inspired by the sophistication of television.

I saw how the media works – who gets to be famous, which stories make the news and, more importantly, which do not. I also saw the D-notice system at play – a device used by government to block any information that is not in their interest. As a member of the animal liberation movement (and one of the first vegans in the country at a time when the number of vegans could be counted on one hand) I informed a researcher friend of a night-time rescue from a vivisection laboratory at Liverpool University, and he arranged for it to be filmed. It was scheduled to be broadcast on *Granada Reports* (hosted by the then unknown Judy Finnigan and her new boyfriend, Richard Madeley, languishing in the graveyard of regional news), but the film was pulled at the last minute since one of the directors of Granada happened to be on the board of the university.

This was my first encounter with the impenetrable glass ceiling, above which presided the secret network of supporters of the system, strategically placed to censor what the people are told. I helped film an interview with a nervous Margaret Thatcher newly installed in Downing Street and was astounded at how she took instruction from her minders, enquiring afterwards as to whether she had 'done OK' before being hastily ushered out.5 I also learned how the stance taken by documentaries was determined prior to any research being carried out.

With the eighties came motherhood, which prompted me to look into vaccination, a bête noire that continues to shock me today. 'Alterative' medicine was just starting to come in when my children were young, so I preferred to consult a homeopath before a doctor. When our daughter contracted whooping cough (cured within twenty-four hours by homeopathic pertussin6), I asked our GP to test her. He stated – with no apparent sense of irony – that 'Since we stopped testing for it, we haven't found a single case.' Meanwhile, whooping cough had been renamed 'viral

[5] Permission to interview had only been granted when we agreed that we would only have one take, thus preventing editing.

[6] Pertussin is the homeopathic whooping cough nosode. It was also given to our other children as a preventative, provoking whooping-cough symptoms for twenty-four hours. It is of note that in the three months our daughter had had whooping cough, none of us had 'caught' it.

asthma', ensnaring a generation of children into inhaler and steroid dependence.

In the nineties, I continued to read spiritual books, including one by medium Betty Shine, whom David Icke had consulted when traumatised by a kundalini awakening, to which the nation was privy via *The Terry Wogan Show*. Shortly after, he published a book entitled *The Truth Vibrations,* which I devoured. I followed Icke, and others, over the next thirty years as they unravelled the dark web of hidden power that cloaks the world. I have had the privilege of learning from enlightened medical practitioners, such Dr Dietrich Klinghardt, and have been inspired by many others, some of whom lost their lives in the doctor cull of 2015.

In 2004, I graduated from a university, which will remain nameless, with a master's degree in natural medicine. The university had insisted that my degree be named 'natural health' rather than 'natural medicine', but due to an administrative oversight my certificate bore the word 'medicine'. Furthermore, I later learned that, although I was acknowledged to have merited a first, I was to be marked down since I had included in my thesis information about the ineffectiveness7 and damage caused by antibiotics. My tutor had naively advised that evidencing my statements with referenced research would protect me.

I had been practising as a clinical nutritionist, naturopath and homeopath since 1994, but in 2020 started winding down my practice in pursuit of what I had hoped would be a hedonistic retirement. In fact, my plans were scuppered by grandchildren and the 2020 alleged pandemic – something that to my way of seeing was a psy-op. I was shocked when alternative practitioners embraced the narrative and when small-business owners colluded in the demise of their livelihoods. I realised at this point that decades of education concerning germ theory, and entrainment into obedience (mostly via the education system and media) had been preparing the population for this moment.

---

[7] Research from several sources shows that antibiotics do not kill bacteria but simply remove the outer membrane, making them invisible to the immune system as this is the location of the presenting antigen. Symptoms abate as the immune system is unaware of their presence. They then club together inside biofilms, which secrete toxins causing chronic disease.

This awakening from the consensus world view to a wider reality set me on a journey in which limitation was replaced by possibility and conformity by freedom. As the kaleidoscope of chaos started to shape itself into a pattern, the world began to make sense for the first time. Politicians supporting untenable policies, managers presiding over systems that were ineffectual and medical treatments that destroyed health had seemed incomprehensible when I thought them the result of poor judgement. However, when I realised that failure had been factored into every structure upon which modern life is based, I was inspired to look for ways of operating outside those structures.

It is true that acceptance by the tribe is hardwired into our psyche, and so questioning the way the tribe operates has at times been an isolating experience. However, I have found that, if balanced by a spiritual philosophy, breaking free from the trance to which most of humanity is enthralled can bring enormous rewards.

Once awakened from the trance, it becomes obvious that we have been corralled into a state of co-dependency. This is aided by a fabricated complexity in the way topics are presented – something that holds us hostage to so-called experts and robs us of our power. However, with knowledge comes choice. Sovereignty becomes possible when you understand how to protect your health or how the financial system works, for example. By embracing a new value system in which simple pleasures replace gratification, I have been able to reconnect with who I really am. I try not to betray my sense of self to societal norms, such as valuing intellectual prowess over intuition or practical skills, and I try to live an authentic life.

I am not pessimistic since I believe in a greater intelligence and in a grand plan that is going to first expose and then – through our empowerment – lead to the disintegration of the control systems that have dominated this planet for millennia. I like to think I have a role to play in bringing in a better world and am grateful for the experiences outlined above that have prepared me for this moment.

EDUCATION

Is there Fakery in Teaching, Learning and Research? Are Colleges and Universities a House of Cards?

DR URSULA EDGINGTON

Ursula completed her PhD in adult education in England before immigrating to New Zealand in 2013. An experienced teacher, freelance writer and researcher, she has qualifications in education, sociology, psychology and law. Her specialist areas include creative assessment strategies and enhancing student-centred learning.

Coming from a working-class background, and living a transient life in council estates, my schooling was disjointed to say the least. Unsurprisingly, I left with little in terms of what others define as 'meaningful qualifications'. But paradoxically, maybe because of the mainly poor-quality teaching I had endured, I harboured a secret desire to teach. It was this idea that motivated me to restart my learning journey later in life, after years of boredom from commercial-sector work in what Graeber defines as *Bullshit Jobs* (Graeber 2018). Being a 'mature, part-time, female student' at a 'top' 'Russell Group' UK University was an interesting experience during the early 2000s. Blair had declared his Government's top three priorities as 'Education, Education, Education' and I was apparently a 'target group'. The University wasn't entirely onboard with this New Labour thinking; scheduled evening seminars were inconvenient.

Many adults are emotionally scarred by the childhood division and prejudice caused by an archaic English Grammar school system, myself included. [8] It wasn't until years later, studying a foundation module of my social studies degree, aged 30, that I was shocked to discover how the whole education system had been (and continues to be) rigged against females. Perhaps even more worryingly, so many people, my parents included, were totally unaware of the mechanisms at play. For instance, the questions within an 11+ exam are not culturally-competent and girls needed to obtain higher marks than boys in order to achieve a formal 'pass'. So, relegated to the local Catholic Comprehensive, I was thus denied the early qualification pathway towards teaching, a career journey that was actively encouraged for my friends at the Grammar School for Girls. Perhaps it was then, more than twenty years ago now - since I am in my fifties - that my worldview began to shake slightly.

Whilst studying further and becoming acutely aware of the corruption deep in the machinery of our society, I worked in a public health research centre. Here, I witnessed for the first time, how an 'academic' paper could be manipulated and edited [described further below]. For, as a humble secretary, I remember being instructed by a senior academic to create a 'new' academic paper about an intervention for patients, by using 'copy and paste' from the body (not the literature review) of an article previously published in a different journal. 'Surely this can't be how it's done?' I asked myself naively. But it was.

Ten years later, when I had completed my PostGrad Teaching Diploma, I was teaching at a city-centre refugee centre, and at Further Education (FE) colleges in the Midlands. These institutions provided insights into the way that education funding policies were seen as hurdles to jump, by (non-teaching) management. Authentic, positive student experiences were often perceived as less of a priority, compared to the bureaucracy that surrounded these experiences. By manipulating the methodologies, language and timing of student feedback and learning outcomes, the data could be presented in a more positive light. Hence funding requirements that sustained income for staff in flash, glass-fronted buildings were built on a house of cards. The reality is, not all students' learning outcomes are 'measurable' in a quantitative way – to claim otherwise is simply absurd. Occasionally, I would connect with like-minded teachers also frustrated by

---

[8] In some counties of England during this time, entry to Grammar School offered a potentially higher-level academic education than that provided by the parallel comprehensive school system; entry was gained via a test taken at eleven years old, hence the term '11+'.

the lack of authenticity in the teaching and learning policies, some were also concerned about the dumbing-down of student activities that risked developing students' critical-thinking skills. The influence of New Public Management (NPM) in education was in full-swing during this time and led to my interest in the impact of NPM on our classrooms. Specifically, I investigated the concept of emotional labour as it relates to adult education (Edgington 2016a).

To explain briefly (because it's relevant to understanding my current situation), the term 'emotional labour' was originally used by Hochschild to describe the performance or 'performativity' of customer-service work. She gave the example of airline cabin-crew whose job demands that staff convey certain attitudes (Hochschild 1983). She argued that these paid jobs are exploitative because it is inherently unethical and shaming to expect those undertaking manual labour to combine this labour with the projection of what appear to be (but may not be) 'genuine' emotions. She went further in stating that, in contrast to practical skills, the more authentic (or 'human') these paid-for emotions are *perceived to be*, the more these individuals are sought-after and valued. In a corporeal example, Hochschild observed how a staff member reacted when a passenger suffering from air-sickness, vomited onto her uniform. In contrast to exhibiting understandably authentic emotions (revulsion, frustration, disgust), the crew-member smiled broadly and reassured the customer that the stinking mess was 'no problem at all.' The concept of emotional labour then, has profound implications today for a generation encouraged to *'fake it 'til you make it'.*

My research confirmed how the phenomenon of emotional labour also exists in Further and Higher Education institutions (FE/HE). It showed, for instance, that when staff 'perform' within their teaching roles they must compromise, or even *betray,* their personal values in order to adhere to (sometimes illogical or even unethical) rules and regulations. Four common (if somewhat 'taboo') examples of such 'unofficial' FE/HE policies (that I have witnessed) include:

1. Recording a student as 'present' on arbitrarily 'important' term-dates when in fact the student was absent/withdrawn from a course (because 'attendance' ensures continued course funding).
2. Encouraging students to record positive feedback on their course evaluations, because the outcomes from these 'surveys' are

reflected in the University's profile 'score' and hence their potential future employment prospects.

3. Not producing transparent assessment grading criteria and thereby enabling students' assignment outcomes to be 'reviewed' in the light of the cohort's results.

4. On being notified of an imminent (Government) inspection eg teaching and learning observations (UK FE, Ofsted), educational institutions instructing their staff to remove any poor quality/incomplete assignments from the spotlight and to send 'difficult' students on short-notice work-placements.

Within these four examples, we can see how staff's emotional labour can artificially prop up the (fake) image of an institution's integrity. This emotional labour can contribute to effective marketing campaigns, producing financial funding and fulfilling contrived auditing requirements. In fact, their enactment becomes a 'necessary evil' in order to retain employment because negative consequences ensue for those individuals unwilling to comply with such coercive policies. Not only can non-compliance lead to alienation and the painful emotion of shame, it can lead to punitive measures such as a lack of promotion opportunities, or even termination of an employment contract and with that, the person's career and vocation (The Secret Professor 2022).

This is extremely serious since emotional labour is far from being innocuous. In my own research, the dangers of this performativity on the individual were evidenced in the form of harms to mental health and wellbeing, when individuals are forced to stray too far, too often, from their authentic Self (Edgington 2016b). A teacher's sense of shame can manifest in acts of compliance that produce a feeling that they are sacrificing fundamental elements of *what teaching and learning is really about*. As I later learned, the concept of shame was exploited by Government agencies, which are victims of regulatory capture in ensuring compliance with the recent Covid legislation. For instance, the behavioural science report *Mindspace* set out recommendations for effective marketing campaigns by Government and specifically commended the use of images/phrases that could encourage feelings of shame, thereby triggering public compliance with authoritarian policies (Dolan et al. 2010).

It was following my immigration to New Zealand in 2013, nearly nine years ago, that I discovered the true extent of the regulatory capture and with that, the conflicts of interest and the power of the unwritten Corporate Playbook. For example, censorship and propaganda are used to *Dismiss, Delay, Deny, Discredit, Deflect, Deceive and Divide* anyone who dares to ask inconvenient questions. The New Zealand taxpayer-funded aerial poisoning of our forests with the highly toxic synthetic poison, sodium monofluoroacetate (1080) has been regularly repeated for over 65 years, despite widespread public condemnation and evidence of harms (e.g. McQueen 2017). And as I investigated the inconsistencies between the New Zealand Government's narrative that presented this poison as 'safe and effective' and the stark scientific realities of this poison, (its lethal instability has caused it to be banned or severely restricted in most other countries) the influence from BigChem became obvious.[9]

That is not all, since just a cursory scrape beneath the surface illuminates how lacking in transparency the scientific peer-reviewed process is, on the topic of 1080 poison use in New Zealand. Articles that get through the censorship filter to publication, are often methodologically flawed and missing essential (human and animal) ethics approval. Moreover, there are often contradictions between research outcomes and conclusions, presumably to appease the funders of the research. The authors perhaps hope that few people will bother to read more than the abstract and in the rare event that a reader *does* spot the contradictions and complain, the usual, highly effective Corporate Playbook can easily be set in motion once again.

Generally speaking, the academic literature on emotional labour discusses the performance of 'positive' emotions such as building rapport and establishing trust, understanding and empathy, observing how these are exemplified in sectors like healthcare, education, sales, customer-service, hairdressing and even sex-workers' roles (eg Price 2001). But what of the emotional labour that emphasises the *opposite* of those emotions – for example the disdainful or hostile emotions towards an artificially defined 'outgroup' (eg Hockey, 2009)? Furthermore, if that same emotional labour promotes a political narrative that is not based on fact, but rather on an *ideology*, it can lead to dangerous discrimination. I believe this type of embedded emotional labour, if unchecked, promotes illogical

[9] For an excellent peer-review of the literature on 1080, see the work of Dr J Pollard et al. at https://1080science.co.nz/

disinformation and becomes a societal norm which can develop into totalitarianism (Desmet 2022).

Reflecting now on the somewhat unfulfilling jobs from my early career, and my later experiences in Further and Higher Education, I can see parallels between my various roles and what lecturers who I interviewed for my PhD research described. For they spoke of carrying out pointless duties that essentially were an exercise in 'jumping through hoops'. Examples included writing contrived lesson-plans that did not reflect the reality of that session's teaching, and submitting the plan *after* a session had taken place.[10] Truth to tell, the distorted definitions of 'best practice' in all sectors of teaching and learning - highly controversial for decades - are widely accepted as having been hijacked for a political agenda (The Secret Teacher 2016). And it's not a coincidence that these educational whistle-blowers are often anonymous. Many individuals have suffered poor health and even committed suicide, trying to align with nonsensical procedures (Adams 2015), procedures that Government agencies regularly admit are meaningless (Ofsted 2012).

However, just as the Covid policy responses such as lockdowns and vaccine mandates are authoritarian and fundamentally flawed (eg Alexander 2021), many staff feel it necessary to maintain compliance by continuing to offer their emotional labour in delivering, or at least remaining unquestioning of, so-called 'best practice' teaching and learning. Caught between a rock and a hard place, some academics feel they must comply in order to retain professional employment, personal recognition and associations with institutional integrity (Honneth 2004). High levels of personal debt – ironically partly a consequence of Blair's promotion of HE, to a population which without student loans, simply couldn't afford it – also provide effective blackmail that coerce staff to comply.

In contrast to undertaking roles that demand compliance, many researchers have highlighted genuine, or authentic human interactions in education. For example, James and Diment (2003) investigated what they described as 'underground teaching' in UK Further Education. The researchers observed student/teacher interactions that took place away from any managerial surveillance, that were honest, rewarding and

[10] Management accepted how these 'planning' documents were simply a paper-exercise for auditing purposes.

intellectually challenging. But I can't help wondering whether in using the phrase 'underground teaching', these authors were complicit in downgrading and marginalising the value of this work. After all, why should the emotional labour offered by teachers in fulfilment of their official duties (the stuff that ticks the various boxes) be 'valued' - whilst simultaneously their authentic interactions with their students remain hidden? Since when did our education system become so Orwellian as to relegate any teaching and learning that happens outside the gaze of Big Brother?

Interestingly, these experiences of genuine learning and teaching may have become even more prevalent during Covid 'lockdowns' when institutions forced policies of distance-learning (McKie 2020). This situation permitted unregulated interactions with students online, sometimes outside the 'endorsed' Virtual Learning Environment (VLE) platforms, and in time-frames not explicitly 'measurable', and this may have led to meaningful opportunities for greater authenticity. This is significant since authentic teaching and learning - *by its very nature* - is creative and does not conform to prescribed curricula, disciplines and institutional policies (Vickers 2010). These interactions could be an antidote to so-called 'bullshit jobs' and their associated emotional labour. That may be because they include *truth telling*: an acceptance of uncertainty within genuine human connectivity (Desmet 2022).

I have described some examples of how NPM has impacted negatively on teaching and learning policies. In addition to these negative aspects, it is worth pointing out that many elements of (well-established) *academic* emotional labour in HE in fact fits with Graeber's definition of a 'bullshit job'. For instance:

- Paraphrasing an already-published article for submission to another journal, because various academic 'brownie-points' are gained with each research 'output';
- Re-working research data outcomes that were collected decades ago (in another context), in order to publish something 'timely';
- Gaining kudos of contrived 'impact' (eg 'reTweets') by using BigTech social media platforms to 'disseminate' research outcomes to Joe Public;

- Manipulating an article's citations to include one or more names of those listed on a specific editorial board, prior to submission to that journal;

- Exploiting PhD students with (ill-advised?) ambitions to be employed within academia, to write a 'co-authored' article that supports his/her government-funded academic-supervisor's theory...and so the list goes on.

Far from being a 'critical conscience of society' then, our universities have lost all integrity and credibility as meaningful and ethical education institutions. This is not due to incompetence or laziness. Over several decades, the valid outcomes from numerous research projects have been systematically suppressed. Evidence-based discussions of climate change, toxicology, democratic rights, gendered roles, colonial history, best practice leadership (Secret Professor, 2022) and many other topics are off-limits because arguments that differ from the political narrative have been conveniently labelled 'conspiracy theories' or 'misinformation'. Researchers who have dared to question their censorship, have been faced with the overwhelming corporate power that is now being exposed to Joe Public (The Secret Professor 2022; Shir-Raz et al. 2022).

In 2020 the disturbing deceptions I had previously uncovered in the aerial poisoning of New Zealand's forests were repeated in the contradictions between Government narratives and the scientific evidence about Covid and then the 'vaccines'. The only difference was that this time the narrative was global and the phraseology and timescales were in lockstep.

In July 2021, many sleepless nights resulted from my effort to come to terms with the way in which my world had shifted on its axis. The increasingly dystopian world that I inhabited saw the mainstream media regularly engaged in reporting the *exact opposite* of the factual information concerning Covid 'cases', hospitalisations and deaths. World leaders would repeat the same phrases, over and again as if this was a neuro-linguistic programming (NLP) session. How could this be allowed? It was a re-telling of the *Emperor has no Clothes,* with numerous people waiting for the child to laugh out loud. But that laugh never came. Days, weeks, months rolled by. By this time, I had left social media (Twitter/Facebook) since those platforms were replete with BigPharma propaganda and much of what I wrote was censored. This shadow-banning meant that I didn't get to see genuine friends and family posts and there was outgroup hatred too, including shills and trolls. It was an unbearable, toxic environment.

I retained my well-established Linkedin profile and made some new connections with others who were speaking out. In October 2021, I saw a post that included Professor Norman Fenton, Queen Mary University, London, talking on Zoom to another academic about all-cause mortality data and the manipulation of statistics by the UK Government.[11] After an exchange of emails, we agreed to chat via Zoom and I vividly remember the relief of discovering (at some Godforsaken hour NZ-time) that I wasn't going insane, and that there were very credible academics who felt they had been let down by colleagues (and Governments) and that we were living in a parallel universe.

It was conversations with academics like Norman, and investigations of research without conflicts of interest, that slowly caused me to regain my confidence and emotional strength. What I needed was that elusive authenticity that has become a constant theme in my life.[12] It was in that spirit of authenticity that in December 2021 I shared an article on Linkedin from the *British Medical Journal* (Thacker, 2021) and my profile on Linkedin was immediately suspended for 'going against community policy'. I realised then, that the Corporate Playbook had matured into a sinister monster and that the suppression of the truth was ubiquitous, across all BigTech platforms.

Little wonder that academic's 'authentic' blogging on non-censored platforms like Patreon and Substack has increased exponentially in the last two years. In my own case, blogging has provided a measure of catharsis for the traumatic challenges that we now face. Yes, technocracy and totalitarianism work in partnership, and algorithms, propaganda and censorship (including self-censorship) can cripple authentic communications and divide society. However, it is human nature to discover creative ways to overcome these challenges; exposing the Corporate Playbook is one way of doing this.

This post-Covid era presents an exciting future of opportunities for educationalists like myself. For many years, we have been 'swimming against the tide', sharing understandings about how fundamentally

---

[11] Details of this research available on the professor's website: normanfenton.com

[12] For instance, see reachingpeople.net for some ideas about debating skills using authenticity.

broken our education systems are. None of us wants a return to 'normal' (even if that were possible). Ethical educationalists aspire to facilitate learning in an atmosphere of mutual trust, in environments free from regulatory capture. Independence from conflicts of interest allows learning to be practical and contextualised, materials free from bias towards corporate profits or political ideologies and policies that are not skewed towards funding streams. Here, learners' 'screen time' with digital avatars are erased in favour of meaningful, authentic, face-to-face communication. There's a growing awareness of how this holistic, student-centred learning experience is a crucial part of our future.

This goal is not an idealistic fantasy. In the school sector, the transformation has already gained significant ground; in New Zealand, parents and guardians home-schooling have increased substantially in the past two years.[13] Kids are taken out of state schools partly in protest at the Governmental overreach, but also for other valid reasons. Many are adopting their own, community home-schooling groups, including creating private mini-libraries and joining the well-established global 'un-schooling' movement (Gatto, 2009).

Now it is time for universities to rise to the post-Covid challenge to provide authentic, student-centred learning. Communities which value democratic rights demand higher-level learning organisations that are without the boredom and restrictions of academic bureaucracies and Government qualification frameworks I describe above. As The Truth University[14] sets out, students can be equipped with genuine critical thinking skills, through high standards of intellectual engagement and innovative curricula free from outside influence or agendas. Re-envisaging and re-creating authentic university education for lifelong learning is an historic and well-overdue paradigm-shift and humanity needs this change urgently.

References

[13] Eg Homeschoolers increase by 80% in New Zealand after a pandemic *Times of India* 17 Oct 2022

[14] www.truthuniversity.co.uk including https://truthuniversitycouk.uk/truth-university-interviews/

See also *The Secret Professor* (2022) pp.192-195.

Adams, R. (2015) 'Headteacher Killed Herself after Ofsted Downgrade, Inquest Hears'. *The Guardian*, 20 Nov.

Alexander, PA. (2021) 'More Than 400 Studies on the Failure of Compulsory Covid Interventions (Lockdowns, Restrictions, Closures)'. Meta analysis, UK: Brownstone Institute. https://brownstone.org/articles/more-than-400-studies-on-the-failure-of-compulsory-covid-interventions/.

Desmet, M. (2022) *The Psychology of Totalitarianism*. London, UK: Chelsea Green.

Dolan, P. Hallworth, M. Halpern, D. King, D. & Vlaev, I. (2010) 'Mindspace: Influencing Behaviour through Public Policy'. Discussion Document. Cabinet Office. London, UK: Institute for Government. https://www.instituteforgovernment.org.uk/sites/default/files/publications/MINDSPACE.pdf.

Edgington, U. (2016a). *Emotional Labour & Lesson Observation: A Study of England's Further Education*. Springer.

Edgington, U. (2016b). 'Performativity and the Power of Shame: Lesson Observations, Emotional Labour and Professional Habitus'. *Sociological Research Online* 21 (1)

Gatto, J.T. (2009) *Weapons of Mass Instruction: a schoolteacher's journey through the dark world of compulsory schooling*. Gabriola Island, BC, Canada: New Society Publishers.

Graeber, D. (2018) *Bullshit Jobs: A Theory*. New York, USA: Simon and Schuster.

Hochschild, A. (1983) *The Managed Heart: Commercialisation of Human Feeling*. Book, Whole. Berkley, CA. USA.: University of California Press.

Hockey, J. (2009) '"Switch on": Sensory Work in the Infantry'. *Work, Employment and Society* 23 (3): 477–93.

Honneth, A. (2004) 'Recognition and Justice'. *Acta Sociologica* 47 (4): 351–64.

James, D. & Diment, K (2003) 'Going Underground? Learning and Assessment in an Ambiguous Space'. *Journal of Vocational Education and Training* 55 (4): 407–22.

McKie, A. (2020) 'Covid-19: Universities Treating Staff in "Vastly Different Ways"'. *Times Higher Education Supplement*, 20 April 2020

McQueen, F. (2017) *The Quiet Forest*. New Zealand: Tross Publishing.

Ofsted. (2012) 'Press Release: Ofsted Announces Scrapping of "Satisfactory" Judgement in Move Designed to Help Improve Education for Millions of Children', 2012.

Price, H. (2001) 'Emotional Labour in the Classroom: A Psychoanalytic Perspective'. *Journal of Social Work Practice* 15 (2): 161–80.

Shir-Raz, Y., Elisha, R. Martin, B. Ronel, N. and Guetzkow, J. (2022). 'Censorship and Suppression of Covid-19 Heterodoxy: Tactics and Counter-Tactics.' *Minerva* Nov.

Thacker, P. (2021) 'Covid-19: Researcher Blows the Whistle on Data Integrity Issues in Pfizer's Vaccine Trial'. *BMJ* 375 (2635)

The Secret Professor (2022) *The Dark Side of Academia: How Truth Is Suppressed*. eBook. UK: The Truth University.

The Secret Teacher (2016) 'I See Ofsted for What It Is – a Purposeless Farce'. *The Guardian*, 20 Feb.

Vickers, M. (2010) 'The Creation of Fiction to Share Truths and Different Viewpoints: A Creative Journey and an Interpretive Process'. *Qualitative Inquiry* 16 (7): 556–65.

Every Day Is a Learning Day

JANE SHERRARD-SMITH

With over sixty years of life experiences, Jane Sherrard-Smith is currently an educator, therapist and small-business owner.

My duty on this evening is to be the responsible adult for an activity for teens in a boarding school. It's Autumn 2020; the school has reopened after being closed due to the pandemic. Extra hand-washing basins are in position all over the school, sanitising hand wash at every door. Obligatory mask wearing for all is a month or so in the future; the vaccines are not yet ready. The pupils are in bubbles by year group; they are encouraged not to mix with pupils outside their year bubble. No sports fixtures against other schools; no trips out to the theatre, art galleries, musical performances or other such cultural enrichment; none of the usual inter-school meetings to debate, or dance, or share a meal and conversation.

The activity is a silent disco, complete with huge beach balls to bounce around the room. It is held in a hall in a modern annex of the school. To accommodate the school's covid-19 measures, the children are to enter the hall by one door and its preceding staircase and leave by an opposite door and staircase. This one-way system is to be strictly enforced to 'reduce transmission' of the virus. For the one hour spent in the hall, the children are to wear a headphone set, which will be sprayed and wiped with sanitiser before the next group arrives. Each year group is timetabled an hour to enjoy listening to the music on their headphones while dancing and bouncing the balls to each other. In between the sessions, the room will be fogged or sprayed with another chemical by a cleaner with a tub on her back, gloves and eye protection, and a spray nozzle to liberally spray the air and balls. The other duty supervisor and I are provided with a box containing sanitising wipes and the spray for the headphones, complete with a risk-assessment sheet and dilution instructions. Unfortunately, the undiluted sanitising chemical has fallen over in the box and spilt, so the paperwork is a sodden mess. I reach into the box and retrieve the instructions, only to realise they cannot be read. My hands are soaked in the chemical.

Not always a teacher, I have worked in several countries, developing skills in food preparation as a cook or chef. At the turn of the millennium, I gained a BSc (hons) in nutrition while simultaneously teaching food safety and hygiene to a variety of adult students. I later completed a PGCE. My interest in science, health and well-being, and food continues. I read scientific papers and books, and attend conferences and workshops while considering the impacts on our future world. The relatively recently discovered world of our micro-biome together with its impacts and connection to our general health fascinates me.

A novel area of interest that continues to require lots of study is the Digital Age, with wireless devices, AI, the Internet of Things, 5G and beyond, and all that this might bring. I am aware of much science regarding the effects of this radio-frequency radiation on the health of all life on our beautiful Planet Earth, the alleged benefits of 'connectivity' and the drive for us all to embrace this technology with little question. Classrooms have transformed from pen, paper, books and chalkboards to laptops, iPads and interactive boards, with the pandemic driving much teaching online. All with little information, consultation, monitoring, regulation or debate. I have questions and concerns.

There is no time to wash my hands now (almost all teachers will agree that one of our greatest skills is the ability to visit the lavatory as infrequently as possible), and this hall is one of the few areas where there are none of the rapidly installed covid-virus-reducing hand washbasins. I dry my hands as best I can. I am aware that these chemicals are harmful to the delicately balance of micro-organisms on and in us. Amid the changeover from one year group to another, the air and balls are fogged, the headsets sanitised, the children directed to the correct doors and stairs in preparation for the next year group. The air is dense with the smell of chemicals and the excitement of the teens about to groove to the music. There are no windows in this hall, and the windows in the corridors outside open only ten centimetres or so due to building regulations – to prevent anyone falling from these heights, but limiting any airflow. The teens dance and enjoy themselves while wearing wireless headsets in an invisible soup of electromagnetic radio-frequency radiation and sanitising chemicals. Who believes these measures are protecting the children's health? Another couple of sessions repeat and pass until my duty ends and I can wash my stinging hands. My skin has shrivelled to that dried-prune look that follows a long soak in the bath. The following morning, the skin blisters and peels, and continues to do so for the next few days.

Due to the mindset that prevails in this and many other schools, no one is concerned that my hands suffer; that the children are breathing in these chemicals, likely damaging the thin mucous layer in their lungs; that there is little if any knowledge of the impact to our sensitive micro-biomes; that the virus is not trained in the one-way system calculated to reduce its transmission; or that the risk assessments are ineffective once soaked and illegible. Reasonably well versed in writing and implementing risk assessments, I am aware of the importance of regularly reviewing and amending them. But we dismiss my concerns to move on to another day of teaching and learning.

Since my return to school after the summer break several years ago to discover the installation of Wi-Fi access points around much of the school, and the start of the integration of mobile devices such as laptops and tablets, I sought to question, inform and debate many of the issues around the accompanying electro-smog, the rise in the debilitating condition of electro-hypersensitivity and the increased vulnerability of children. Over several years I occasionally provided the ever-expanding IT department with occasional studies, articles or clips of conferences and official committee hearings to justify my questions on safety, impact on health, the environment and the learning experience. Judging by the responses, I was not seen as highlighting potential concerns, but instead I was considered a troublemaker; and indeed, eventually these concerns contributed to a disciplinary hearing in 2021. Several months later, due to the irretrievable breakdown of my relationship with the Senior Management Team, I left after fourteen years, having had an (until then) unblemished record with that school. I learnt to keep my head down and silently lament the effect on schools as they followed the business-driven model of today, losing so much of the holistic approach to care and support for their charges they used to have in days gone by, not so long ago.

Interestingly, at the later date of July 2022, the Upper Tribunal (Administrative Appeals Chamber) ruled that East Sussex County Council must provide an educational setting free from wireless technology for any child who is electromagnetic hypersensitive. This is a giant leap forward in recognising the condition. A 'white-zone' environment with hard-wired connections would facilitate learning without the risk, yet with all the benefits, of modern technology. All being well, enlightened schools will learn to embrace hard-wired technology to provide a safe environment, protective of pupils and staff alike.

Working in schools, we are charged with supporting children to realise their fullest potential, including their health and well-being, and equip them for participation in their adult life. As a teacher, I was used to some pupils being fully engaged, while from time-to-time others passed notes, doodled, daydreamed, or read an off-topic magazine or book; now, with so much of their learning behind a screen, I am frequently unsure what they are engaged in. The world is set to embrace info-technology; what implications will there be for our children in their adult lives? 'Greater connectivity' is the mantra behind the relentless drive for 5G, the Internet of Things, etc., but at what cost to us as electromagnetic beings – human that strive for and thrive with real (not virtual) connections to our fellow living beings? Many enjoy dancing and physically playing games and sports together – activities I took for granted as a child and as an adult, but largely denied to our children at times during the pandemic. From the early stages of the pandemic, it was clear children would most likely recover from the covid illness, which in turn would provide a degree of immunity. Instead, most schools and their staff instilled fear.

Yesterday I visited the local library with my mother, aged eighty-eight. She obediently used the technological machine at the door to scan the book codes and her library card to return her books, and again when she borrowed some new ones. All without any human connection. All without a word from a fellow human being. On the other hand, I went straight to the friendly librarian behind her desk and the obligatory covid protective Perspex screen and struck up a conversation. She asked whether I would like her to show me how to use the machine. A polite but firm 'No, thank You – I would rather you kept your job and we have the pleasure of chatting about books.' We engaged in a chat concerning the book that I returned and had thoroughly enjoyed, and she informed us that it was now a film.

This led us to discuss how passively watching films rarely matches the vivid journey of our imaginations in reading a book. It was a small conversation and connection that I enjoyed, and one that my mother, who now has very few interactions with the outside world apart from her family, missed out on due to technological advances in our local library. Not just that, but her life has been drastically altered due to the pandemic. Her volunteer role of many decades in a local hospital, as an interface between visitors, staff and patients, was closed to her on the grounds of her age and the risk of covid-19 to her health. She misses the interactions; her compassion and care have been made superfluous on the grounds of her health and safety. She now suffers from feelings of worthlessness, anxieties and low self-esteem.

This reflection regarding my personal journey – the events of a single evening activity within a school, and the current downturn in my mother's well-being – leads to questions about health care and covid measures. And the looming future of a technological age – artificial intelligence, algorithms and robots – leads me to me to question the very meaning of connection. My belief is that we are losing our connection to truth, to health and well-being, to compassion, to curiosity. Who should we trust? Where should we seek information? Who defines misinformation? What are their intentions? Is profit, power and gain for the corporations and the elite few, in the name of advancement, more important than the right for an individual to live their life without harm, injury or fraud to their self, possessions and others? How do we find a balance?

I am awake to several disasters in the recent history of our ever-advancing world: the tragedies that accompanied the Big Tobacco industry; thalidomide from Big Pharma, asbestos, mercury, DDT, glyphosate, etc. It took years, many experts and campaigns to raise awareness of harms, and eventually we have come to a more truthful consideration. I am aware that the verdicts are not yet complete on the pandemic measures, nor regarding the future of mankind in the technological era.

For many years I have been aware enough to question information we are fed, and the paths on which we are led. A key skill has been Critical Thinking – a skill that I endeavour to foster in all, children and adults alike. I feel blessed to have the curiosity to learn from a wide range of sources, together with the courage to debate and question. Every day is a learning day. It is within each of us to seek and preserve our real connections, to our inner self, to our intuition, to our fellow earthlings, to the beauty and wonderment of Mother Nature, to our joy of family and friends. I trust in God and pray for a bright future for mankind.

HISTORY

My Journey of Enlightenment

JOHN HAMER

John spent most of his working life as a corporate slave to the IT industry, before seeing the light and becoming a full-time author. His books to date include The Falsification of History *(sold 75,000 copies),* Behind the Curtain *(a huge two-volume, 600,000-word exposé of the fraudulent worldwide monetary and banking systems),* JFK: A Very British Coup, The Falsification of Science, *and* Welcome to the Masquerade: Prelude to the Coming Reset.

I was born and raised in a small village in the Pennine Hills in *Last of the Summer Wine* country, in rural West Yorkshire in the north of England, but now live on the beautiful North Yorkshire coast, overlooking the North Sea.

I spent most of my working life as a corporate slave to the IT industry, before seeing the light and finally escaping from the dreary soul-destroying confines of the corporatocracy over twenty years ago. Since then I have been a full-time professional geopolitical researcher, analyst, public speaker and author, having written and having had published eight books to date. I have appeared on several hundred broadcasts, including radio and TV as well as innumerable podcasts, and I have spoken at many 'live' events on a variety of topics.

My journey to becoming 'awake' began just over twenty-five years ago and was triggered by the suspicious death of Princess Diana on August 31st 1997. It happened in this way:

The weekend following Diana's untimely death, my wife and I met with some friends who had been in Paris over that fateful bank-holiday week-end, for a coffee and a chat. During the course of that conversation, one of them just happened to mention in passing that they had experienced something really strange and they were still trying to come to terms with it. In fact, they had both witnessed, on a late-night French news TV broadcast, the aftermath of the crash – and clearly saw film images of Princess Diana *walking* into an ambulance. At the time they assumed that she was shaken up but clearly lucky to survive, and also that she was probably just being taken to hospital as a precaution.

They were, of course, then both extremely shocked to wake up to the news that Diana had been fatally injured in the crash and had died in the ambulance on the way to hospital. In fact, the whole episode had really unsettled them and they were in a state of disbelief themselves, wondering if they had imagined the whole thing.

Of course this piqued my own curiosity. I have always been one who questions things and never take anything at face value, so I began my own investigations on the (at the time) fledgling Internet.

During the following few years this research took me down some very deep and complex rabbit holes concerning not just the death of Diana, but across the full spectrum of the vast deception taking place on just about every topic one can name.

The following year (early 1998) my wife began a job as a secretary to an author named Stephen Dorril in the small village where we lived. This involved, amongst other tasks, sifting through excerpts in various books provided by Stephen himself for the purpose of finding quotes for his new book on the life of Oswald Mosley. Some of those books, whose titles and authors' names now escape me after the passage of a quarter of a century, I found extremely shocking. They related what would now commonly be referred to as 'crazy conspiracies'. But, as some would say, this label is just a mainstream tactic to deflect and discredit them in order to protect the untruths of the establishment.

I clearly remember spending several evenings utterly fascinated by the contents of these books, and I became even more determined to seek out the truth having now seen for myself exactly to what lengths the powers-that-be will go in order to present an entirely fake or at least distorted reality.

Then in 2001 the 9/11 event occurred, and this further served to awaken many thousands of others and open up even more avenues of research for those of us who had already embarked on our journeys of Critical Thinking.

And so my long, tortuous journey to enlightenment began. It has been an extremely rocky and at times traumatic ride. I have lost *all* of my lifelong friends along the way, as well as my wife of thirty-seven years, whom I still miss dreadfully. But on the positive side I have gained many new friends too, some of whom I cherish dearly. I cannot now imagine life without their love, friendship and support.

When I look back now on that period of my life, I was totally alone in my beliefs and had no one to turn to – no one with whom to discuss my work or my research. Not a single person that I knew was actually on the same page as myself. All my efforts to 'educate' people fell on deaf ears, and I was the subject of much scorn and ridicule – even from my own family at that time.

But having now seen the light, it was utterly impossible for me to un-see it; and so I blundered on and on, trying to uncover and record as much truth as I could whilst feeling persecuted by almost everyone I knew and loved.

My lifelong interest in writing now began to come to the fore, and as the Internet rapidly grew in popularity and proliferated widely over the course of the first few years of the twenty-first century, I began writing articles on various topics, mainly for my own gratification and as a form of catharsis. I eventually contacted various website owners and asked if I could write short articles for publication. In this way I gradually gained a reputation as a competent researcher and writer and realised that this was where my main interest lay. As the years passed, I began to gain confidence and eventually found that I was in demand for my written work, and also at this time began speaking on podcasts and radio broadcasts. I was even invited as a guest of Theo Chalmers on two occasions on Edge Media TV (SKY channel 200), which is now sadly defunct.

Then in 2009 I had the seemingly overambitious idea of writing a book for publication, and I would eventually title it *The Falsification of History*. From this small germ of an idea, a best-selling definitive 'conspiracy' book was realised; and now, more than thirteen years and 75,000 sales later, looking back, I now understand that this book was a great turning point in my life, enabling me, as it did, to become a serious professional author.

Of course the process itself was very far from simple. I had no idea at this juncture how to even go about writing a book, let alone have one published. I found the whole idea extremely daunting, but persevered with it in the optimistic belief that it would all eventually come together successfully – somehow or another!

Serendipitously, I hit upon the idea of simply taking many of my previous stand-alone articles and stitching them together, thereby creating a coherent whole. This seemed to work extremely well, and I have indeed been complimented many times on the format of *The Falsification of History* (published 2012), which many people seem to agree is the ultimate 'conspiracy reference book'. *TFOH* was, and continues to be, a great success. It established my reputation as a writer of 'real' history, as opposed to the usual lies we are fed on a daily basis by the puppet masters and their totally controlled corporate media in all its forms. Of course, the controlled media is only one element of the mechanism used to subtly deceive us all. Another huge player in this regard is the entirety of the educational establishment, which somehow succeeds in not only propagandising us from the age of four until graduation, sometime in our early to mid-twenties, but also clandestinely mentally prepares us for a lifelong servitude to our masters and the corporate machine. And the student loan scam also guarantees our servitude to the system, by snaring us in huge debt as soon as our adult lives begin.

So, it was from those small beginnings that my writing career blossomed, and from there I embarked on some extensive research into the real *Titanic* story, culminating in two books on the topic: *RMS Olympic* (2013) and *Titanic's Last Secret* (2014) – a novel based on the factual *RMS Olympic* book. Both these books propound the theory, backed-up with copious evidence, that it was not RMS *Titanic* that sank on that freezing cold April night in 1912, but her identical twin sister, RMS *Olympic,* and they outline in great detail the reasons for the gross deception, and exactly how the hoax was facilitated and subsequently covered up. This enabled possibly the greatest insurance fraud of the twentieth century, facilitating as it did J. P. Morgan's efforts to rid himself of the debt burden incurred by the collision with HMS *Hawke* that rendered *Titanic*'s twin, RMS *Olympic,* a virtually useless wreck.

And the sinking of the *Titanic/Olympic* additionally enabled Morgan to rid himself of serious opposition to the formation of the Federal Reserve Bank. Three of the greatest opponents of this nefarious scheme to wrest the control of money from the US Government all 'coincidentally', and conveniently for Morgan, died on the ship that sank to the bottom of the deepest part of the Atlantic in 1912. Bearing in mind that more than ninety-five per cent of all first-class passengers survived, what are the odds that all three of those individuals – J. J. Astor, Benjamin Guggenheim and Isidor Straus – would actually die?

The bodies of Guggenheim and Straus were never recovered, but Astor's body was picked up several days later and was identified only by the contents of his jacket pocket, his face having been battered to an unrecognisable pulp.

In May 2016 I published the largest book to date in my rapidly growing portfolio – *Behind the Curtain,* a huge two-volume, 600,000-plus-word exposé of the fraudulent worldwide monetary and banking systems that prevail today and the people who run them with an iron fist encased inside a velvet glove. This book outlines precisely how those who are able to create money from thin air are able to use that fraudulent money to control almost everything else in the world, and how they (the international banker-gangsters in concert with the ruling elite) have distorted history and science for centuries, to pursue their own sordid agenda and create a false reality for humanity.

My next work was a new take on the JFK assassination – *JFK: A Very British Coup* (2019), which names and shames the British Crown as prime movers in the plot. And then, following on from that, *The Falsification of Science* (2021) is a sister volume to *The Falsification of History*. This is a huge volume of work, edited by and with significant contributions from Shannon Rowan, exposing all the anti-science tactics employed by the draconian powers-that-shouldn't-be in their never-ending agenda for the total subjugation of the human race.

Finally (for now), *Welcome to the Masquerade (2022)* was written in conjunction with my aforementioned very good friend and writing partner, Shannon Rowan. This is a detailed dissection of the great 'plandemic' of 2020/21, outlining how just about every aspect of this event was gross deception and exactly how, by whom and for what reasons it was perpetrated.

So what does the future hold?

Shannon and I are about to commence work (in early 2023) on another blockbuster, which will detail the next stages in the plan for total subjugation of humankind and the march towards mass depopulation and transhumanism (or Human 2.0).

And personally, I plan to embark in tandem on another lone project which will concentrate on Agenda 21 and 2030. This is the long-term plan of the demons who believe they own the Earth and all its peoples to further subjugate the masses by the use of psychological operations such as fake pandemics, genocidal vaccination programmes, fake climate change, proxy wars and transhumanism.

Looking back on the last twenty-five years, my life has been turned completely on its head in so many different ways. Had my forty-five-year-old self been visited that first weekend of September in 1997 by my seventy-year-old future self in some inexplicable temporal short circuit, never in my wildest dreams could I have ever believed the story of the next twenty-five years of my life, which he would no doubt have related to me. 'Surrealism' does not even begin to cover it.

The 'Brave New World' described by Aldous Huxley in his book of that name does not have to be a dystopian one. If the spiritual awakening of the whole world is to take place, as I believe it will, as 'good' is a far more powerful force than 'evil', then this will surely facilitate a much fairer and more equitable world for our descendants. I envisage a world where reality will no longer consist of satanic inversion. Health care will not destroy health for the benefit of a small clique, and politics will facilitate a much more benevolent society, where everyone will be assured of sharing all aspects of the fruits of human endeavours.

Currently the world is run by a small band of multi-billionaires whose primary goal is to subjugate and bend humanity to its iron will. The key to a brighter future is to quell the power of these maniacs. We know who they are, and we are slowly but surely gaining the upper hand. We are many and they are few. We do have the power, both individually and collectively, to change the world and shape a fairer, more abundant future for those who will come after us. Let us harness that power wisely and put an end to the millennia of slavery that our ancestors and ourselves have endured throughout the entirety of human history.

References

John's author page: https://www.amazon.co.uk/-/e/B00B8X4CB6

John's website: http://falsificationofhistory.co.uk/

John's channel is 'John Hamer Official': www.bitchute.com

Through the Looking Glass

WENDY WENDORFF

Wendy Wendorff has run several successful businesses and travelled extensively in Britain and overseas.

For much of my life, my computer was tethered to my office and used exclusively for work. However, the advent of a new laptop, more free time and being introduced to Facebook and other social-media platforms created opportunities to dip in and out of an unlimited field of information at any time of the day. What I discovered was a breadcrumb trail of mysteries and questions about our true history and the nature of our reality which gradually became a living adventure and, before very long, my main motivation. One day, when I was scrolling through the Internet, an article caught my eye about a megalithic complex at Puma Punku in Bolivia (Image 1).

Image 1: Puma Punka, Bolivia

'Pre'-history

Puma Punku contains structures of such size and accuracy that it is said that it would be almost impossible to recreate them with the technology available today. They also appeared to me to be cast from geo-polymer or some sort of concrete, but this doesn't fit with the dates given for the building of this site, which are 13,000–17,000 years ago. The questions surrounding its construction, location, placement, purpose and so on were ones to which I was unable to find satisfactory answers. I then discovered that within established archaeology many dating mechanisms are circular – fossils found in certain layers are such and such age because that is the age of that sedimentary layer; and conversely, the sedimentary layer was dated according to which fossils were found in it. It seemed there was a lack of real information, and I needed to search further.

Finding out about the existence of Puma Punku led me to research, and later to visit, many other sites around the world, including the Pyramids (Image 2) and the Sphinx (Image 3) in Egypt, the Bosnian Pyramids, where I was an archaeological volunteer (Image 4), and a pyramid in Israel (Image 5). I discovered that pyramids exist in most countries in the world, including one in Rome and one on the Balmoral Estate in Scotland!

Image 2: Pyramids (bent pyramid of Daschur)

Image 3: Sphinx

Image 4: Bosnian Pyramid

Image 5: Pyramid in Israel

Amongst other places, I visited Petra in Jordan (Image 6), Baalbek in Lebanon (Images 7 and 8), the Plain of Jars in Laos (Image 9), Angkor Wat in Cambodia (Image 10), Felsenmeer in Germany (Image 11), Sigiriya in Sri Lanka (Image 12), Daorson (Image 13) and the stone balls in Bosnia (Image 14), Derinkuyu underground city (Image 15) and Mount Nemrut (Image 16) in Turkey. I discovered that there exist stunningly beautiful star forts in virtually every country, and impossibly symmetrical and intricate 'temples' and stepwells throughout India. Closer to my home in the UK, I visited Stonehenge (Image 17), Silbury Hill (Image 18) and the Avebury complex (Image 19), and many other megalithic stone circles and placements are to be found around Europe and Sweden (Image 20). There are so many sites worldwide that due to their apparent age, size and complexity are completely inexplicable within the 'established' historical paradigm.

Image 6: Petra, Jordan

Image 7: Baalbek, Lebanon

Image 8: Baalbek, Lebanon (photo credit: Sylvia Freidler)

Image 9: Plain of Jars, Laos (photo credit: Sylvia Freidler)

Image 10: Angkor Wat, Cambodia

Image 11: Felsenmeer, Germany

Image 12: Sigiriya, Sri Lanka

Image 13: Daorson, Bosnia

Image 14: Stone Balls, Bosnia

Image 15: Derinkuyu, Turkey

Image 16: Mount Nemrut, Turkey, (photo credit: Petra Dagenhart)

Image 17: Stonehenge

Image 18: Silbury Hill Avebury

Image 19: Avebury

Image 20: Ales Stenar, Sweden

For example, how is it possible to explain the vast size of the blocks in the quarry in Baalbek or the jars in Laos? If we take the jars in Laos and consider what a normal ratio is between a large jar (give or take, say, twenty inches in height) and a person (say, six foot), then the height of the jar works out at approximately one fifth the height of a person. Now, since some of the jars in Laos, which are scattered over an area of 300 square miles, are up to eight feet in height, this would suggest that those responsible for them may have been around forty feet in height – six to seven times the height of current human beings!

This enhanced height may in fact hold the key to understanding some of the extraordinary remains at the other sites, and can possibly be corroborated by a mystery that exists in Washington, USA. Documented articles, including photographs, from nineteenth-century newspapers, report that many giant 'human' skeletons had been discovered at that time and were on show in the Smithsonian Museum. Subsequently, these displays were dismantled, and the giant skeletons hidden away in the vaults. In time, their very existence has been strenuously denied. However, a recent legal case has apparently forced the Smithsonian to admit to having these giant 'human' bones in their vaults. This then begs the question – whose bones were they and why were they hidden and denied?

The prehistorical mysteries do not end there. For example, the fact that there are many megalithic structures and cities located below the sea – in some cases, thousands of feet below – indicates the probability of altered sea levels. There is a vast undersea bridge or road linking India to Sri Lanka, undersea pyramids near the Azores and in the Bermuda Triangle, and sunken cities off the coast of Okinawa in Japan, in the Mediterranean, the Aegean, Egypt and many other places. What could have caused the sea level to rise (or the land to sink) and when? Official history does not appear to have answers to this question, and this made me aware of significant gaps in our knowledge.

What were we to make of the giant megalithic walls in Siberia, Japan, France, Sicily, Peru and elsewhere? Google Earth shows unexplained structures in the middle of nowhere, with thousand-mile-long completely straight 'roads' in what are now desert areas. What are we to make of these? And what of the Nazca Lines in Peru, and the presence of what look like ruined cities and dry riverbeds at many other deserted and unpopulated remote locations?

The questions did not stop there. Indeed, Anatoly Fomenko, senior professor of mathematics at Moscow University, and full member of the Russian Academy of Sciences, caused further ripples when he recently released the findings of his twenty-five-year study into the New Chronology, which shows convincingly that 1,000 years were added to our timeline.

I found it astonishing that we did not learn about any of this while we were at school, and I asked myself why today's school history syllabus focuses on the very recent events of the First and Second World Wars when there exists such a vast panoply of fascinating structures and, by extrapolation, builders, former occupants, and societies, to decode and understand.

'Modern' history

It was not just gaps in prehistory. Recent discoveries bring modern history right up to date, including the recent release of over 100 weather-modification patents dating back to the 1920s, the observation of chemtrails in our skies, and the experience of extreme weather events happening around the world and being blamed on climate change. This made me wonder, since it is not unreasonable to perceive a connection between these weather-modification patents and the extreme weather events happening now and in recent times, whether we could be witnessing attempted weather (and societal behaviour) modification by governments to justify their stated goal of combating climate change.

At the same time, a mass of information has become available concerning the manipulation of information about world events that may not have been as they were presented to us. For example, the sinking of the *Titanic* in 1912, which resulted in the death of John Jacob Astor IV, the richest man in the world at the time and an outspoken critic of the creation of the Federal Reserve. Drowning alongside Astor were two other opponents of the Fed: Benjamin Guggenheim and Isa Strauss. Coincidentally, this happened in the year before the Federal Reserve was created. This private institution, owned by a handful of bankers, being neither federal nor holding any gold reserves, was set up solely, some argue, to control and manipulate the financial system of the US and the rest of the world via taxation, currency-fixing and the lending of fiat money to create debt. We may need to be patient to discover why, on 6 November 2022 a ten-foot-high wall was erected around the Federal Reserve Building in Washington.

In September 2001 another landmark event played out live on TV screens, and it is now apparent from the vast amount of work that has been done to understand the causes of this by an independent multinational organisation called Architects and Engineers for 9/11 Truth that it may not be an open-and-shut case. This organisation presented evidence and argued that this was a deliberate demolition event. Some commentators were claiming that this event was meticulously planned by governments and intelligence services to provide a justification for invading the Middle East. One notable exception to the meticulousness of the planning – and consequently a smoking gun pointing towards a deliberate and planned destruction by the establishment (rather than by Arab terrorists) – was revealed when the BBC's Jane Standley, Fox News and CBS News all reported on the collapse at 'free-fall speed' of Building 7 on public TV twenty-six minutes *before* Building 7 in fact came down and while it was still visibly standing in the live image behind the talking heads of the presenters! These revelations alone gave me cause to doubt the findings of the official inquiry into the event.

Some years later, I could not help but perceive the similarities between the sinking of the *Titanic* and the downing of Malaysian Airlines flight 370 in 2014. This plane had on board four of the five patent holders of a semiconductor patent that may have been the same patent used in the creation of the covid-19 jabs. The fifth patent holder, Jacob Rothschild, was not on board that flight and therefore became the sole owner of the patent following the crash.

Then, a mere five years later, the covid 'vaccination' operation was launched worldwide. It is reported that the same semiconductors mentioned above play a vital role in the linking of data from the 'vaccinations', via 5G and the Internet of Things, to usher in AI and the 'Singularity' – a term coined in 2005 by Ray Kurzweil, Google's director of engineering, referring to a hypothetical future where technology growth is out of control and irreversible. We need to be patient to see whether there is any truth in this hypothesis.

On a side note, the plane that 'disappeared' as flight 370 was, in several accounts, remotely flown to an airbase in Diego Garcia, where the passengers were murdered (possibly with poisonous gas) and left strapped to their seats. The same plane then allegedly reappeared two weeks later in a field close to Ukraine as Malaysian Airlines flight 17. The reports from those on the ground were of stinking, rotting and decomposing bodies, which would not have been the case had this been a normal plane crash, but does fit with the notion that the plane involved in flight 17 was actually the same plane as was used in flight 370.

What conceivably could be the purpose of disguising the Malaysian Airlines flight 370 plane and then flying to Ukraine as Malaysian Airlines flight 17 to be shot down? Reports in the alternative media were suggesting that this second event using the same plane could have been for distraction purposes, to destabilise Malaysian Airlines and to get rid of the bodies/plane. Some even suggested that the alleged downing of Malaysian Airlines flight 17 was used to foment the Ukraine conflict and lay the blame on Russia.

It is worth a mention here that although the Internet is regularly 'sanitised' with inconvenient information deleted, there exists an Internet archive called the Wayback Machine which can find almost anything that has ever been on the web.

So much for history past and recent. It was time to move on to other fields, with food and health being the most pressing.

Food and health

Two other areas where my investigative journey caused me to question the mainstream were food and health. Regarding food, we know that there has been a drive in the past fifty years towards mono-cropping and pharmaceutical dependence within agriculture. For example, we know that glyphosate, a common systemic weedkiller marketed as Roundup, is now sprayed on virtually every cereal crop just before harvest for the stated reason of desiccating (drying) the grain. It is a fact that this carcinogenic poison causes many bowel problems commonly referred to as 'gluten intolerance'. Also, and just as seriously, glyphosate causes permanent harm to the entire ecosystem (especially to bees and other insects, on which ongoing food production is utterly dependent)! Roundup is a poison, so why is it being sprayed on our food?

This brings us to the Codex Alimentarius (Food Law or Code), a massive multi-nation agreement concerning food and ingredient labelling. This agreement sits under the auspices of the United Nations and is the central part of a programme by the Food and Agriculture Organisation (FAO) and the World Health Organisation (WHO). Since the protection of human health is part of the brief of Codex Alimentarius, and since it is an acknowledged fact that glyphosate is sprayed on to the grain just before the harvest and will remain there, why does the Codex not require glyphosate to be listed as an ingredient? Other concerns were being voiced as well – for example, that the range, depth and complexity of this Codex provides ample opportunity for labelling food in ways that do not represent normal, accepted definitions, thereby allowing ingredients to enter our food chain without the people being alerted to them.

This is extremely concerning since the alleged purpose of the Codex is not only to protect consumer health, but also to promote fair practices in food trade. This means that any producer wishing to sell their products abroad must sign up to it. As I dug deeper, I realised how easily this system could be used to push out small producers, since it would take an army of lawyers to fully interpret the Codex – a cost that would be easy for multinationals to bear (not least because they are probably party to the writing of the definitions), but impossible for small producers.

Is this all bad news? Well, not necessarily, since many of those becoming aware of these discoveries are now taking direct responsibility by producing their own food – organically, at home, in their gardens. It is possible to feed a family for a year with a plot of under 100 square metres, provided that the 'old ways' are utilised, such as composting, seed saving, crop rotation and companion planting plus bottling and jam making to preserve the glut at harvest time. Even smaller areas can be equally productive if aeroponic systems are used. Why is this a good idea? Because traditional methods preserve the natural biome and ecosystem and are self-replenishing, providing highly nutritious organic food.

I have already touched on health in relation to food labelling and production, but there is also the mainstream 'health system' to consider. My research showed me that those working within today's medical profession are educated to a different curriculum from that of their forebears. Food and nutrition, for example – arguably the main factors in health – typically account for only two hours of instruction during six years of medical-school training. On the other hand, a massive proportion of medical students' time is devoted to pharmaceutical products. Once qualified, doctors are lured into incentives such as 'medical conferences' in exotic locations and bribes to administer certain drugs.

The covid injection (while in its trial stage) earned UK-based doctors £12.58 per two doses, which went up to £15 for omicron per person injected – a substantial addition to their salaries when you consider that according to official figures overall forty million people received the first two jabs and over thirty-six million the third. Although there are around 39,000 GPs in the UK, only a proportion of jabs were administered by them. However, their compliant participation in this mass roll-out of an untested trial injection gave people confidence to participate. It seems to me completely inappropriate and a serious conflict of the Hippocratic Oath for a doctor to be financially rewarded at all for delivering a *trial* vaccine with no knowledge of the ingredients and absolutely no test results or any information regarding possible side effects!

I was wondering why, with so many subsequent side effects and 'sudden deaths' of healthy young and middle-aged people being discussed in the news, there are so few doctors offering, at the very least, a theory that these tragic events might be linked to the hurried roll-out of an untested trial jab.

Of course, once again, even with evidence that the 'health system' is a misnomer, there is an upside. People are taking their health care into their own hands and researching natural methods to maintain optimum health. There is renewed interest in plant and herbal medicines and an emphasis on prevention rather than cure. We are beginning to understand the importance of water in its purest form and structure, and why organic fruit and vegetables are so good for us. This awareness will be at the forefront of a resurgence in health for those awake to these matters.

Conclusions

It seems to me that a societal power structure has existed since records began. Can we ever be sure that what we read or are taught is the truth when 'truth' can depend on the perspective of the person telling it? The historical records that survive in this top-down controlled system are those written by those in control, at the top of the social system. We therefore need to maintain an open mind regarding what has been written. We have been indoctrinated to believe that in the UK, for example, there is an immutable class system, and that it is not possible to alter the position within society that we were born into. What a perfect example of the 'rulers' providing the information with which humanity can create a collective reality to maintain a status quo and thereby be more easily controlled within a top-down system of rule!

There is so much to be investigated, reconsidered and understood using the insights we have gained. Do all our accepted historical parables and current social structures demonstrate a controlled society? The Adam and Eve story? Cain and Abel? Moses? Noah? Nimrod? The Egyptians? The Romans? The Roman Catholic Church? All organised religions? Royalty and the aristocracy? Governments and presidents? Could it be that those who appear to hold positions above the population – i.e. ruling over or guiding humanity – were in fact simply controlling the consciousness of humanity? What if those visible 'rulers' were merely the puppets of another layer of control, which remains hidden but pulls the strings? What if we the people are being farmed like sheep and cattle within a self-created and maintained matrix version of a reality that *only* suits those in control? It is certainly beginning to feel like it these days!

In summary, once awakened to the knowledge that things are in fact so significantly different from the way we were taught, told, and believed as to be almost the reverse (hence the through the looking glass reference), it was not only impossible to go back to sleep, but it was also impossible to stop questioning.

There is a saying that 'with knowledge comes power' and I like to think that having looked at things differently I have a better understanding of what I am up against and therefore am much better able to prepare and protect myself against the various top-down control systems imposed at ever increasing speed. Using critical thinking allows the individual to take full responsibility for him or herself. There is no longer the need to rely on the protection or support of Governments because they do not have our interests at heart. So, it is a coming-of-age, a stepping into our own power and I can say from personal experience that this is a wonderful feeling - self-governance, self-sufficiency, and open-minded learning - what a gift!

POLITICS AND CONTEMPORARY AFFAIRS

Breaking Free: How EMF Harm Led to Mental Liberation

SHANNON ROWAN

Author of WiFi Refugee: Plight of the Modern-Day Canary, *Shannon Rowan was raised on the east coast of the United States, and lived a number of years overseas in Ireland, France and Turkey. After a broad liberal-arts schooling and obtaining a Bachelor of Fine Arts in 1995, little by little her trust in the mainstream crumbled as she witnessed manipulation in the advertising industry, the loss of a friend in 9/11, the failures of the EMF regulatory system and the failures of politicians. Ultimately, these changes in perspective have been liberating. They produced an ability to look afresh at information and led to a major lifestyle change, taking her ultimately to the wilds of the northernmost part of California, where she now lives off-grid with her partner enjoying a healthier low-tech, nature-centered existence. (Readers can find out more about her work or contact her at www.wifi-refugee.com.)*

In early 2014 my world completely shattered after I returned from Bali, Indonesia, to Washington DC, USA. I had travelled for thirty consecutive hours, with all that time spent on airplanes and in airports. Upon returning to my apartment, I collapsed and was bedridden for nearly a week. I do not remember much from those days; it was as if I was only half alive – barely conscious.

After I began to slowly recover and return to work and my daily routine, I noticed that holding my smartphone caused strange sensations in my body, starting with electrical-pulse-like shock waves jolting through my hand and travelling up the length of my arm. The sensations persisted for up to an hour after only a five-minute texting session.

Holding the phone to my head was even worse. While I had always noticed a slight heating phenomenon occurring behind the ear to which I held the phone after a few minutes' call, the heating sensation was now intensified and the whole side of my face nearest to the phone felt numb and partially paralysed for a long time – even after very short calls.

I had never been prone to headaches before this time, but now they became a daily part of my experience, often building to debilitating twelve-hour migraines. I noticed intense chest pain when I stood near Wi-Fi routers and a crushing, squeezing pressure in my head when I was approaching cell towers while driving on highways.

Chronic insomnia, joint pain and night sweats were now my constant companions. And I noted that I could now feel when someone had a transmitting phone hidden on their person when standing in close proximity to me or when entering my apartment. And I was alerted to incoming texts and calls on a friend's phone by way of an electrical jolt through my body seconds in advance of the beep or ring announcing the digital message's arrival.

I began to research my symptoms online and confirmed what I already had been piecing together – I was experiencing what was now called electro-hypersensitivity or electro-sensitivity. I learned that the condition was previously known as microwave sickness or microwave injury and that the term was used to describe similar symptoms seen in radar and radio operators in the 1930s–1950s, experienced by the small subset of the population who were exposed to microwaves and radio waves on a regular basis.

Now these waves had become ubiquitous and an integral component of the myriad of our communication and entertainment technologies, and we were all swimming in this wireless radiation soup. But some of us (estimated from two to ten per cent of populations all over the world) were beginning to feel the effects of being slowly boiled alive, like the frogs in the proverbial pot. The frogs will not jump out if they do not notice the subtle rise in the temperature. This accurately describes what is happening to most as they get sicker with once rare – now increasingly 'normal' – diseases due to prolonged periods spent in the radiation soup.

I had not noticed living in the pot either until the temperature under my section was turned up quickly to high. This is how I describe those thirty hours of cooking in the most electromagnetic-radiation-saturated environments one can find – in airports and on airplanes, where radar and radio antennae, Wi-Fi and thousands of microwave-emitting devices abound, all inside metal EMR-conducting containers.

I had also recently switched from an old flip phone to a fancy new 'smart' phone and my electric utility company had covertly installed a bank of 'smart' (radio-frequency-pulsing) utility meters on my apartment building. If that were not bad enough, my city had just turned on the new 4G cellphone networks.

For me personally, the pot was now on full boil and I could feel it. I did not want to feel it; I did not want to acknowledge the relationship between wireless tech and my physical pain – it was not exactly convenient for me to do so. But I finally had to admit it. As a result, I gave up my beloved not-so-smart-after-all phone and began to spend as many nights as possible sleeping in the woods outside of town, where the signals were weakest. When I went into the woods and was able to get away from the electromagnetic fields, I felt enormous relief. All of my terrible symptoms rapidly eased.

Because living full-time in the woods outside our city was not an option, in under a year from my first EHS (electro-hypersensitivity) pains, my partner and I packed up and moved 3,000 miles across the country in order to find a location free from the ever present fast-encroaching wireless grid.

In the eight years since, we have been made to move several more times as the net of the new *net*-works tightened in. During these years I also engaged in extensive research on the EMR/EMF topic. In my research I uncovered another network – one of vast corruption and collusion, of revolving doors between the FCC (the regulatory agency for radio-frequency communications grids) and the wireless-industry lobbyist groups. Through these doors the chair of one the groups became the chair of the other (for example, Tom Wheeler after heading up the wireless lobbyist group CTIA for several years went on to take the helm of the FCC). I found that the FDA (Food and Drug Administration), which regulates product safety, did not require updated safety studies to prove the safety of wireless products, and that the only safety study that had been conducted was based solely on thermal heating effects, and not on other biological effects, even though both are most definitely occurring in human, plant and animal life.

This single study had been carried out in the early 1990s using old technology and exposure from only one phone equipped with an eternal antenna pointed away from the mannequin head in question, and it was tested for a duration of only six minutes with the cellphone held nearly half an inch away from the plastic head. The head itself weighed eleven pounds and the dummy represented a six-foot-two-inch 200-pound male – not exactly representative of the average cellphone user today (some of whom are pregnant women or even toddlers). They called the mannequin SAM (Standard Anthropomorphic Male), which ironically happens to be the name of my partner (Sam), who has stood by my side throughout this whole near-decade-long ordeal.

To date, the SAR (specific absorption rate)[15] is the only standard used for regulating wireless radiation exposures – one that bears little resemblance to the reality of our exposures today – with the average person exposed to multiple wireless devices, multiple Wi-Fi signals, 'smart' appliances, 'smart' meters, antennas and towers, everywhere, on a regular basis.

In the uncovering of this web of corruption and deceit, the veneer of my own personal bubble or shell began to crack a bit more. And the splinter in my mind (as described by the character Morpheus speaking to the character Neo in the 1999 Hollywood movie *The Matrix*) began to grow. The sense of this splinter and the first crack in my shell had in fact begun many years before. I had studied photography, communications, world religions, foreign language, writing, literature, the humanities, art and philosophy (with the main emphasis on design and photography) at university and exited with a Bachelor of Fine Arts (BFA) degree. I had been a thoughtful questioning child and student, interested in discovery and truth.

Upon graduation, my degree helped me obtain employment in New York City in the field of commercial photography. As a result, I learned first-hand from behind the scenes to just what lengths advertising art directors and their hired studio photographers would go to in order to manipulate and deceive audiences into buying (often cheaply made, sometimes dangerous) products.

Disillusioned by the commercial advertising world, I moved on to journalism. Being young and idealistic, I thought I could help change the

---

[15] For more information about the SAR test, seehttps://ehtrust.org/sar-test-inadequate/.

world for the better by capturing and publishing provocative images of newsworthy but under-reported struggles and events. As a caring, compassionate, nature- and animal-loving person, I naturally gravitated towards involvement with conservation and environmental protection, and animal- and human-rights activist groups. I undertook freelance work as a photojournalist and writer for PETA (People for the Ethical Treatment of Animals), the Animals Agenda, the Human Rights Campaign, the *Baltimore Sun* and many others. Over the years, this work took me to New York City and Washington DC in the US, and Istanbul, Turkey and Paris, France, abroad.

I had a strong sense of right and wrong, but my high moral compass was often used against me when I was taken in by politics, believing the left right, and the right wrong – liberals good, conservatives bad. This was an easy trap within which to become ensnared during the Bush Jr presidential years and the concurrent US invasions of Iraq and Afghanistan. My 'camp' seemed to be the only side protesting against these horrific and unjust military operations, while the other cheered the oppressors along, shouting 'America is Number One!' all the while.

But several cracks to the veneer of my aforementioned hard-shelled bubble gradually eroded my sense of being on the right side, of belonging to a 'correct' and infallible political group or movement. I had been suckered into voting for Obama and even celebrated in the streets with the rest of the equally duped masses when the election results came in, but it did not take long for me to see how I had been fooled when Obama's many campaign promises proved empty – leading to another crack.

The cracks occurred at various times and to varying degrees over many years and for many different reasons. The first truly significant crack occurred when I questioned the religion within which I had been raised during my early years at university. The questioning led, within a few short years, to my leaving the organisation, and led to my rejecting all organised religions after trying out a few others. However, my religious zealotry still found an outlet in political groups and movements, as mentioned. It took a long time to see how one had served to replace the other and that I was still actively engaged in black-and-white thinking and not engaged in the Critical Thinking for which I felt I was striving.

The second serious crack, of truly megalithic proportions, came with the destruction of the World Trade Centre buildings in New York City, on the fateful day of September 11 2001. From the year 1999 to that infamous day, I had been living in Istanbul, Turkey, working for various magazines, covering a wide variety of stories – ranging from Istanbul nightlife to Gypsy camps, to camel-wrestling events and to nature and marine-life conservation topics. My then husband was a well-known Turkish photojournalist, whose assignments had taken him to war zones, primarily to Afghanistan, on several occasions.

We were downtown when the news broke, and quickly joined with a group of other curious passers-by to crowd around a television screen at a nearby bar. We watched in stunned disbelief as the footage showed a plane hitting one of the towers, and then the two towers collapsing, played on repeat. It was surreal, and we almost laughed because it seemed like it could not be real. Something about it looked fake. However, as the realisation that my very close friend worked high up in the first tower sunk in, any impulse to laugh was soon replaced by horror. Hours later the call came. A friend simply told me that Adam was 'missing'. I knew what that really meant, but I held on to hope for as long as possible that he really was missing, that he had gone into work late, that he had not been in the building at the time.

That hope turned out to be futile. Adam was gone forever. The biggest news story and American tragedy of my time translated into a tragedy on a very personal level. I did not accept the official story about who was behind the attacks and how the buildings had come down. So many things about it did not seem to add up – especially the quick cry to arms and subsequent rapid invasions of Iraq and then Afghanistan. And my Turkish husband and I knew that American investors had unexpectedly and inexplicably pulled out of Turkey only a few months prior to the event (nearly collapsing Turkey's economy overnight), it seemed in a move to destabilise the country, paving the way for NATO troops and their use of Turkey's air-force bases for their Iraq invasion. Although Turkey never relented, as was hoped, we realised that these military plans had been laid out well in advance of the 9/11 attacks, which naturally led to the idea that 9/11 must have been planned in advance as well. Because of my very personal loss on that day, the event nagged at me, haunting me, as did the ghost of my lost friend, for many years to come.

More cracks in my shellac bubble crept through as my subsequent years of covering anti-war rallies and hearings on 'the hill' in DC bore testament to the corruption within journalism as well. My photographs were often grossly misrepresented in magazines and newspapers due to cleverly crafted captions meant to mislead subscribers. Yet again disillusioned, I moved away from journalism to wedding photography, and found the same forces at work within that industry, as starry-eyed couples were robbed blind by a voracious capitalist appetite that saw the world as comprised only of a mass of consumers – a world in which no one and no place or thing was sacred. This was painfully evident when I repeatedly witnessed a wedding couple's special day hijacked by wedding-industry vultures who did all in their power to turn a sacred event into a stressful nightmare. Every aspect of the day was craftily micromanaged and cashed in on, leaving the couple exhausted and bewildered by the day's end.

I spent some years involved with the New Age spiritual movement as well, joining drum circles, meditation groups and yoga retreats. I tried my hand at 'positive-thinking manifestation', which required the adherent to block out and repel any so-called 'negative' thoughts. It did not take me too long to realise both the impossibility and the folly of this practice. Without addressing and talking about 'negative' subjects there can be no critical thought and there can be no acknowledgement of problems, which also means no real solutions discovered.

More fissures in my bubble.

When I became microwave-injured and forced to leave my latest career (leaving behind my budding new dog-walking business), friends, family and home city, another deeper crack initiated full-on crumbling of my protective shell and I began to finally see the bigger picture, to connect the dots and to question . . . everything.

Soon after, I met geopolitical author and researcher John Hamer. I had come across his work by chance, or perhaps by destiny, and reached out. His book *The Falsification of History* further contributed to the necessary shattering of my illusions – the ones I had been conditioned to believe from day one – and ultimately led to our collaboration in co-authoring *Welcome to the Masquerade* after the biggest crack of them all manifested in the worldwide events of 2020 to 2022 which were rolled out under the guise of protecting public health.

When I became microwave-injured, I thought people would want to hear about the dangers of EMFs, of the risks of severe harm, brain damage, tumours, cancers, diabetes, autism, etc., but they did not want to hear it. My warnings were most often met with disbelief, distrust, disapproval and dismissal. In short, I was completely 'dissed'. And I found that people *liked* living inside their comfortable-seeming bubbles – ones that protect them from harsh truths better left undiscovered. For outside is an unknown place – one that requires stepping up, and demands self-discipline and self-responsibility.

When first breaking free of our prisons, of the many bubbles, it can feel painful, like a newborn chick breaking out of its warm cocoon of an eggshell—newly naked and exposed, the outside world can seem terrifying and strange. But freedom is worth the pain of the rebirth. Freedom of thought, freedom to ask questions, any questions – and to be open to answers (ones you yourself get to sort through and reject or embrace) – is priceless. It is what gives us the opportunity to grow as individuals, to realise individuation, to grow into our own selves. It offers us a chance to realise our true potentials – ones that have been robbed from us our entire lives.

Outside our shells, regaining lost freedoms means that we can no longer easily be deceived and manipulated by forces profiting from our continued imprisonment and enslavement. Not knowing about the hazards of EMFs or prescription drugs does not protect the ignorant from harm or premature death or loss of loved ones to the same. Ignorance is not bliss; instead it sets the ignorant up for abuse – physical, spiritual, emotional and mental.

I no longer subscribe to left over right or right over left. I see that both sides are manifestations of the same problem, that they are playing their parts in a drama orchestrated by the elite puppet masters from behind the curtain. And I understand that the drama is just part of the distraction, meant to keep us from finding the wizard behind that same curtain.

This is why I am no longer affiliated to a particular political group or movement. And I do not consider myself to be 'awake'. Rather I understand myself to be on a path of *awakening*, or, in other words, of critical thinking, of discovering, of growing, with no end to this unfolding. In the same way, a Buddhist understands that 'enlightenment' is not a single event or a place at which one arrives, but rather a continually unfolding process – a journey upon which one decides to embark.

To think of oneself as 'awake' or 'awakened' is another trap, another bubble, that prevents us from continued self-realisation, and from maintaining an open receptive state of humility. If we are to continue to seek out truth, to expose deception in all of its guises, we have to first seek this out within ourselves. In order to think critically we have to be ever wary of traps and be willing to break out of our own bubbles.

Being on this path for me means that I must do all in my power to discover and uncover hidden truths and to share what I learn with others who also want to learn, grow and free themselves from remaining forever unborn, stuck within a fragile eggshell.

When we cease to place our unquestioning trust in official narratives, we begin to shake off the shackles of naivety, and afford ourselves the opportunity to think critically.

If our nations' governments had told us that we would be required to carry at all times on our persons a health-destroying, mind-altering, wireless-radiating, transmitting surveillance device that would track our every move and monitor our personal conversations, purchases and Internet searches, and require us to foot the bill for the device *and* service to boot, there would have been worldwide outrage and protest.

However, this is exactly what has transpired. Nearly every citizen in both 'free' and dictatorial-ruled societies carry with them such a device; and in the case of the 'free' citizens, they do so willingly, while individually paying for the 'convenience' – the pretence under which these dangerous surveillance devices were sold to us, but which really describes the 'convenience' with which governments and industry partners monitor us as a result of our compliance. The only difference between 'free' and 'enslaved' nations lies in the *consent* given for technological enslavement in the former group over the latter. Each time we purchase and utilise surveillance-technology devices or software, we 'agree' to the terms of service, which, increasingly, are rewritten to allow a further surrender of individual liberties.

Today's wars are increasingly waged as covert operations which infiltrate and undermine our democratic systems. So stealthy are they that most targeted citizens are woefully unaware of being attacked. We consistently surrender our rights to the enemy with each acceptance of innocent-seeming cookies while surfing Internet pages, and with each wirelessly transmitted communication. But the enemy cannot defeat us without our consent. If we simply decide to forgo the many 'conveniences' (really trappings) of surveillance technology incessantly and aggressively offered under this disguise, wrapped in shiny, enticing packaging, and not purchase 'SMART' (which is really an acronym for Self-Monitoring And Reporting Technology) phones and appliances, and opt out of SMART utility meters, we could not be contact-traced and we would not provide personal information that can be used against us to detain, imprison, medicate and oppress.

Without these alleged conveniences we cannot be made to carry and present digital identification and proof of vaccination for the 'privilege' of travel, socialising, working or engaging in commerce. And without access to the 'news' (propaganda machine) 24/7 that harasses us from these same devices, we cannot be so easily misled and mind-controlled. By withdrawing our consent from these applications and devices, and by refusing to expose ourselves to the harmful electromagnetic fields inherent to them, we can regain our privacy – which forms the basis and foundation of any liberty, including that of freedom of thought. We can also reclaim our health.

It is up to each and every one of us. We personally and individually hold the keys to unlocking our prisons – the cells of our cellphones. We have the right to say no. If we do not exercise this right, we will ultimately inevitably lose it, as we are seeing happen as more people relinquish their rights in favour of these devices. What was once optional becomes essential in order to gain access to banking and other necessary digital platforms. But we still have time to say no. Each time we are locked out of a service or venue for our unwillingness to consent to contract, we can protest and demand access another way.

In lieu of consenting to 'SMART' phones we can opt for older 'non-smart' cellphones, although these are still harmful to health and allow for some level (albeit less intrusive) of surveillance. What we really need to do is demand continued access to landlines or they will be taken away completely, as is proposed for the UK by 2025 unless an existing campaigning group is successful in stopping these plans.[16] In the US, landlines are also disappearing, but the FCC (the US telecommunications and radio regulatory agency) is facing a hefty lawsuit17 over its misappropriation of hundreds of billions of tax dollars taken from landline users intended specifically for the improvement and expansion of both landline-based telephone and Internet. Instead, so the applicants claim, these monies were funnelled into expanding and improving wireless communication networks. Without this massive theft, the wireless networks and services would not have proliferated as they have done nor been so profitable. Therefore, it is our right to demand access to what we have already paid for.

Once upon a time, not too long ago, public landline telephones were readily available to the public at affordable rates (no device purchase or subscription rates necessary). The phones also dotted the highways at mile intervals for emergency use. Now, in their place are cell towers on the highways and Wi-Fi hotspots in cities. Landlines were not only healthier and more secure, but they did not fail during storms as wireless networks do, providing true emergency-use benefits often far superior to wireless counterparts.

It is up to us to take a stand before the enemy has won and completely dissolved our democracies and replaced them with dictatorships. It is not until we see that we are being deceived, that we are giving consent without truly being informed of the implications of this consent, that we can effectively fight back. And this fight begins with critical thought.

My own journey (detailed above) that served to open my mind to critical thought is also what motivated me to write my part of the aforementioned book with John Hamer and to solo-author my own book about my experience as one of the microwave-injured masses in *WiFi Refugee: Plight of the Modern-Day Canary*, and to continue to work on

[16] However, it seems that the proposal is to replace them with fiber-optic connections, so at least it will still provide a wired connection over wireless; but the connection will be digital instead of analog, which may not work during storms and also may be less secure and cause some ill-health effects in sensitive people. For more information, see https://www.bbc.com/news/technology-58233420. (The article also explains that by 2022 forty per cent of UK citizens had stopped using landlines, making their upkeep more costly.)

[17] To learn more about the lawsuit, one can visit www.irregulators.org and also purchase Kushnick's *The Book of Broken Promises: $400 Billion Broadband Scandal & Free the Net* on Amazon.com.

forthcoming books on a variety of important topics related to health, liberty and corruption within politics and industry. In addition to my own rejection of 'SMART' surveillance technology and my decision to opt out of tyrannical pandemic policies and never to 'accept cookies' or access the Internet wirelessly, I hope to keep freedoms alive through my writings and through the exercise of critical thinking.

How The Truth Began to Dawn

DAVID HENRY

David Henry is a former schoolteacher and college inspector who has taught in London and Africa. A former Conservative supporter, he later joined UKIP and then the Brexit Party.

Well, it wasn't really new, was it? Firstly, some years ago my wife told me about what the Kalergi Plan, fomented in the 1920s, aimed at, and it was scary! What she told me was that there were evil people in the world making plans to steer the world towards a totalitarian future rather than the free-thinking one we thought we were encouraging, certainly in the sixties. The Kalergi Plan aimed to mix white Europeans with other races by manipulating immigration (Coudenhove-Kalergi, 1925). Kalergi predicted that in the future a mixed race would arise and that today's races and classes would gradually disappear. According to the plan, the Eurasian–Negroid race of the future would replace the diversity of peoples with a diversity of individuals.

Secondly, when we were canvassing for Brexit – the only alternative to endless and excruciating payments of billions of pounds to unelected bureaucrats to run the affairs of what was once a proud nation – a lady came up to my wife and started pontificating on the great things Barbara Spectre and others were doing to help rid countries like England of their monocultures and replace them with a multicultural society. Spectre and others favoured allowing floods of immigrants to cross the Channel – something that had been happening for many years and still continues in 2022, when this account was written.

Thirdly, and quite by chance, my wife found a YouTube video in which Aaron Russo, Bette Midler's manager, who was dying of liver cancer and had nothing to lose, talked to Alex Jones about Rockefeller's plan for a cashless society in which we would all be controlled by the bankers and the globalists. Mentioning these highly worrying aspects to friends elicited some interesting replies. They told us that this was true, and that alerted us to other scary things that were planned for us. It soon became clear that many of the people we were talking to, including some friends, were very much aware of what was going on. It was clear that the so-called pandemic was being used as a mask to hide the headlong rush to a cashless society, side by side with the erosion of free speech. Could this be true?

A short while after this – and fourthly – I was rereading *The Trap*, written by James Goldsmith, founder of the Referendum Party, which later became UKIP, a political party campaigning for Britain's exit from the European Union. The book mentioned the same idea – namely, that there was a plan for a new world order, a world ruled by elites. Policies such as those concerning welfare and green energy don't actually benefit ordinary people. They do, however, make billionaires like Bill Gates even richer.

When Covid arrived, we asked what was going on. People walking around outside in masks, stores putting up directional arrows and notices imploring people to 'socially distance', governments holding daily broadcasts with a select cabal of so-called eminent doctors whilst other eminent doctors had no say and were effectively cancelled, a ban on foreign travel or even travel to neighbours' homes . . . Was any of this logical? Pubs were required to close at 10 p.m., as though for a curfew, but why not 10.30 p.m.? Where was the evidence for the effectiveness of these measures?

What was the justification for scaring people even more day by day through the mainstream media? Statistics were repeated concerning the mushrooming numbers of people catching seasonal flu (renamed covid), and flawed computer modelling showed that thousands would die or at best need to be put on ventilators in hospital. The effects were clear enough: swathes of the population were paralysed by fear, locking themselves inside their homes, often wearing masks, closing windows, getting groceries delivered and abandoning infected deliveries at the front door.

But where was the *real* evidence? Had a virus even been identified or isolated? How was SAGE, a so-called wise group (with one of its members, Susan Michie, an allegedly lifelong communist with a £2-million house in Central London), able to wield such influence with the UK Government?

SAGE, the government's advisory group of hand-picked scientists, also included Sir Patrick Vallance, who owned half a million shares in Pfizer. Why were dissenting scientists and doctors ignored or drummed out of their jobs? Why were groups like SAGE, who took over government policy for lockdowns, vaccine mandates and so on, not allowed to brook any dissent? And why did they ignore common sense? Who was pulling their strings?

Were these people really giving us impartial news? Can the BBC still be considered an impartial source of news when it (and other broadcasters other than GB News) steadfastly refused to question the pernicious ideology, which ruined the economy and many innocent people's health? This behaviour by the BBC confirmed my wife's growing realisation that the agenda was a plot against the people, cast in the name of health, the clue was to 'follow the money'. Where was the sense? Where was the logic? Where was the common sense in shutting down the economy? Bars, cafés, restaurants and other businesses, like clubs and barbers, were forced to close whilst still needing to pay rents and business rates. Bankruptcy was looming for many, exacerbated by higher taxes and the drive towards 'net zero'. And inflation was ratcheting up.

Then my wife showed me videos from Catherine Austin Fitts, an experienced American investment banker and political commentator. Austin Fitts graphically showed how the richest globalists would be buying up bankrupt businesses, such as cafés and small sole traders in the USA and other countries, and then using the repossessed land for their own profit. Later we heard of Mr Gates buying up millions of acres of farmland. Why? To depopulate the planet? There was a TED Talk from 2010, in fact, in which Gates speaks of vaccination as doing a great job in halting the increase in population. Here are his words:

> The world today has 6.8-billion people. That's headed up to about nine billion. Now, if we do a really great job on new vaccines, health care, reproductive health services, we could lower that by, perhaps, ten or fifteen per cent.

Was he really advocating a reduction in population through vaccines or, as Reuters suggested, were his words interpreted out of context?

As the country steadily closed down, teachers' unions were complicit in ruining children's education by forcing them to learn from home, studying syllabuses and curricula that were not impartial or balanced. For instance, new science textbooks, eagerly snapped up by ideologues in the classroom (hot from universities that had abandoned both impartiality and free speech), stated that (covid) vaccinations were a great thing (never mind the thousands of reported adverse reactions) and that climate change was mainly our fault and needed to be arrested through a green agenda (though there is no consensus amongst scientists and the proposed measures would cripple the world's finances). Despite the falsehoods parroted in the school textbooks, this agenda was keenly adopted as policy by governments of all colours! Build Back Better!

How was it that politicians from all over the world, royalty and the mass media spoke the same language at the same time – Build Back Better? Why did things need to be built back better if they weren't broken in the first place? My wife was smelling a lot of ratty smells and I was beginning to as well! What she was telling me was that the globalists were doing the very opposite of this slogan in their policies and prognostications! Cut the world's population, spread more viruses, cut down access to medical services, including GPs, postpone vital operations, close banks and force people to go online, lock people down as much as possible in their homes, don't let them talk to each other, get rid of motor cars so people can't escape . . . What was going on? And then there are the petrol shortages, the supply-chain problems, the slaughter of millions of healthy food animals so that in future people could not only eat bugs or chemically engineered synthetic food – a campaign spearheaded by Mr Gates and his friends.

I was not yet convinced, but I saw that the globalists were successful in their efforts to cancel the views and opinions of those smaller than themselves, whether it be ex-President Trump or a little old lady who found she couldn't pay her bill because PayPal didn't like her politics! My wife asked why 5G was being rolled out so quickly and whether the same people were behind this as were behind the roll-out of the so-called covid virus? What was their agenda? Was it to depopulate the world even more by means of radiation?

Very luckily, watching the new GB News channel every day and subscribing to daily emails from *TCW* (*The Conservative Woman*) made me more inclined to believe my wife, and so more inclined to believe that we were being duped, taken for a ride. This was reinforced at least once a week by the like-minded groups we chatted to and the huge London marches where we had our suspicions confirmed. There's safety in numbers! We were steadily coming to reason, rightly or wrongly, that we, the twenty per cent being classed as traitors or misfits, were in fact the majority, and we believed we knew what was really going on, and what game the globalists were really playing! Their plan – parroting the mantra of Klaus Schwab, head of the World Economic Forum (WEF) – was for us to own nothing but nevertheless be happy!

As we talked to more and more like-minded people and read more and more evidence-based books, like *The Real Anthony Fauci*, we were more and more convinced that we would never change our minds; we would never surrender our freedoms!

References

Coudenhove-Kalergi, R. N. 1925. *Praktischer Idealismus,* Vienna-Leipzig: Paneuropa-Verlag

Kennedy, R. 2022. *The Real Anthony Fauci,* Children's Health Defense, New York: Skyhorse Publishing.

Finding a Voice

ANNIE CURRIE, BA (Hons), ADGE, ACCP

Anne Currie is a teacher and psychotherapist.

Picture a long hospital ward. A gloomy brown dado separates the spinach-green walls, and curtains flap at the windows, wide open to a gale. It is November 1939 and I am three years old. I've swallowed a hairgrip and I've been rushed to hospital for cotton-wool sandwiches to make it go through my tummy without hurting. I'm sitting up in one of the cots, ten on each side. We all have a little plump eiderdown. Mine is blue, and at the bottom, where the legs go, a pretty tin tray for the dinners. I do like my new teddy, but I'm missing my mangy old Buster.

Across the ward there's a little boy with ginger hair. He's very noisy and he's holding on to the bars. Now he's pulling himself up and rattling his cage and stamping on his tray, shouting and crying. I watch him, fascinated. What a wonderful idea! So I get up too and start to stamp on my tray as well. It makes a lovely tinny sound and I yell, yell, yell. 'I want my Mummy!' Screech, scream, cry.

Along comes Matron. She looks cross, like a very fierce lady lion. She says we're very naughty children and tucks us in very tightly so we can't do it again. All the other children look frightened, but I'm feeling really happy.

* * * * *

And so I remember vividly my copycat rebellion – outwardly docile, yet inwardly rejoicing in the heightened energy produced by anger expressed. I was later to recognise that feelings in our household were not encouraged; my parents were, after all, Edwardian. You might cry at a pinch, but were quickly hushed or soothed with a sweetie and told to be a brave soldier or a big girl now. But the expression of anger was a big 'no no', unless it belonged to Father. He was kindness itself when he was not troubled, but we never knew what would upset him next. You might think there were few advantages in growing up with an irascible parent. However, it taught me to keep a careful eye on the weather mood and to recognise that appearances can be deceptive. And thus I've lived most of my life in two worlds: the seen and the unseen, the public and the private, the overt and the covert. A latent scepticism was hiding within, and this training by Father was to prove useful later on.

Throughout my childhood, the local doctor was a remote, hallowed figure, always male and rarely seen, since a visit cost half a crown. My faith in medicine and doctoring was thus absolute, based, as it was, on the mystique of reputation and absence. Then, in 1948, the NHS was formed. Hurray! Mr Bevan's mantra 'Free health care from cradle to grave' meant we were safe for ever.

Forward to 1963, when my comfortable suburban state received a jolt. As a young mother expecting my second son, I began to hear rumours of babies born without limbs and with other deformities. Two of my friends, who had taken thalidomide for nausea in the first trimester, produced babies who were so badly affected that they died at birth. Later we learned that thalidomide, developed in the 1950s and pronounced safe and effective, was withdrawn in 1961, but was still available on prescription. My faith in doctors and medicines began to falter, and having discovered homeopathy and osteopathy, both equally effective for me and yet dismissed by the medical profession, I began to feel like an outsider. How puzzling! Why were these systems considered to be hocus-pocus, a threat to allopathic doctors, when their healing qualities can be so potent? Thankfully osteopathy is now welcomed in doctors' surgeries. Things have moved on.

Then into the eighties, when as a languages teacher I found myself particularly interested in those pupils who couldn't manage an academic approach. This, and a change of personal circumstances, prompted me to train as a psychotherapist, and this is where memories of Father came to the fore. The grounding he gave me in gauging minute signals of mood and fluctuations in atmosphere helped me to discover material which was hidden, through shame and fear, within both myself and others.

To couple this training, I went to work at a childcare centre. The atmosphere there was toxic. Almost all the young people were described and treated as wilful troublemakers or downright evil. No one seemed to be interested in what lay beneath their behaviour. Containment was all.

Then in 1987 the floodgates opened. Over time it became apparent that most of our children in the care home had been abused, sexually or by way of neglect – hence their behavioural difficulties. Sexual abuse was not then an everyday concept – something that it has become this century. It was a taboo topic or else not recognised as existing at all. It was then that the Cleveland Abuse Scandal became a cause célèbre. News reached the local and national press that two consultant paediatricians in the Middlesbrough Hospital had used a new one-size-fits-all method for establishing whether the sexual abuse of local children had occurred. One hundred and twenty-one of those tested were summarily removed from their homes, often in the middle of the night, and placed in childcare establishments such as ours, foster-care and even a hospital ward. Family members were left to face allegations of having perpetrated these crimes.

Such information was gladly seized upon by editors, and the story ran and ran. Day after day, headlines and articles filled the newspapers. For many members of the public, these stories came as a surprise. They could not conceive of this type of abuse happening on such a wide scale and necessitating investigations when children visited the hospital for routine physical ailments such as an earache or a wounded knee. People were awakening to the possible widespread incidence of child sexual abuse.

In 1988 the Butler-Sloss Inquiry into the affair found that most of the diagnoses were incorrect, so ninety-four children were returned to their homes. The paediatricians were criticised and the ensuing Children's Act of 1991 was implemented, partly as a result of the inquiry. Seven years later, a TV documentary suggested that very many of the diagnoses were in fact correct and that there were still children who were at risk. Moreover, Beatrix Campbell, the author of a book concerning the inquiry, described it as compromised by establishment guile and bad faith. So the extent to which the establishment was acting in the interests of children was called into question.

We did not realise that decades later we were to become embroiled in a parallel division which, though different in substance, reminded me of the uncertainty and uncomfortable feelings I'd encountered in that era.

Psychotherapy requires an interest in the subterranean; and very soon, in the course of my experiences, I found that I had developed a nose for what I would vulgarly call bullshit. Any display of the inauthentic would cause me to develop an uncomfortable feeling in the stomach, and this has become a useful facility for assessing everyday life – one that I trust and value. It was to be much tested when we reached March 2020, for, almost overnight, life changed and became full of mind-screwing paradox. For after several months of our watching it spread across the world, and despite all the warnings, covid-19 was no longer a high-consequence infectious disease (HCID). Yet within a few days we were in lockdown. A curious juxtaposition. The official explanation: the downgrading was merely a technical classification and had no bearing on governmental action. Life 'through the looking glass' was coming closer, where words can mean what you want them to mean. My inner sceptic was alerted.

At first, the lack of traffic in lockdown seemed to provide a relief from the hectic nature of modern life. That relief was short-lived. Government plans were swiftly brought out in a sewn-up fashion and yet, at the same time, seemed to be shambolically organised. A restrictive, even tyrannical, emergency Coronavirus Act was rushed through Parliament on a Thursday afternoon. Despite all of this, interestingly, I felt no fear of this virus whatsoever. The BBC news talked of nothing else and even ignored a massive earthquake in Russia, which would normally have been a major headline event. I began to question everything. There were so many anomalies and rumours. The rules were legion and confusing. Even the police were muddled. One neighbour, cycling to his allotment half a mile away, was accosted by an officer who threatened him with a fine on the spot. Helicopters followed lone cars travelling along deserted roads. We seemed to be living in a police state.

I dutifully wore a mask for a few weeks and developed blepharitis, involving headaches and inflammation of the eyelids. It was a consequence of breathing in my own toxins. Exemption contributed to my feeling like a pariah, as folk moved out on to the road to avoid this old woman without a mask. Or were they obeying the order to protect the elderly? Interesting when you realise that the inevitably tiny holes in even the best-fitting masks are larger than any virus!

Meanwhile, mothers held their children close and shielded them from other human beings. As a boy went off to buy an ice cream, his mother even shouted, 'Don't go near people!' We know that connection is a vital ingredient for mental health and well-being. Its deprivation lies at the centre of many heartbreaking family-separation stories: children warned not to kill their grandparents, old people peering through care-home windows. Above all, we were restricted in our movements. We could not travel in this country or abroad. Schools were shut, exams cancelled. People found the injunction to use cards instead of cash a convenience, not realising the implications of creeping government control.

Questions needed answering, and the first one for me is usually Cui bono? – 'Who's to gain?' Since governments all over the world seemed to be acting in unison (a rare enough concept) there must surely be some bigger overriding manipulation – some corresponding bribe or coercion must be at work to produce such cohesion. The World Economic Forum (WEF) fitted the bill. As an unelected non-governmental agency, founded by Klaus Schwab, the WEF openly declares its mission to do away with the democratic process and to give all ownership and control to the deep state via what they call the Great Reset. The private, unelected World Health Organisation (WHO) seems to be equally powerful and equally suspect.

And then there is the problematic UN. Massive amounts of energy and resources were being expended in promoting a fear-driven enforced obedience in surprisingly abject global populations. In the UK, despite panicky news items about overflowing wards in ordinary hospitals, large emergency Nightingale hospitals, built in days, lay empty. Meanwhile, very many people, including Members of Parliament, were growing richer from the contracts for masks and PPE. It is always wise to follow the money.

Daily bulletins were established from government officials, allegedly based on 'the science' – a much vaunted mantra. But true science requires a heavy dose of scepticism, not algorithms. The nation was beginning to divide into two groups: the first consisting of those who followed every regulation put out via the media, and the second consisting of those popularly known as 'conspiracy theorists'. They were very far from popular, but what if a conspiracy really did exist? Life could be made very uncomfortable for people who didn't go along with the government's diktats based on this emphasised 'science', and the divisions in society accentuated the problem.

Through the latter part of 2020, we heard excited talk of the search for a vaccine, and it was claimed that the British version was developed in a weekend. Eureka! A likely tale, since it usually takes years to establish the efficacy and safety of regular vaccines! I was surprised to read accounts of vaccines prepared in advance for a potential pandemic, and so deduced that someone may have known it was coming.

And whatever had happened to flu? I did not hear of a single case. I also noted the contrast between the habitually un-pushy invitations to have a flu vaccine and the much more forceful and urgent approach to the covid-19 versions. Then the results of the celebrated PCR test, invented by Nobel prize winner Kary Mullis, for lab purposes only and not for diagnosis, were often suspect. Operatives had only to allow the tests to pass the recommended number of thirty-eight cycles to ensure confirmation of a positive result. Along with all these leaked stories, the murky provenance of the disease in Wuhan did not inspire confidence. Who knew what to believe?

In all this, I was wondering what had happened to my stomach-ache signal. Even that was being tested as a guiding measure. It suddenly surfaced when I heard the following: as soon as the medical profession discovered that ivermectin, a cheap and long-established drug, was an effective cure for covid-19 symptoms, it was removed from general availability. It became an expensive product, available only on the Internet, if you knew where to look. Hmm! One poor husband was forced to secrete a second dosage into the hospital for his wife to take, since her own had been confiscated by staff. And this in Great Britain, Land of the Free?

Soon, almost every conversation would begin with an enquiry about one's vaccination status. Then, if you were declining the vaccine, what followed were covert or actual expressions of disapproval of your selfishness in being unwilling to protect your friends and neighbours. The situation came home to my partner and me when our fellow Quaker worshippers found our position in refusing the vaccine difficult to accept. This resulted in the need for much relationship repair work. It was particularly disappointing when you consider the history of Quakers' resistance to the injustice of many social norms. Of course, no one knew where the truth actually lay in this situation, and luckily the love which we feel for one another helped us to survive the impasse.

Gradually, throughout 2021/2, a few people we knew began to 'confess' that they had begun to guess at what seemed to be happening behind the scenes. We found comfort in the formation of a small group of a dozen or so whom we meet every week with the purpose of supporting one another and trying to prepare for an uncertain future. By now we were sharing information from many eminent doctors, virologists, immunologists and journalists who were beginning to surface on websites to speak out about the bogus nature of the experimental vaccines, their poisonous ingredients and the purpose of persuading the populace to take them without informed consent. This latter was in contravention of the regulations formulated after the post-World War II Nuremberg Trials.

The possibility of covid passports hovered. If the WEF, for example, were to succeed in their aims, this would harm populations globally in as yet inconceivable ways. And so the thirteen or so richest families in the world, along with Big Pharma, would further enhance their power and wealth. Thus occurred our gradual realisation that there may be a bigger picture showing accelerating domination by means of a fraudulent corporate takeover.

At last there arrived the person who was to rouse people from their slumbers. John O'Looney is a funeral director with fifteen years' experience who has a unique view of events. Whistle-blowers are usually people whose moral compass will not allow them to stay quiet about what is happening around them. To come clean is a perilous option, since they risk losing their livelihoods, reputations and even their lives. Because of these factors, I believe their evidence is likely to be truthful.

It was John O'Looney who convinced many that there was sinister intent behind the introduction of the allegedly gene-modifying vaccines. He is at the sharp end of the process when he receives the bodies of those who have died, and he is able to compare the government's claims with what has actually been happening. A body does not lie. A worrying story unfolded of old folks in care homes who were dying in unusually high numbers.

What was happening there? And why was the drug midazolam being administered in care homes – especially to those residents ordered there by the Health Secretary from hospitals where they were being treated for symptoms of what was described as covid? The symptoms of covid-19 allegedly include respiratory problems; and yet midazolam is a drug associated with respiratory suppression and respiratory arrest, and can lead to death. This drug could have been a major factor in the sudden spurt in deaths in the UK that was used to justify lockdown.

Further, there were the allegedly gruesome effects of the mRNA vaccines on people's bodies, causing sudden death in increasingly younger age groups. These even included numerous babies of vaccinated mothers, and O'Looney spoke of the NHS dealing with the bodies and not passing them on to funeral directors who could blow the whistle on the elevated levels of infant deaths. The media outlets seem to have shut their eyes to these apparently abnormal events.

As I listened to John's passionate caring for his clients and his obvious disgust at their treatment, I too was convinced of his sincerity and that he was speaking the truth.

I urge those of you who, up to now, have believed what the government tells us via their announcements through the BBC and other media channels, to take a chance and listen to what John O'Looney and others have to say. It may encourage you to ask questions.

What can we do? As a child, I was told that our hands on earth are God's hands. He can turn evil into good when we act. Since a digital currency is fast approaching on the horizon, I suggest there is one small positive action in which we can join, all pulling together, whatever our views: pay for as much as we can in cash. In this way, we will retain some of our freedoms, privacy and individuality.

A small Quaker aphorism:

In essentials, unity;

In non-essentials, liberty;

In all things, charity.

God bless us all.

References

Esteemed doctors, virologists and journalists questioning the mainstream narrative:

Dr Aseem Malhotra, Dr Simone Gold (of America's Frontline Doctors), Dr Dolores Cahill, Dr Bryan Ardis, Dr Tom Cowan, Dr Zach Bush, Dr Rashid Buttar, Dr Vernon Coleman, Dr Judy Mikovits, Dr Reiner Fuellmich, Dr Mike Yeadon (erstwhile chief scientist for Pfizer).

Follow-up information from all these and others may be found at bitchute.com, brandnewtube.com, rumble.com and their own websites. Visit the UK Column for livestreamed news.

Freedom Fighter to the Last

JEFF WYATT, written by his friend Jill Turner

Jeff Wyatt, May 1964 – September 2022, was an entrepreneur, political campaigner and racing driver.

Jeff and I spent hours talking as we drove up and down the country to countless rallies. Below is my take on Jeff's realisations over the last couple of years as he told them to me and often shared his thoughts at talks and speeches.

Right up until the day he left us, he never stopped resisting, defying the tyranny and fighting for our rights!

> 'Good men and women have to stand up for the truth. If that's anarchy, then it's anarchy'
>
> –*Jeff Wyatt*

Jeff often spoke of his journey of increasing questioning as leading him to a sense in March 2020 that a runaway freight train had hit him. As Boris Johnson was giving the nation instructions to stay at home, Jeff instantly knew something was amiss. In his own mind, this was nothing to do with a 'deadly virus' and he sensed that a big fight lay ahead. His sense that civil liberties were being removed really touched a nerve with him, and so his activism began with earnest.

His questioning had been progressive. During the Brexit campaign, he became aware of the Foreign and Commonwealth document written in April 1971 - 'FCO 30/1048' - that contained information that was not released to the public under the thirty-year Official Secrets Act rules and so was not released until the beginning of this century, in 2001. His reading was that this FCO document clearly revealed the loss of British sovereignty that would follow Britain's membership of the then European

Economic Union (EEC), with the end of the document stating, for example, that entry into the EEC would give way to increasing integration, leading to, in the words of the document, the '*consequent decline of the primacy and prestige of the national parliaments*'. He was outraged that this information was kept from the public until 2001 and felt that the British public had been misled.

He would pull out quotes that he'd saved to make the point. For example, he told me that in June 1971, a White Paper was sent to every home in the UK, promising: 'There is no question of Britain losing essential sovereignty.' Then, he told me that he'd read that in a TV broadcast in January 1973 to mark his signing of the Treaty of Rome, Edward Heath, the then Prime Minister, went even further saying that

> There are some in this country who fear that, in going into Europe, we shall in some way sacrifice independence and sovereignty. These fears, I need hardly say, are completely unjustified.

In Jeff's mind, these moves allowed the political classes to press ahead with Britain's accession to the EEC.

His thinking did not stop there. He told me that in January 1972, the Treaty of Accession was signed by Prime Minister Edward and the European Communities Act 1972 enacted on 17 October 1972 and the instrument of ratification deposited on 18 October, coming into force on 1 January 1973. This was the point at which Britain's membership of the EEC came into effect and he told me that some people had said, Ian Stuart for example, that the transfer of British sovereignty to the EEC that took place at that point was not only treasonous under the Treason Act of 1702 but also killed off the office of sovereign Queen. He told me that he took the view that this left her as a private citizen of a new entity, the United Kingdom, a legal entity under which she was given the title of 'Head of State'. According to this way of thinking – and who knows how correct it is -the absence of a signature and Royal Assent on statutes by a reigning monarch meant that all statutes issued since 1973 were neither legally valid nor binding.

Jeff was also concerned about possible encroachment on British territory of United Nations (UN) Troops. He told me many times of his concerns that young, able-bodied men were arriving illegally on British shores and might be used as a UN fighting force which might first appear benign but might then turn on the people once they became aware of the treachery that had been perpetrated against them on many fronts. His first instinct was to acquire information and then use this to petition the government.

As a former political candidate and campaigner, Jeff was not new to petitioning the government, so it was no surprise that he was to be one of the first wielding a homemade placard (they quickly became infamous in the Freedom Movement) to exercise his liberty. His uncompromising booming voice – 'We are all free people in this country and we need to reclaim our freedoms!' – and provocative placard won him the attention of the police (who, in lockdowns and early protests, far outnumbered the protestors). Despite Jeff's declaration of his non-consent – 'I am a free man; I do not consent' – after some lengthy harassment by London's Metropolitan Police, on May 16th 2020, he was to become one of the first to be arrested at the epicentre of free speech, Speakers' Corner in Hyde Park, for having the temerity to exercise his right to protest whilst he was in a group of more than two people. Jeff did not miss this opportunity to loudly proclaim his rights as he was led away, handcuffed, through the crowd as they were chanting, 'This is fascism!' and 'Shame on you!' to the Metropolitan Police.

I had only known Jeff for a short time at this point, but I remember that day well and it truly set the scene for the next two years. I was not fit enough to join Jeff and his friend Paul Watson that day, so I watched Twitter and the online live feeds and was elated to find that Jeff was trending on Twitter with one of his infamous placards: 'I am a free man, not a number.' Naturally the tweeters were hurling abuse at him and others, but Jeff simply did not care what people thought. He stood firm in his personal belief that the government was using the fear of the pandemic to control and intimidate the population. Later that day, word got round that Jeff had been arrested and spent six hours in Charing Cross Police Station. Who could believe that this law-abiding Englishman would be kidnapped by the state at Speakers' Corner for simply stating that he was a free man?

Jeff handled his arrest and pending legal battle, to avoid conviction, with his usual stoicism and determination. He faced the challenge with a glint in his eye and used it as an opportunity to both expose what he perceived to be a corrupt judicial system and challenge it with common law. And challenge it he did! Jeff chose to represent himself, majoring on the Bill of

Rights and the Magna Carta, and asserting what he considered to be his inalienable right to free speech. He even enlisted the help of Professor Dolores Cahill as his expert witness, to give evidence to underpin the view that the covid restrictions were unlawful. Despite this, he was handed a criminal conviction with a conditional discharge, effectively for walking in a public park with a placard.

His experience gave people an insight into the workings of the judicial system in the UK and how common law rights have apparently been ridden roughshod over by government. After this sense – in his thinking a Light Bulb Moment - that people's inalienable rights were under attack, Jeff and I frequently discussed his view that the people who prosecute criminals in the UK could be described as criminals themselves.

From the moment of his arrest, Jeff really grasped how serious the fight we were facing was. He became a regular at covid-restriction protests up and down the country, often with me in tow. During our travels he frequently and fondly referred to his late father as his inspiration. He spoke of how his Dad brought him up to speak his truth. Without fail, Jeff would get emotional sharing stories of their strong bond and his sadness caused by his father's passing just four years ago.

Jeff was relentless in his commitment to fighting the tyrannical overreach by the government, and he was never happier than when he had a mic or loudhaler in his hand. It didn't take long before Jeff was well known in what we refer to as the Freedom Movement; and despite his resistance to the calling, he was to become the everyday man's accidental leader – something the people were looking for.

He was one of the best orators in the so-called Freedom Movement that emerged, and his fearless approach and straight-talking manner won him legions of fans whilst also attracting some haters. On many occasions Jeff was accused of being 'controlled opposition', which he guffawed at. There was never any evidence to support this, and that kind of thing is typical of any movement when someone continuously puts their head above the parapet.

Jeff felt strongly that we should accept that *agents provocateurs might be* amongst us, stirring up trouble, but he took the view that people should not let that distract them from the fight against the World Economic Forum's plans for the future – the so-called 'Great Reset' – and should resist attempts to impose global governance on the world, what some refer to as ‘the New World Order’. He said that people must put aside differences and concentrate on the central issues that people can agree on; otherwise, he would say, people are doing the other side’s work for them, leaving people divided and demoralised.

The seed that stoked his interest in politics was a conversation with his daughter when she exclaimed, ‘Dad, you can’t say that!’. Jeff would say that kids, by virtue of going through the education system in this country, are not always presented with evidence-based information and so cannot be blamed for not perceiving what he considered to be the truth. Jeff came to feel that he had grown up with the erroneous belief that he lived in a free country. This was a personal belief but one that he felt strongly.

As a former political candidate with UKIP and deputy leader of ‘For Britain’, his experience served him well as he soon realised how party politics was used as a means to create division and discord among the people. He remained staunchly independent and vocal about how the left–right divide had facilitated what he described as ‘descent into tyranny’, and this led him to form close bonds with those on the opposing side of the political spectrum from himself. In many of his speeches, Jeff would share another of his favourite quotes:

> ‘The most important political office is that of the private citizen’
>
> – *Louis D. Brandeis.*

Jeff saw his role as being to encourage as many people as possible to perceive the injustice of the alleged pandemic and to take action, no matter how small but his frustrations at many people’s general apathy was taking its toll. I remember that one Christmas – 2020, to be exact – he found things extremely tough and he spoke of how difficult it was for him to talk about his concerns with friends and family who were reluctant to listen. During those bleak winter months, Jeff, myself and other people spent hours in the freezing cold building a vegetable garden to prepare for what he saw as the eventuality of food shortages. He said that he looked into the subject of weather modification and was surprised to find that there are military patents on this over a long period, allowing the creation of rainfall, droughts, hurricanes, tsunamis, forest fires or geoengineering in the sky. Some of this he said he’d gleaned from the website of Dianne Marshall that discussed ‘Weather Wars’.

When I expressed surprise, he told me that he had read how US$3 million was spent from 1967 to 1972 as the secret project sought to make the monsoon season longer and flood the Ho Chi Minh trail, which was being used by the North Vietnamese as a supply route. He told me that it was hoped that the extra rains would cause rivers to flood cutting off bridges and crossings, as well as landslides, and that reports on the use of weather manipulation appeared in the mainstream press, for example the *New York Times* and the *Washington Post.*

Despite all the hard work that he did, he always enjoyed drinking beer in front of the fire with like-minded people who were willing to question government policy and use their inquiring minds to understand the truth behind events. And in spite of his larger-than-life presence and love of public speaking, Jeff did not engage in his public work in order to build a platform for himself. On the contrary, he was only interested in speaking the truth and honouring the memory of his grandfather, who was dodging bullets on the beaches of Normandy in 1944, fighting for our freedoms.

It is thanks to courageous and outspoken people like Jeff that we have been able to enjoy the freedoms (of sorts) that we have today, and it is now up to us to build upon the good work that he has started and that he continues to inspire so many to partake in.

One of his favourite quotes, which was adorned on one of his many placards and can be seen in countless videos and footage of protests from 2020 to 2022 was 'When the law becomes tyranny, rebellion becomes duty.'

And that is exactly how he lived his life, right up until the day he left us so prematurely, in September 2022.

CONTEMPORARY CULTURE

My Journey into a New Way of Life

MARK DEVLIN

Mark Devlin is a UK-based club and radio DJ, music journalist and author. As a DJ he has played gigs in over forty countries. In 2010 he had a new awareness of what's really going on in this world. His special area of interest was how this ties into the mainstream music industry, and the way in which A-list artists have been used to manipulate and mind-control the masses in line with much larger agendas. He now presents public talks on these subjects, as well as appearing on radio, and producing two regular podcast series. In 2016 he published his comprehensive book Musical Truth, *with the second and third volumes following in 2018 and 2021 respectively. His allegorical novel* The Cause & The Cure *appeared in early 2020.*

Thinking back with the benefit of hindsight, it seems that it was always on the cards for me to stray from the crowd and take an anti-establishment approach to life. I just could never have known, until a few years ago, that it could have led to quite the kind of career that I seem to have stumbled into.

A good start in this regard would appear to have come from my Dad. Leading by example, he always taught me that it was OK to stray from the crowd and not be a part of mainstream consensus. Being a quiet loner at school who didn't fit in with the popular kids, I took this as welcome advice. Although working class and 'uneducated' in the accepted sense, Dad had been an alternative thinker from as far back as I can remember. He had come across the books of Erich von Däniken in the 1960s, resulting in him, as my Mum puts it, 'going a bit funny'. Several authors later he had moved on to the books of David Icke, and it was his encouragement of me to read them that truly kick-started my journey in questioning.

There were a couple of other early indicators as to the approach to life I would eventually take. I remember from a very young age questioning the legitimacy of a monarchy, and wondering how, if we lived in a fair and just society, one family could be afforded all the wealth and luxury that the royals were, while others went poor, homeless and starving. (It hadn't occurred to me then, of course, that we *don't* live in a fair and just society!) I also remember being horrified when first discovering that animals were actually slaughtered, while young and healthy, for their meat, and this drove me sometime later to become vegetarian.

My full questioning of reality and our purpose on earth didn't come until embarrassingly late in life, however. Having followed my dreams to become a magazine writer, then a club and radio DJ, the career that this spawned kept me busy and distracted from more meaningful pursuits for many years. My full-time DJ'ing career was a whirlwind of overseas travel, non-stop parties and an unhealthily nocturnal lifestyle that lasted twenty years. It wasn't until around 2007 that I started asking some deep questions about the things that really matter: Who really runs this world and is pulling the strings of every aspect of our daily lives? What, even, is the purpose of these lives in the first place? And what, really, is *here* – this world in which we spend the entirety of them?

As the months wore on these questions troubled me more and more, eventually leading me on the path to devouring books in pursuit of the answers. By 2010 I was seeing the world in an entirely different way, and it was as if a light bulb had been switched on in my mind. My passion for truth discovery spawned a phase where I became zealously evangelical, spouting what I'd learned to anyone who would listen. Thankfully this period was short-lived, and I came to realise there were far more effective ways to communicate this information.

This involved drawing on the experience and skill set that I'd spent the previous twenty years building up; and while in retrospect those years can sometimes feel like wasted time, what was actually happening was that I was equipping myself for when my *real* work in this life would begin. It was all grounding. My years of presenting radio shows and conducting interviews was getting me ready for the podcasts I would put into the world; my time spent writing and researching for business and music magazines was training me for the writing of my books; the years spent travelling the length and breadth of the UK and beyond for DJ gigs was getting me ready for the same process, only now involving public talks and conference presentations. This plus the mature and sober approach to life that hitting middle-age brings once all the fun and foolishness of youth has been cleared out of the system. This wasn't 'wasted time' at all, it turns out; and while I sometimes wish I'd got my start much earlier, I now accept that nothing happens until its time has come.

My grounding in the music industry was the perfect preparation for what I would become well known for speaking about. Since coming to a grudging acceptance that the world – and life – is nothing like we've spent our entire lives being conditioned to accept it as, I set about studying how this dynamic filters down into the aspect of life that interests me the most. My furious delving into never-ending rabbit holes made me realise that what the music business represents and the agendas it's used to push serve as a microcosm for organised society generally.

By 2015 I was confident enough to self-publish a book containing everything I'd come to learn up to that point, and that became the first of my *Musical Truth* trilogy. I've since carved out a reputation for myself as 'that music-industry guy'; and while it's hugely gratifying to reflect on the degree to which my work has been so enthusiastically received, it's also very humbling. Through all my years of DJ'ing, driven by ego, I sought fame and recognition of the type that I only received once I'd stepped back from all of that and embarked instead on work which has some true value to others. As much proof as I could ever have needed that I'd finally got on my rightful path and was doing what I'd incarnated into this life to do.

Besides gaining an appreciation of 'real world' issues, my process of questioning also evoked some deep spiritual values within me. Following a long period of cynical atheism, I regained my faith in a Creative Force, and a realisation that all in apparent 3D existence is actually universal energy vibrating at an endless array of different frequencies, and that we, as living conscious beings, are expressions of that universal energy; we are spirit-souls having a brief but meaningful experience in this apparently physical realm, before we leave these bodies and our consciousness returns to its source.

I learned about what's been referred to as natural law, and specifically the dynamics of consequentialism and cause and effect, sparking the revelation that what happens in this world *does* matter, because it has implications for the spiritual evolution of humanity generally. My recognition of what true rights and freedoms really are, and our inherent sovereign nature, has spurred me on in combatting evil and tyranny and exposing lies and deceptions wherever I've found them, and has coloured the nature of the work that I've put out.

Here, for example, is what I wrote in *Musical Truth,* volume 1 (2016):

> There are two stances that I generally take with those sceptics who automatically scoff and dismiss any suggestion that the world could be just a little different to what we're being told, on the basis that it can't possibly be true because it 'doesn't sound right.'
>
> One is to ask them to use their imagination and put themselves in the place of an 'elite.' For this, they need to forget all about how they themselves would act in any given situation, and instead, take on the mindset of a psychopath – one whose mental condition makes it impossible for them to empathise with the feelings of others, thus leaving them free of any qualms whatsoever about how their actions might cause others to suffer.
>
> Their priority is to maintain their position as a ruler and controller over the rest of the population, and this must be upheld at all costs. Imagine also that you happen to be a satanist, and immersed in dark energy that allows any act of evil to be fair game. With these tenets in place, now consider what tactics you would employ.
>
> *Would* you seek to install obedient governmental leaders around the world that would do your bidding and adhere to your agenda?*Would* you instruct these governmental leaders to present an innocent and benevolent-sounding cover story for their actions to disguise their true nature? (Telling the public that you are invading an overseas nation to 'protect the people' while you slaughter the population and steal that nation's land and natural resources would be just one of a multitude of examples that would apply.)
>
> *Would* you bring all the main media outlets – newspapers, television and radio news, prominent internet sites – under your control, and shape and mould the content to give the masses the versions of events that suit you, while completely ignoring and side-lining those subjects that you don't want the people to know about?
>
> *Would* you coerce the public into eating food and adopting lifestyle habits that bring on cancer and other diseases, then deliberately

> suppress known natural cures and criminalise their use, instead offering pharmaceutical drugs, chemotherapy and radiotherapy, knowing that these treatments are actually responsible for killing off many of the patients even quicker and causing the very diseases they're claimed to cure, while at the same time creating an industry worth billions every year to those that run it?
>
> *Would* you seek to introduce a worldwide financial system that keeps the population in perpetual economic slavery to the bankers that run it, and that keeps the people of the world needing to constantly work for the majority of their lives just to be able to afford to live?
>
> *Would* you create religious systems that keep vast groups of people controlled by creating a belief that they will suffer eternal damnation and separation from their 'god' if they dare to disobey the rules and regulations set out in a particular book?
>
> *Would* you seek to create a paradigm in which what's considered 'normal' or 'possible' is what suits your ongoing agenda of control, and of cutting people off from a recognition of their true spiritual nature and potential, in which anyone who deviates from these 'norms' and tries to tell others that there's another way of looking at things is immediately demonised and branded as 'crazy?' [p.9]

I can say for myself that I would certainly do all of the above. Is it really too much of a stretch to imagine that this might be exactly what has happened?

Consider also the type of public reaction that would most suit the dark controllers in such a scenario. Would it not be a widespread scoffing condemnation of any information offered regarding their true nature on the basis that it 'can't possibly be true'? Dismissing information on this basis without doing any independent research of your own whatsoever is *exactly* the type of response they would rely on.

The other stance is to ask people whether they can afford to take the chance that the above scenario might be true, given the implications for human freedom that it brings. Yes, the idea of a worldwide conspiracy spanning generations that has prevented human society from taking what would have been its natural course if left free of these manipulations *might* be a load of old bollocks. But then again, it might not.

And, with doubts being cast by so many researchers into the subject, and evidence presented at every turn to suggest all might not be as it seems, can you afford to take the chance? Through adamantly refusing to look at the evidence, despite the free abundance of it now available through the Internet, by your tacit cooperation are you allowing this system of human subjugation to continue unimpeded? It's a question I would suggest everyone owes it to both themselves and their families to ask.

Many people are kind enough to tell me that my output has resonated deeply with them and helped them see the world in a different light. No one could ask for any more proof that, though far from an easy ride, they are truly walking the rightful life path that – just perhaps – they themselves in a higher form of consciousness, before they got here, chose to undergo.

And there is a great deal of information to take on board. Where the popular music industry is concerned, I wrote this in *Musical Truth,* volume 1 (2016):

> The dark manipulations of the music business are as old as the industry itself, and early examples of the dubious calling cards evident in the contemporary scene are equally present in its formative years. Mind-control, military 'intelligence', paedophilia and occult fascination are, it seems, nothing new.
>
> Many feel overwhelmed by the dark nature of these subjects, reasoning that the control system has been so deeply embedded into our reality for so long, that deconstructing it step-by-step seems impossible. Those of a New Age persuasion, meanwhile, will argue that paying any kind of attention to a dark or negative subject only helps to keep it manifested in reality, due to the energetic connection that individuals make when applying their conscious attention.
>
> This is ultimately a cop-out and an abdication of personal responsibility, since the first step towards resolving any problem has to be an understanding of the full nature of it as far as it's possible. Only then can any solution come. And attempting to dismantle the hugely complex and multi-tiered control system brick-by-brick clearly is impractical. The real solution lies elsewhere. [p.476]

In my view, solutions include a change in the human mindset as I pointed out in the same volume. Here is what I wrote, and I would endorse this thinking today:

> And so, it becomes clear that a major change in the human mindset — brought about by a radical shift in consciousness — is vital if this world is to ever come close to being a just and moral place to live. Losing the fear of what others might think is the first change that has to happen on a major scale. But an understanding of the moral laws of the Universe — on a scale that rivals the knowledge that's been hoarded by the dark occultists who have held humankind in slavery for so long — is also essential. [p.487]

Reference:

Devlin, M. (2016), *Musical Truth,* vol 1

Waking Up to Woke

NIALL McCRAE

Dr Niall McCrae is a registered psychiatric nurse, social commentator and refusenik. He has written five books, including The Moon and Madness *(2011),* Echoes from the Corridors *(with Peter Nolan, 2016) and* Moralitis: A Cultural Virus *(with Robert Oulds, 2020). A regular writer for the* Daily Sceptic, The Conservative Woman, *the* Gateway Pundit *and* The Light, *Niall is a frequent panellist on George Galloway's* Kalima Horra *debate show.*

As a large rally against the covid-19 regime approached the parliament building in Wellington, New Zealand, a gathering of masked counter-protestors awaited them. Having experienced some of the harshest restrictions in the world, Kiwis have good reason to complain, yet their procession was met with chants and placards accusing them of racism and homophobia. A banner asserting that New Zealand is 'no place for hate' seemed at odds with the good-natured cross-section of society that it was aimed at. The smiling faces on the freedom march contrasted sharply with the unprovoked self-righteous rage of middle-class youth.

During the purported covid-19 pandemic, I wasn't surprised that the younger generations (particularly the more educated) uncritically accepted the official narrative, despite the draconian curbs on socialising, festivals and travel. The regime of lockdown, closure of schools and universities, masking and obligatory vaccination seemed to suit their outlook of interdependence and compliance. As a senior lecturer at a leading London university, I saw how this segment of society was primed for moral panic, as induced by the mass psychological manipulation of covid-19.

Lecturing in mental health, I was disillusioned by students' lack of scepticism about the system. Few had heard of the anti-psychiatry movement of R. D. Laing and Thomas Szasz, or understood the harm of the medical model. For example, when discussing the relentless rise in antidepressant use, I failed to persuade students that an unholy alliance between government and big business was pacifying the populace. I could imagine that several students were taking the very pills that I presented as scientifically and ethically dubious but profitable for Big Pharma. Indeed, the ineffectiveness of these drugs would increase their profitability since their promise of offering a cure for depression would provide a lasting crutch. So, instead of challenging what could be seen as a manufactured dependence, students appeared to put mental-health problems on a pedestal of vulnerability – something that it seems they regarded as a positive attribute.

These students appeared to pride themselves on holding the progressive values of identity politics – values that stand in opposition to those of the Enlightenment. I say this since in identity politics freedom of speech is reinterpreted as a licence for 'hate' while democracy is rejected on the basis that 'populism' delivers the wrong result. Indeed, one of my nursing students opined that Brexit demonstrated that uneducated people should be deprived of the vote. So it is that equality before the law is perceived as problematic since it is conceived as reinforcing inequalities.

This point came home to me in class discussion concerning the tragic random killing of a white man outside his front door as he went to post letters announcing the recent birth of his daughter. He was stabbed by a psychotic Nigerian man; and while I expected the students to engage in discussion about risk management in psychiatric care, the class turned it into a study of racism in the newspaper the *Daily Mail,* in which the story appeared.

This incident caused me to reflect on what might be occurring here. I was fully aware that adherents of radical race and gender theory could be described as having attitudes that were 'woke' in nature, since two years earlier Robert Oulds and I had explored this ideological onslaught in our book *Moralitis: A Cultural Virus*. We argued there that ideas could spread rapidly on the Internet with a small number of proactive zealots spreading the ideas or 'contagion', and the majority picking up on these ideas as 'carriers'. The key question was how a contagion, often a warped ideology, could in fact make such a dramatic impact?

To answer this question, we need to go back to the counter-protestors in Wellington, who, the reader will recall, were masked. While it might be assumed that their faces were covered for reasons of public health, in fact leftist agitators have used face coverings since the turn of the millennium and one can fairly assume that this was for two reasons: firstly to prevent identification and secondly to convey something symbolic. For a face covering conceals individual identity and thereby conveys a collectivist one; and this may serve as a device to avoid dialogue with opponents, who are thereby dehumanised.

Through reflections such as this and observing the tactics of those bearing Antifa flags, waving fists for Black Lives Matter or insisting on transgender pronouns, it appeared that we were not observing groups that were upholding liberal values. On the contrary, they appeared to be engaged in a mindless onslaught, the effects of which would be to tear society apart.

At the time that I was mulling this over, I had a vague appreciation that the woke phenomenon was a progression from the cultural Marxism of past decades, but reading *The Strategy of Maoism in the West* by professors David Martin Jones and M. L. R. Smith (2022) showed very clearly how an uncompromising form of Marxism practised by Chairman Mao and his henchmen in the People's Republic of China was exported successfully to the liberal West. Suddenly a light bulb was switched on in my mind.

In a land steeped in Confucius and Buddhism, Mao Zedong targeted the 'four olds' – old ideas, old culture, old habits and old customs – in other words, lingering traditions in China that perpetuated what was deemed to be a false consciousness. So, the battleground was internal, with Mao seeking to remould minds and implant ideology in the fear that even the keenest fighters might regress. His antithetical *Little Red Book* was held aloft by the shrill youth of the Red Guards, and exported to student revolutionaries in the West.

What is the relevance of Maoism today? Well, although current social-justice warriors may have a limited grasp of history, they share with Mao's youth a similar fanaticism – one that leads them to produce displays of violence against professors on American university campuses. As Martin Jones and Smith note, 'From Peking to Pomona may seem a tenuous intellectual connection, but the resemblances are striking.' The reality is that Western society is being forced into undergoing its own version of Mao's Cultural Revolution, but is hardly fighting back.

How have things reached this point? I wondered. Where China was concerned, Mao came from a peasant background in Hunan province and, although not intellectual, was probably influenced by Western ideas. His fellow revolutionary Deng Xiaoping, who later succeeded him as leader of China, had studied in Paris. When the Frankfurt School of critical theory was founded in the 1920s – a school that taught that as long as an individual had the belief that his divine gift of reason could solve the problems facing society, then that society would never reach the state of hopelessness and alienation that they considered necessary to provoke socialist revolution – it was understood that a Bolshevik revolution in the West would fail if driven solely by Marxist economic theory. Indeed, the founders of the Frankfurt School realised that nothing really changes unless the culture changes.

And discussion of culture change focused on profound changes in societal attitudes. So, the school recommended (among other things) the creation of racism offences, continual change to create confusion, the teaching of sex and homosexuality to children, huge immigration to destroy identity, the promotion of excessive drinking, the emptying of churches, an unreliable legal system with bias against victims of crime, dependency on the state, control and dumbing-down of media, and encouraging the breakdown of the family.

A revolution in attitudes such as this demanded time, and so the radical socialists who drove this needed to be patient. Their time came in the 1960s with mass protests against the war in Vietnam and an outbreak of emancipatory movements, including the 1968 student demonstrations in Paris. This wave of protests showed that a restless younger generation was ready for revolt.

By this time, the USSR had lost its shine as a socialist star among Western scholars. Avant-garde philosopher Jean-Paul Sartre pursued a more humanistic Marxism, and, like his postmodern Left Bank peers, he was more drawn to the thrust of China and Mao's mass mobilisation of the people. Straightforwardly dogmatic, Maoism was fresh and unburdened by intellectual verbiage. As Jones and Smith remarked, 'the Chinese Marxists made the European Marxist thought of the Lukács, Frankfurt School and Althusserian varieties seemed increasingly abstruse and impenetrable'. Indeed, China appealed for its mystical 'otherliness', detached from their own national context, as a blank slate on which to build a socialist utopia. To have a sense of pro-Chinese thinking in the France of 1968, I recommend Bernardo Bertolucci's film *The Dreamers*, which depicts the delusional worship of Mao among Soixante-Huitards.

So, the youthful New Left departed from the materialism of Karl Marx to focus on self-expression and identity. As the authors explain, 'The affluent student products of the post-war recovery found the successful, stable Western democracies that they inherited intolerably repressive.' In California, critical theorist Herbert Marcuse attacked mass consumerism and its illusions of choice. More significant was the undermining of parents and authority figures. According to Theodor Adorno in the *Authoritarian Personality* (1950), the bourgeois family preserved the psychological conditions for oppression. The crisis of modernity, as Jürgen Habermas argued, was not economic, but cultural, with society stifled by linguistic norms.

While Jacques Derrida preached deconstruction, in China Mao was applying it – brutally. But in the West, the lure of violent uprising faded in the 1970s. Graduates of a growing and increasingly politicised university system embarked on careers in the professional bureaucracy, and strove to change society from within. German student activist Rudi Dutschke coined the phrase 'long march through the institutions', referencing Mao's Long March to revolution. My reading of Jones and Smith illuminated this strategy.

What is more, it seems that Mao was aware of his popularity among Western radicals, whom he indirectly supported through the propagandist 'United Front in Cultural Work'. He planted a seed that grew into the triffid-like monster that dominates Western life today. Mao died in 1976, but his legacy is remarkable. His Red Guards are our woke warriors, whose activities are not as organic or spontaneous as they may seem to a bewildered public. Social tensions and moral confusion caused by militant racial consciousness and transgenderism are part of a strategic destruction of the societal structures of faith, flag and family.

Just as Mao's shock troops ransacked museums, burned books and humiliated teachers, so do current agitators topple statues and erase cultural artefacts for the merest association with the slave trade of 300 years ago. Language is a battleground, and woke is winning. Each tranche of initiates pushes further than the last. Puritanical identity politics, based on spurious evidence of discrimination and relativist notions of justice, are a Maoist polarising tactic. As Jones and Smith explain, 'Grassroots activists in Red Guard style raise the consciousness of the alienated and repressed,' and they also highlight the necessity for an enemy.

I asked myself who that enemy could be. In reality, Mao perceived liberalism to be more of a threat than reactionary conservatism, but he maintained a disingenuous alliance between the two. Ask any young progressives for the destiny of their espoused progress, and the probable answer is a vague ideal of equality and diversity, but they are merely being led by a Pied Piper. For Maoist practice is to advance by exploiting values and rights while actually having no respect for those values and rights. Indeed, just like the Jesuits, a priority is to indoctrinate from the youngest age. For older students, Western universities have become finishing schools teaching radical ideology. So, what appear to be hallowed institutions and hives of liberal culture are actually falling prey to cultural vandalism.

In these times of technological advance, I learned that technology can be a boon to revolutionary activism. Why do I say this? Well, the Internet facilitates the efficient operation of the thought police, and the younger generations who spend most of their lives on online social media via their cool and convenient smartphones have abandoned privacy in favour of constant contact. Then a spontaneous comment, perhaps in jest, but deemed offensive in some confected way, is enough for a student to be harangued or ostracised by woke peers. In my current role as a trade-union representative I repeatedly deal with disciplinary cases arising from tweeted 'wrong-think', and I have personally opted to move away from Twitter to avoid its giant spider's web.

Of course, I can well imagine that Mao would have loved this powerful tool for surveillance and incitement. In this modern resurgence of the lynch mob, redolent of the persecution of alleged witches in past centuries, students are unwittingly acting for rather than against the system. Just as the authorities pushed the witchcraft inquisition, vice chancellors and senior administrators (particularly in the human-resources department) ensure that everyone below their level slavishly follows the latest show of piety, whether it is directed towards BLM or Ukraine. As Jones and Smith observe, the milieu has become a minefield not only for staff of a conservative bent (a tiny minority nowadays), but also for anyone of classical liberal or a common-sense perspective.

What is more, I know from bitter experience that objective enquiry has given way to ideological doctrine. Whatever the course, whether it is travel and tourism or applied mathematics or whatever else, critical race theory and gender politics are crowbarred into the syllabus. Most educators are not Marxist, but are unwilling to challenge radical assertions which soon become official policy, such as the 'decolonisation' agenda. Fearful lecturers may tell themselves that BLM is a necessary leg-up for disadvantaged persons of BAME background, and that gender-neutral toilets are inclusive, but they should know that such incursions are just the thin end of the wedge.

After decades of peace, comfort and convenience, the intelligentsia lack backbone, keeping their heads down as the revolutionary wrecking-ball swings. Whereas conservativism is to conserve and liberalism is to reform, Maoism strives to smash the structures of society, using rage rather than rational argument. The revolution appears to be endless. It seems clear to me that we are not advancing towards social harmony, but rather to division and hatred, escalated by activists who claim to be fighting *against* division and hate. The irony is palpable.

There must be something wrong in society for this destruction to happen. The West withstood Bolshevism, but has fallen to Maoism. I asked myself why society appears to have lost its resilience and wonder if the demoralisation in society has been achieved through a range of techniques, ranging from alienating architecture to the undermining of the truth (a reminder of George Orwell's *Nineteen Eighty-Four,* in which the people were taught that 2 + 2 = 5). The moral decay of the West has been unwittingly facilitated by liberalism, through its unprincipled tolerance of dangerous, illiberal Marxists – led by the Frankfurt School – and intolerance of conservatives.

Who are the beneficiaries of the social turmoil that has been created? Arguably, when Mao's Cultural Revolution was launched in 1966 the purpose was not primarily ideological, but to quash potential rivals in the Politburo, whose revisionist tendencies surfaced after the disastrous preceding strategy of the Great Leap Forward (as Jung Chang described in *Wild Swans*, the people were ordered to kill sparrows, leaving insects to thrive, resulting in crop failure and famine). After his Cultural Revolution inevitably led to factional chaos, Mao restored order with the army, and consolidated the centralised command of the party. Mao had in fact deployed the mechanism of problem–reaction–solution.

The relevance to our society? Just as true medicine seeks the cause of illness rather than simply treating the symptoms, so the cause of the woke-inspired problems in our society appears to be Maoist-inspired woke radicalism, with Frankfurt School dogma as part of its foundations.

This has produced the 'moralitis' as Oulds and I described it (2020) – a symptomatic pattern or syndrome in our society. The underlying disease is difficult to treat, especially since the last three years of the covid-19 crisis have indicated pathological levels of the disease. Jones and Smith name the beast that is attacking society as Maoism – a phenomenon that has a wider reach than simply serving as a vehicle for race and gender politics. As David Icke explained in *Perceptions of a Renegade Mind*, 'The reason for the Cult's Chinese revolution was to create a fiercely-controlled environment within which an extreme structure for human control could be incubated to eventually be unleashed across the world.'

In terms of my personal intellectual journey, I regard the twin Trojan horses of covid-19 and climate change as engineered crises that assist this control, with useful idiots such as Extinction Rebellion activists used as instruments of social disruption, to justify global control and government. I have heard the view that the West is modelling itself on China since it developed as an interesting hybrid of a rapacious capitalist economy in combination with communist discipline. This is perhaps not as strange as it may sound at first since some say that fascism and communism are two sides of the same coin. The goal is technocracy, and China, having learned much from the decades under Mao, is at the vanguard. Sadly, the woke cannot see that their destiny is not emancipation, but enslavement; and since awareness is a precursor to resistance, my closing question is 'Can enough people wake up before it's too late?'

Our political system is not favourable to a gradual enlightenment. In the UK and most Western democracies, two major political parties compete for power, with little prospect of a newcomer breaking through. Covid-19 showed that the country is governed by a uniparty, with the opposition just as keen on lockdown and vaccine coercion as the incumbent. In the recent midterm elections in the USA, California governor Gavin Newsom was re-elected by a margin of fifteen per cent, despite imposing one of the strictest pandemic regimes in the world. Putting to one side any allegations of vote-rigging, we can only imagine that it is based on the will of the moneyed and the meek consumers of mainstream media, as also the views of the woke. It would seem that whole swathes of society still believe that their government is protecting them from a plague.

My journey exploring the origins of the woke agenda has revealed that the hidden hand of the Frankfurt School and then of Mao's China may have attempted to subvert Western society. I can believe that a growing number of people are the minority – we are slowly but steadily growing. It is neither realistic nor necessary for us to convert over half of the populace: history shows that a successful force for change may be as small as five or ten per cent (much greater than the self-appointed elite who deign to control us). This is not a democratic situation, but a crisis for humanity. Instead of wasting time on trying to convert cultists, we should lead by example. We should develop and maintain a parallel society, living alongside the majority, but disengaging from systems that deny our fundamental freedoms and rights. Unlike the woke, our cause may be summarised by a chant at the huge anti-lockdown protest in Berlin in summer 2020: *'Frieden! Freiheit! Keine Diktator!'*

References

Jones, D. M., and Smith, M. L. R. (2022), *The Strategy of Maoism in the West*, Cheltenham: Edward Elgar.

McCrae, N. And Oulds, R. (2020), *Moralitis: A Cultural Virus.* London: Bruges Group.

Awareness of Frequencies and Other invisible Influences on Society

NICHOLAS MARTIN

After attending City of London School and the Guildhall School of Music Junior Exhibitioner Scheme, Nicholas read economics at Brunel University and subsequently worked for large international packaging companies, initially Unilever and then the Smurfit Group. The opportunity arose to join a management buy-out of an SME (small or medium-sized enterprise) in an unrelated industry and he then ran that company for a number of years. He is committed to local democracy and is a local councillor in Berkshire.

A philosophical view of life

The life that we experience is strange, isn't it? All of us are in the same soup – experiencing pleasure and pain, and then death comes along at the end and says time is up. It not only removes all the things accumulated over a lifetime, but it takes us away too.

After leaving university, personally I wanted to find out what all this is about, 'Alfie'. Having been brought up without any religion, organised or otherwise, I decided to go to the Church of England and get baptised since that seemed to fit with the culture I had been born into. I did all that for a time and then felt sorry for 'God' insofar as He had to listen to a small group of people singing often out of tune, week in, week out. It seemed to get me nowhere fast in terms of providing a truly sacred dimension to life, and it all seemed so frightfully mundane and routine. What is more, it was inordinately boring – at least that is how it all seemed to me.

So I turned to a monastery to see if that would give me a glimpse of another aspect to life. I became an oblate – a person who lives in the world, but who is attached to the monastery. And the monastery building was marvellous – originally designed by Edwin Lutyens for the exiled Russian Dolgoruky family. The order there was Benedictine and it was moderated by the Church of England Catholic rite, although not accepting of the Pope.

That particular life had its own fascinations: the beauty of the building and the grounds, the peaceful order of the seven services a day, the plainsong hanging in the air and the greater silence after the evening meal when no speaking was allowed till the morning.

One day the man who was called my spiritual director there – a really honest and insightful person – advised me not to become a monk 'if you would like to find truth'! So I didn't. And at around the time he said that, I saw an advert in Kensington Public Library for a Gnostic lecture, so subsequently joined a Gnostic spiritual school where I learned to give up meat and learned too about a totally different version of Christianity – very similar to Buddhism in that there is reincarnation until the mind matures and sees the necessity of a change in consciousness. Shakespeare, in inimitable genius, summed this up when he said 'Ripeness is all' and 'The rest is silence.'

Without doubt I learned a great deal in that spiritual school, including about such things as the priceless wisdom of Lao Tse and the journey of the Pistis Sophia. Some of my fellow Gnostics there knew of a philosopher, J. Krishnamurti, who at the time was giving talks in Hampshire. So several of my Gnostic friends, two of my relatives and I went to listen to him. I listened with great interest and thought it was all very well – but not relevant to me, a Gnostic.

Following the talk, however, someone saw Krishmamurti walking back and grabbed my arm and said, 'Let's go and thank Krishnamurti for giving his talk.' This is something that it would never have occurred to me to do, but the person grabbed me with such intent that I found myself momentarily standing next to Krishnamurti. I then realised, without any words exchanged, and in an immediate space of time, that it was utterly obvious that this man had travelled very far in terms of human consciousness. You could feel a very powerful field of energy about his being, full of benevolence and with a sense of righteousness. That's the best way that I can think to describe it. Having said that, not a word was needed in that instant.

The Gnostic school I was at the time connected to spoke of the need for a change of consciousness, and yet the one person I had just encountered, someone clearly living in a different state of consciousness, was not a member of the Gnostic school. So I left that school, grateful to have been part of it but grateful also to have left it.

At that point, I read as much of J. Krishnamurti's philosophy as I could and came to perceive the truth he pointed out, that thought and all thinking (our consciousness in time and of time) are obstacles to a real understanding of life rather than a vehicle for it. After all, we as humanity have been thinking for millennia, but understand nothing for the most part as to what life is and why it is. He also pointed out that there is an altogether different energy for mind, different from the energy of thought alone – 'the energy of the absence of thought'.

Of course, he pointed out that thought has its place, but he indicated that it should not be the controller of the human mind. If it is, the ensuing consciousness is, in his view, limited. In fact, he had an insightful saying: 'A wise man does not rely on thought alone.'

A good friend of mine who knew Krishnamurti put it well in my view: the works of Krishnamurti can take the listener by the hand, as it were, and to the edge of the lake of eternity, and leave the listener there. Then you can either stay on the shores of life or jump in and find out if silence and the energy of the absence of thought is truth or not – first hand.

It may be more intelligent not to think than to think, but the reality of this is without meaning unless thought is actually absent. And no one can do this for another person.

Life is indeed altogether a very strange business, isn't it? Maybe we could say that if you want to be unburdened by life then when you see something that is wrong you should take it upon yourself to do something about it – or else you will experience a lack of integrity which could eat away at your mind.

I personally don't want to live with any such feeling, and so will do as much as I am able to fight a wrongdoing seen. Then, when my time comes to die, I will be able to say that I did my very best to detract from the disorder of our society. If what I did was futile, that will not disturb me as long as I know I could not have given it an ounce more.

Microwave-in-air radiation – Wi-Fi, smart meters, 4G and 5G and mobile phones

Life has made it clear to me (and to many, many others, of course) that microwave-in-air technology as we have it today – which is 2G, 3G, 4G and 5G, smart meters, Wi-Fi and mobile phones – is a technology that can harm human health. That is unacceptable to any rational and sensitive mind, isn't it?

I had come across the case of a person who installed Wi-Fi and subsequently noticed tingling in arms and legs, but didn't associate that with the recent Wi-Fi installation. The GP told him not to worry about it, and the person ignored the symptoms. Some years later that person had to be rushed to hospital in the middle of the night, unable to move and racked with pain. Cortisone was administered to help mobility, and morphine to dull the pain. That person then was forced to use a wheelchair and was unable to operate anywhere near their former normal standards of mobility.

I did my own research and realised that Wi-Fi – which affects all people – can have extreme effects on some of us.

I realised too that education about all of this would enable people to use some of this technology safely, and that in fact there is no need for microwave-in-air wireless computers at all. We can use wired broadband systems, which give better download and upload speeds and do not harm human consciousness and physiology. By the same token, people can be taught to use a mobile phone on speakerphone and to switch it to airplane mode when it is in their pocket.

I am glad to say the person affected by Wi-Fi is now back to normal mobility, no longer wheelchair-bound, after installing wired broadband in their property.

The harm caused by microwave radiation is not in dispute. Indeed, Dr Martin Pall, world famous biochemist, has collated thousands of papers all saying that microwave radiation is harmful to human health. Most radar is microwave radiation, and it is likely governments are aware too that there are papers linking radar to cancers in radar operators.

And 5G microwave weapons used by governments all over the world kill people – otherwise they would not deploy them as weapons, of course.

LED street lights and 5G

Many LED street lights have 5G antennae in them for smart-city technology, and this is a form of urban radar that most people are unaware of.

The IoT is the Internet of Things and is 5G – in that many emitting devices can be picked up and the data backhauled to a control. All the emitting sources in a field can be picked up with the scanning beam of 5G, and then the data picked up is sent back to a control in what is called backhaul.

That aspect of backhaul was referred to in the literature of Harvard Technology – a one-time LED-street-light supplier. Documentation in relation to Telensa (now called Signify, which was formerly known as Philips Lighting) refers to antennae / small cells to improve 4G and 5G coverage and to the facility to receive signals from such lights and relay them to a control centre.

What is different about 5G?

Speaking of 5G, the fundamental difference about 5G is that it is a beam or collimation of energy within a densified microwave field. 4G and below is radial wave technology which obeys the inverse square law of physics, which means the further you are away from the emitting source the safer you are. Those 5G focused beams of energy can travel miles at high intensity, and this is part of how scanning/target-acquiring microwave 5G weapons work.

What does the WEF want to do?

The WEF-style agenda of the Fourth Industrial Revolution was summarised by a US publication, *Forbes m*agazine, as follows:

> *When the Internet of Things (IoT) connects with your body, the result is the Internet of Bodies (IoB). The Internet of Bodies (IoB) is an extension of the IoT and basically connects the human body to a*

network through devices that are ingested, implanted, or connected to the body in some way. Once connected, data can be exchanged, and the body and device can be remotely monitored and controlled.

To implement the Internet of Bodies, you need the scanning target-acquiring technology, which is 5G. This technology, as we can see from the street lights, can pick up data from many emitting devices in the field and send the information back as backhaul to a control. Once a human being has the technology described in the patent below, for example, they can be scanned with a 5G beam and their biometrics, including heartbeat, blood sugar level and so on can be backhauled to a source – they are subject to technology known as telemetrics.

The way the Internet of Things (IoT) gives way to the Internet of Bodies (IoB) is well shown in the patent below:

Publication number: 20180328884

Abstract: The present invention generally relates to injectable electronics. In some aspects, the present invention is generally directed to systems and methods for interfacing an electrical cable with electrical elements, such as nanoscale wires, that are injected or otherwise introduced into a subject. The subject may be living or non-living. In one set of embodiments, electrical elements introduced within a subject may be placed in electrical communication to a circuit board using a plurality of electrically isolated contacts that the circuit board can clamp or otherwise connect to. The electrical contacts may be in electrical communication with the electrical elements using a joining portion. The circuit board can also be connected to an electrical cable that can be attached, for example, to a computer. In some cases, the electrical cable can be attached or detached to or from the circuit board, e.g.

Type: Application

Filed: May 11, 2018

Publication date: November 15, 2018

Applicant: President and Fellows of Harvard College

Inventors: Charles M. Lieber, Thomas Gerard Schuhmann, Jun Yao, Guosong Hong, Tian-Ming Fu, Jungmin Lee, Hong-Gyu Park

Publication number: 20180328884

Telemetrics is apparently what the WEF wants to use in the course of remotely monitoring and then ultimately controlling humanity.

The question then arises – as human beings, do we want to be remotely monitored and controlled? If not, then it is up to you and me to do something about it – but never with violence, of course. For violence is an attribute of a deranged mind, it might be said. Society and its state are not separate from our consciousness, and we are all responsible for it.

As JFK said, 'Our problems are man-made. Therefore they can be solved by man. . . . No problem of human destiny is beyond human beings.'

Can society change?

So what can be done to bring about a society in which humanity is not controlled and manipulated – in other words, to bring about a genuinely free society?

In my view at least, the prerequisite is the fundamental necessity of freedom of speech. That means a mass media that does not censor and does not impose narratives – but rather one which allows intelligent, open and Socratic debate on the whole range of issues that confront us all at any given time.

And that debate must be completely open – so that if indeed there are strings being pulled in any area of society, in any organ of our society, people can see those strings.

As an example, take research in our universities. If such research is being conducted in a university, then we should see – shouldn't we? – who funds it and what agenda such a funder might be trying to bring about in our society. As an illustration, at Harvard it has been alleged that a team of scientists was funded by Jeffrey Epstein. It is legitimate in a free society that this should be fully and widely scrutinised by the media to establish the veracity (or otherwise) of it.

It is entirely right to ask and to find out if and why that should be true; and if is true, then to ask why a man like Jeffrey Epstein, who was allegedly identified by a prosecuting attorney as an intelligence asset, should be connected with this particular type of research in an internationally respected university.

And Thomas Scripps penned an article for *OffGuardian* on 26 June 2019 stating that the minutes of the Ministry of Defence (MoD) meetings have confirmed the role of Britain's *Guardian* newspaper as a mouthpiece for the intelligence agencies. If all this is so, it means things are being covertly orchestrated by secretive agencies – the sort of thing JFK warned about as being inimical to a free and open society.

Another aspect of control of information in our society, it might be said, relates to Ofcom, which has a dual function in regulating TV and radio stations with regard to content, and also in regulating the airwaves with regard to wireless communications, including microwave-in-air technology such as 5G.

There has been an incident relating to 5G where it might be said Ofcom showed both these controls operating in tandem.

The scientist Dr Diana Wojtkowiak said the following:

> The aim of this paper is to clarify the problem which is currently the topic of a heated social discussion and explain whether it is accidental that the location of the new 5G network has overlapped with the biggest outbreaks of the COVID-19 pandemic in the first months of 2020. This paper shows that in relation to viral infectivity and aggressiveness, kinase pathways used by the predecessor of SARS Cov-2, i.e. SARS-CoV, are the same pathways which are activated by microwaves in healthy animal and human cells. This knowledge, based on experimental studies, has already been described in scientific literature many years ago by multiple scientists. [Diana Wojtkowiak, Gdańsk ,Poland, 7 May 2020 – abstract.]

Rather than allow an open, public and scientific debate on this, the attitude of Ofcom as expressed by its then CEO, Melanie Dawes, was – as quoted in the *Daily Mail* – as follows:

> Social media giants had taken some steps to stop the spread of fake news and she warned of 'some very persistent incorrect mes-

saging' such as the debunked conspiracy theory that 5G technology is related to the corona virus.

As far as I am aware, Ofcom did not supply any independent scientific data to support their stance as reported by the *Daily Mail*. In fact, I did write to ask them to do that, but received no such science.

Public awareness of all of this sort of activity is the key perhaps to rightful change. In fact, a general public awareness that this type of thing might be going on has its own potency, its own action, its own doing. By analogy, knowledge of Prince Andrew's association with Ghislaine Maxwell and Jeffrey Epstein, seen by the public at large, was enough to effectively remove him from his former prominent role in public life. Awareness at large is a most potent thing, it seems.

It might be said that this awareness is a disinfectant for our society; and, as we said, society is not separated from our consciousness. That unfettered flowering out of public awareness is something which might create, naturally, a rightful societal environment – a healthy soil, so to speak, for all the roots of all the organs of our society.

A soil in which just organs of society can develop sui generis and operate in a way that is utterly coherent with compassion – and coherent too with the innate decency of being which characterises the noble values common to all of us as free and equal humanity.

References

Scripps, T. (2019), Exposed: The Guardian's collusion in State Censorship. https://off-guardian.org/2019/06/26/exposed-the-guardians-collusion-in-state-censorship/

CULTURE AND PHILOSOPHY

My Journey through an Academic Cult of Ugliness and the Awakening of a New Thirst for Beauty

MATTHEW EHRET

As a journalist, and historian, my comfort zone has tended to revolve around commenting on the world around me (and prior to me) as an objective process in space and time. Rarely have I been asked to speak subjectively about my own experience within this lived history. Since comfort zones don't make for fertile soil for growth, I will embrace this challenge with ardour.

My particular set of experiences which have brought me to my present outlook and sense of mission in life began in large measure with my confrontation with a certain set of uncomfortable facts pertaining to the truth of the events of September 11, 2001 during a dense and traumatic period of life at the start of 2004. I was then a twenty-two-year-old studying film animation at Montreal's Concordia University and found myself on what I believed to be a rather banal group assignment to compose a short film about 9/11.

My sense of reality at that time was no different from that of your average person without any conviction of principle or historical sense of being. The shock of encountering a series of lectures and research reports by eminent architects and engineers on the impossibility of three buildings free-falling after two planes had struck them caused a deep pain that I couldn't un-see. Hell, I never even heard of the third building falling on 9/11.

In the wake of this violent cognitive barrage on my comfortable sensibilities, I soon found myself consuming lectures, books and documentaries with an obsessive energy I had never before thought possible. This exercise increasingly helped me situate a new higher narrative of history that better explained how we were brought to our present dire circumstances.

But despite having come to grips with the notion of a multigenerational bankers' conspiracy, intelligence-agency-managed coups, assassinations and cover-ups both domestically and abroad, I still lacked a sense of true understanding. I could feel a sort of shallowness within my new-found sense of reality, since I still lacked a sense of causality. If the notion of a trans-generational conspiracy were to be maintained, then what would animate this elite? Did they hold a secret that a lowly pleb like myself could not possibly understand? Were the countless deaths caused by genocide, famine and war deemed necessary by the elite? Was it possible that the very notion of good and evil was merely an illusion caused by my impoverished intellect's inability to break free of dualisms? These were extremely important questions that I could not easily answer. It became increasingly difficult to maintain my commitment to the tasks of fine art as it was taught within the postmodernist environment of my university.

Despite my efforts to compose artistic productions that would in some small measure express the thoughts and sentiments that I was working through, I was troubled to discover that those professors who managed the young souls within the arts department tended to react in a surprisingly hostile manner.

I recall the head of the department delivering a lecture in which he publicly criticised one of my projects because it failed to accomplish what he saw as art's primary purpose: to render an audience uncomfortable. Here he didn't mean a form of discomfort caused by the mind's exposure to uncomfortable realities conveyed by rational narrative or supported by facts, for that is what I had been attempting. This professor meant something very different.

He explained that the primary purpose of true art is not found in the communication of intelligible thoughts, but rather in the *deconstruction* of thoughts. He explained that it was only when an artist could cause an audience to squirm uncomfortably in the face of the ugliness and irrationalism of existence that 'true art' could be said to have been attained. This professor was sadly not alone in this view.

I don't know how many of the poor malleable young students who had been processed through that institution came out undamaged with their creative and moral energy intact.

For myself at least, I can say that the obliteration of a naïve world view caused by my new-found introduction to the reality of conspiracies past and present and my dual encounter with this cult of ugliness masquerading behind an academic veneer within the university posed a fundamental question deep within my gut. That question was 'Why are societies around the world embracing the ugliness and lies that have brought us step by step closer to a hellish dystopia of pain and injustice?' Why, for instance, are we in Britain accepting the growth of a surveillance state?

Are we simply stupid by nature? That is one possibility. Perhaps we are just an anomalous accident not ultimately fit for survival. For no other species seems to be wired to destroy itself, and so the possibility that humanity is merely a mistake couldn't be easily discounted.

But of course, unlike other species of the biosphere whose behavioural patterns are shaped almost entirely by genetic and environmental conditions, human beings had this additional factor of culture which shaped our identities. Culture of course is a strange and powerful invisible thing which can be made healthier and can be made sicker, and upon close inspection we find that it isn't unidirectional. It is something which in turn is both *shaped* by individuals with ideas and *shapes* individuals with ideas. It is like the soil within which seeds grow. Except these seeds are metaphysical.

And if soil receives proper sunlight, water and vitamins, seeds will grow fruitfully. When soil is barren, neglected and dry, seeds will either grow sickly, or fail to manifest the fruit they were destined to produce. So it must be with a society whose cultural and aesthetic values have been permitted to rot.

If ugliness is celebrated as beauty within the domains of 'high culture', or if mediocrity is sold as excellence within the domain of 'popular culture', then any seeds (aka individuals) attempting to grow within said soil will find themselves in deep trouble.

If it is true, as modern relativistic academia asserts, that a Bach motet can be judged as no more beautiful than a Lady Gaga tune or if a Rembrandt cannot be deemed superior to the splatterings from the brush of a Jackson Pollock, then how can any objective standard of truth exist? If ugliness becomes indistinguishable from beauty then how could anyone distinguish a lie from the truth? For certainly lies are ugly *only* if truth is considered a thing of beauty.

And so, when I saw this postmodernist Gestapo pressuring young students to abandon their reason and conscience for the sake of worshipping at the altar of ugliness I gained a powerful experience that gave me an insight into the deeper causes of society's tendency to fall into corruption. For it wasn't in the domain of logic alone that the problem resided, but in the domain of the spirit.

When I began reviewing the history of education and cultural norms over the centuries, with a look towards the Ancient Greeks as my baseline, something new began to take form, giving me the context I craved. With a growing appreciation of a conspiratorial framework of history, and with a longer perspective from which to begin reconstructing my scaffold, my soul found food and my mind found insights the likes of which I had never thought possible.

My searching for a mode of thinking that would allow for a sense of solution to our modern crises brought me to read like I'd never read before, and among those authors in whom I found the highest value were Plato and the American philosopher Lyndon LaRouche (1922–2019).

Despite having left this mortal coil over 2,300 years earlier, I can say that Plato became my closest friend. This friendship started in the summer of 2006. Speaking through the character of his martyred teacher, Socrates, Plato's dialogues taught me that I was not alone, and that a society's slide into corruption, sophistry and demagoguery was not unique to my world.

Plato taught me dialectic by releasing me from my tendency to crave finished didactic answers to questions. He taught me to appreciate the subtle axioms underlying the intricate web of opinions upon which our convictions and identities are built. In reading (and re-reading) the works of Plato, be it his *Gorgias, Meno, Phaedrus, Cratylus , Philebus, Protagoras, Apology, Theatetus, Imaeus, Crito, Phaedo or Republic,* I realised that just as the poison of a seed will express itself through every branch emerging out of it, so too the poison of a false assumption will express its hollowness within every opinion built upon it. Far more important than acquiring 'the right answers' is a spirit of humility and love of truth that precede this. All this I learned from Plato.

Plato also taught that the only pathway towards a healthy mode of thinking lies in the examining of assumptions and the rigorous testing of new hypotheses. This involves pressing the internal mental mapping of reality on to reality itself with concrete examples to save us from the dangerous waters of hypertrophied ivory-tower abstractions. Ontological paradoxes emerge when assumptions and explanatory models break down in the face of reality. These are the causes of the rich ironies embedded throughout the dialogues. These were the singularities that stood out from the norm and the fruit upon which substantial 'eurekas' were built.

The more I studied Plato, and Platonic thinkers who applied his method over the millennia, the more I discovered that the internal dialectic process that great artists have with themselves coincides with a form of dialectic between thinkers separated by vast chasms of time.

On one level this internal/external dialectic refines our own powers of judging beauty and ugliness, and it creates a profound appreciation of the dialectic we all have with the entire universe. When an individual follows Plato's path and rigorously awakens a love of truth, beauty and goodness, we find muses awakening the hearts of scientists, artists and statesmen, urging them to go beyond the mediocre limits expected of them in those times and places in which they find themselves.

When ideas of a truthful character are put into action, we find the universe responding by giving humanity greater potential to sustain a greater number of people, of ever higher quality, as they make and apply new discoveries that bring about scientific and technological progress.

This profound relationship between mind and matter that hinges upon truth and morality is at the heart of the nature of the meaning of humanity. It also represents a source of great fear for oligarchical systems. The lack of exposure to this mode of thinking is at the heart of the loss of wisdom suffered by societies that fall prey to oligarchical modes of culture and learn to acquiesce in their own 'bestialisation'.

To the degree that a society's moral attitudes and cultural standards remain healthy, the creation and application of new discoveries is both good and beautiful. When this happens, we find time and again the divide separating science from art to be just an illusion. The work of great minds like Johannes Kepler, or educational reformers like Moses Mendelssohn, Friedrich Schiller and the Humboldt brothers, who recognised the dance of art and science, can only be properly appreciated from this perspective.

The fact that all of the aforementioned great souls explicitly understood that ideas of good and evil shape the contours of our political reality is also no accident. Reading the original works of such great thinkers made me realise that they were all Platonists. If they were Christian, they all tended to be Augustinian. (Augustine himself created a form of Christian Platonism that towered over all the splinters of Christianity that came into being over the centuries.)

Dante Alighieri's' *La Divina Commedia* and *De Monarchia* contained not only seeds for great Renaissance works after his death, but also Platonic dialectics of a pure nature. The same could be said of Renaissance humanists like Erasmus of Rotterdam, Thomas More and Jonathan Swift, whose *The Battle of the Books, A Modest Proposal* and *A Tale of a Tub* contain some of the most brilliant attacks on oligarchical thinking of the eighteenth century.

Beginning with my association with the LaRouche Organisation (which had a small branch of ten or so people in Canada), I was exposed to a form of humanist education that was otherwise absent in our oligarchically influenced society. This was an educational process that emphasised not only a rigorous working-through of the original works of great thinkers, but also a strong focus on constructive geometry.

Through an immersion in constructive geometry, I began to appreciate why the memorising of formulae to pass tests in maths was merely a poor substitute for true knowledge, and that this knowledge can only be won by working through constructive geometrical proofs that gave birth to the formulae which school taught us to memorise. This gave me an appreciation as to why my younger self was so repulsed by maths in high school. I had been led to believe that I was merely 'a right-brained artist' who wasn't made for science. Finally, I began to realise that I wasn't actually stupid, but entirely capable of thinking scientifically if I were taught properly. The wall separating left and right brains no longer seemed so real.

Studying the comic sections of *Apollonius* was a breath of fresh air which made me realise where elliptical functions, parabolic functions, hyperbolic functions and even trigonometry and algebra itself emerged. Constructing the five Platonic and thirteen Archimedean solids, and seeing how they could organically fit into each other, helped me appreciate the cause and purpose of the golden section itself.

Seeing these processes unfold by studying Plato's *Timaeus* helped me appreciate the works of Leonardo da Vinci, Luca Pacioli and especially the great astronomer Johannes Kepler, whose *New Astronomy* (1609) and *Harmonies of the World* (1619) revived the Pythagorean/Platonic hypothesis of the music of the spheres and, from this potent idea, revolutionised all known physics.

This process of self-education guided by the insights of the wise old man LaRouche was sometimes messy and haphazard, often lacking the mentors with the knowledge and structure to lead such a process properly. However, it was enriching beyond anything available in our current culture of mediocrity and oligarchical control; and despite my having to part ways with the LaRouche Organisation in 2017 due to unresolvable conflicts with certain personalities that created a toxic office climate, the experience is something for which I am eternally grateful.

During my ten years volunteering with that organisation, I attempted to apply this method of thinking about thinking to navigate through the dark narratives, lies and myths shaping the structure of our history. The concept of a history of science premised upon ideas was thus kindled in a way I had never dreamed of. Conspiracies for good or evil, to shape the world into ideal blueprints, shaped literally all of human history; and the question was always 'Are those ideas of good and evil which animate those conspiratorial actions in harmony with or in defiance of natural law?'

From this perspective it becomes ever more clear that the ideas of Platonic humanists like Benjamin Franklin or Thomas More were of a diametrically opposing character to the ideas of those oligarchists who wished to maintain systems that kept humanity locked in systems of mental, spiritual and material containment.

Where Plato outlined a challenge for future statesmen to create a society led by Philosopher Kings who could actualise on earth laws that would reflect ever less imperfectly the unchanging laws established by the Creator, Thomas More both amplified this concept in his *Utopia* and devoted his life to bringing such an order into actuality. Ben Franklin's lifelong efforts advanced this mission further than any had ever taken it by establishing for the first time on Earth a constitutional republic premised on 'a more perfect union'; and the consent of the governed as the basis of law's authority reflected this powerful concept in our modern age.

As a Canadian activist and researcher, I began to realise that many of the modern myths organising my world were entirely invalid.

I realised for instance that the British Empire continued to exercise vast influence over world affairs through a certain type of coup that took control of the USA after the murder of young John F. Kennedy. Scratching the surface of the official narrative of Kennedy's murder with an appreciation for the Anglo-Canadian intelligence networks centred around Louis Mortimer Bloomfield's Permindex based out of Montreal, NATO's Operation Gladio and the CIA–MI6 axis helped me to make sense of the darker truth behind the 'lone gunman' narrative. Not only was this a demonstrable lie, but when re-evaluated from a holistic perspective, Kennedy's murder actually reflected a broad takeover of the US Government and a purging of the last residues of patriotic anti-imperial resistance within the corridors of power of Washington.[1]

Of course, the USA was not alone in this coup process as similar purges of anti-Malthusian statesmen across the entire transatlantic shaped much of the 1960s, including a Rhodes Scholar-led overthrow of a Canadian prime minister in 1963.[2]

I realised moreover that the very Canadian socio-political landscape I lived in was little more than a contrived fraud. I had been taught by my British liberal educational experience that Canadians should be proud of not being like the unwieldy Americans down south. We were told that while they were of an imperious stock, we Canadians were distinguished by our loyalty to Crown, and required no sacrifice or revolution to achieve those freedoms which patience and a benevolent monarchy would inevitably bestow upon us. How misguided I was!

As I used this Platonic method amplified by my studies of LaRouche to piece together a higher appreciation for Canadian (and world) history, it became ever more apparent that the failure to accept Ben Franklin's challenge of 1776 to join as a fourteenth colony in the Declaration of Independence created a tradition based on lies and synthetic beliefs of nationalism for over 240 years.[3] The realisation that Britain had used its control over Canada as a chess piece in the Great Game explained how the US Deep State had been created and maintained since 1783 and how the assassinations of leading American presidents involved British intelligence agents firmly planted in Canada.[4]

This included the Montreal-based plot to murder Abraham Lincoln, which was effected by British–Confederate operations run out of St. Lawrence Hall, Montreal (the Confederate intelligence northern headquarters throughout the Civil War). From this platform, not only did John Wilkes Booth receive his orders and pay for the ugly role he was assigned to play on the stage of history, but continuous terrorist attacks against the Union from the north made Lincoln's efforts to carry out the war increasingly difficult.[5]

Doing this work as part of my *Untold History of Canada* book series[6] made me realise that British Intelligence had not one North American Confederate operation deployed to subvert the Union, but rather two such operations. Only the southern version failed, while the northern confederacy succeeded after Lincoln's murder. The British North American Act of 1867 (drafted in 1864) established the Confederation of Canada, which kept Britain's northern colony as a chess piece in the Great Game; and this subversion of Canadian aspirations to become a republic while working with Russia and the USA as partners in global industrial development was a tragedy understood by too few today.[7]

Perhaps the most important of the insights into the shaping of world history which I made beginning in 2012 was driven by a new appreciation as to the role, origins and purpose of two interconnected eugenics-based think tanks. The first of these was the British Fabian Society, based in the London School of Economics, and the second was the Rhodes-Milner Round Table Movement with its associated nests of Rhodes Scholars sculpted within the halls of Oxford. The role that these two organisations played in shaping so much of recent history cut through many popular narratives of Canadian history that have been crafted to deflect the minds of inquisitive researchers from those involved behind the scenes.[8]

Not one war, assassination or coup of the twentieth century could be understood without an appreciation of the role these groups played both within Canada and especially within the USA with British-run operations like the Council on Foreign Relations. Generations of loyalist tools masquerading as patriots have kept the British fifth column intact within the USA from its earliest days after 1783 to the present precarious moment in history.

Any value that I find in the research that I've done and small discoveries I've made in the field of history is entirely due to my traumatic experiences post-2001. These experiences were accompanied by the impetus to heal the sick intimidation of the postmodernist academic ethic – an impetus that led me to discover Lyndon LaRouche's writings and their special emphasis on the mind of Plato.

NOTES

1. For a brief outline of the programme JFK fought to bring online in opposition to the Malthusian Deep State that carried out his murder, I invite you to read 'Remembering John F. Kennedy's Vision for the Future That Should Have Been', by Matthew Ehret, first published in the *Canadian Patriot Review* (2019) and *The Clash of the Two Americas vol. 2.*

2. 'John Diefenbaker's Northern Vision Sabotaged by Rhodes Scholars', by Matthew Ehret, the *Canadian Patriot Review #4*, 2013, and *Untold History of Canada vol. 3*, 2018.

3. For more, see 'Why Canada Failed the "Ben Franklin Challenge" in 1776' published in *The Clash of the Two Americas vol. 1: The Unfinished Symphony.*

4. For an introduction to the British-controlled Deep State within the USA during the nineteenth century, see 'America's Forgotten Constitutional Traditions Needed to Stop the Great Reset and WW3', by Matthew Ehret.

5. For more, see 'Understanding the Tri-fold Nature of the Deep State', by Matthew Ehret.

6. https://canadianpatriot.org/untold-history-of-canada-books/.

7. For the full story, see 'The Imperial Myth of Canada's National Policy: Its Contemporary Implications', by Matthew Ehret.

8. See 'The Origins of the Deep State in North America parts 1–3' for more on the growth of the Rhodes-Milner Round Table and the Fabian Society with a deep exposition of their role in shaping the twentieth-century Deep State in both Canada and the USA.

A Study in Evil

NEIL KRAMER

Neil Kramer is a British teacher, writer and speaker, specialising in the fields of theology, esotericism, and philosophy.

Introduction

Is normality truly normal? Is it a good thing? Is it legitimate and organic, or has someone messed around with it? Could normality be an artificial construction, something painstakingly crafted to bring people into line? Is it even possible to control something as apparently nebulous and all-encompassing as normality? These were the questions that catalysed my early spiritual inquiry.

I used to think that normality was just the way things were – the unplanned, natural, median reflection of human society. It's what most people freely thought, what they openly did, what they impulsively felt, what they watched, what they wore, what they ate, what they believed, what they agreed to. It simply didn't enter into my head that normality could be routinely and systematically manufactured. Yet, when I looked carefully, I started to see this process demonstrably taking place. My starting point was to examine what normality actually is.

The word normal derives from the Latin *normalis*, meaning 'in conformity with rule'. This comes from the Latin *norma* and Greek *gnomon*, meaning 'a carpenter's square/rule, standard, line, indicator on a sundial'. So the technical definition of normality is the state of conforming with a predetermined rule. That's quite a different meaning to our accustomed understanding of the term. This is the first key. Normality is not what most people naturally think and do. It is what most people are told to think and do.

In an attempt to change how we perceive reality, words like normality, diversity, discrimination, vaccination, hate and truth are being slowly redefined in order to propagate a new preferred world view. Words have power. They are like incantations with spring-loaded mechanisms that create impressions in the mind when we speak them. This is why the constant repetition of such words, along with their new meanings, is omnipresent in popular media and culture. Every time you look at a mainstream news website, every time you listen to the radio, every time you switch on the TV, the normality template is being disseminated.

Dark provinces

My first suspicions about normality were glimpsed through the dim mirror of my teenage years. I could feel something was horribly wrong with the world. I had a creeping awareness that it wasn't warped by accident or incompetence. There was a design to it. An intention behind it. I can't say whether my observations were due to a particular set of circumstances, or some youthful spasm of acuity, or natural adolescent blues, or what. But everything just seemed *off*. For a while, I wondered whether it was just me – my brain, my house, my village, my family, my patch of sky, my way of life. None of which were conspicuously awful. But deep down, I knew it wasn't any of those things. It wasn't just me and my little world. It affected everyone and the whole world.

I remember standing on a windswept Cheshire hillside staring down at my high school and feeling an epic wrongness seeping from every godforsaken brick. That dark provincial penal colony – disfiguring the glacial terrain like an open wound – was meant to be a bastion of vibrant learning, inspiring discovery and wholesome edification. In reality, just like four thousand other secondary schools across England, it was a government facility for grooming teenagers into their impending life sentence of soul-crushing nine-to-five serfdom

It's no secret. All honest students, regardless of social class or academic ability, witness first-hand the giant incongruity between the noble educational service advertised and the actual work training received. It's quite a shock at first. The grim succession of dysfunctional teachers, the superficial treatment of subjects, the transmission of blatant falsehoods, the onerous workloads that kill the pleasure of learning and contemplation, and the dangerous disinformation concerning sexuality, gender, class, ethnicity and heritage. All the while, students are attempting to survive the brutal haemorrhaging of precious time they are coerced into accepting as par for the course. Untold hours squandered on circus-trick recitations and futile token exercises, as opposed to nourishing scholarly study and independent critical thinking. Sooner or later, the honourable pupil confesses to himself that mainstream schools and universities exist to standardise and flatten minds. Rarely, if ever, do they expand and uplift them.

This is not a modern phenomenon. During the final years of the Second World War, the dubiously named Ministry of Education was tasked with administering compulsory education across England. Its primary goal was to set people to work in offices and factories, with the products of their labour focused on rebuilding Britain and Europe, ultimately fuelling the long-planned borderless European superstate and the gradual blurring of distinct and homogeneous nations. The enrichment of the mind for the refinement of the individual was already obsolete. The ministry's secondary objective was to eliminate any future questioning of mainstream political messaging, such was the rising tide of anti-government sentiment following the palpable deterioration of English society after apparently winning the war. To meet these two goals, it was decided that the principles of wartime psychological conditioning through film, TV and radio would be extended indefinitely across the population to ensure the ongoing pacification of British society.

Hiding in plain sight

It is a matter of record that MI5 (Military Intelligence Section 5), the domestic British intelligence service, was intimately involved in selecting staff at the BBC for decades. The impact of this cannot be overstated, especially considering that the BBC was the only TV channel in Britain until 1955, and the only legally permitted radio broadcaster from its founding in 1922 right up until 1968. For a long time, the MI5-controlled BBC had a total monopoly of the airwaves. As intended, this state-sponsored programming profoundly influenced British social attitudes for generations. If you wanted the latest news about events in the world, it was the BBC. If you wanted to listen to the radio, it was the BBC. If you wanted to watch TV, it was the BBC. The BBC *was* the mainstream media. Consider the scope of that effect on ninety-five per cent of British citizens, who never left the British Isles and never heard truly independent broadcasts. It is well known that even ITV, the only other main British TV channel from 1955 to 1982, and then, later, Channel 4 were both overseen and populated by intelligence-service operatives.

So, it is an indisputable historical fact that the British mainstream media was an intelligence operation from the outset, designed to appear sensible and beneficial whilst actually being totally disingenuous and innately deceptive. MI5 involvement in mainstream media had very little to do with national security. Its raison d'être was to create and steer narratives to manipulate society towards passive compliance. Even with the explosion of satellite, cable and Internet media over the coming years, an alarmingly small number of organisations (currently six) own and control the entire global mainstream media outreach. Those regulating the content and distribution did not arrive in their positions by accident.

But it wasn't just about lowering IQ, seeding narratives and breeding indifference. I observed a much more disturbing thing. Internationalist factions within the intelligence services were instructed to use the mainstream media to slowly and deliberately degrade morality, marriage and spirituality in British society from the middle part of the twentieth century to today. A truly catastrophic enterprise. Why would they do that? Here's the first part of the answer: because immoral, fatherless, secular people are much easier to control. Moreover, an ideological assault is cheaper and more effective than a traditional kinetic war with bullets, bombs and boots. Better to deceive and numb the population, rather than bully and coerce them. This technique represents an actualisation of Huxley's *Brave New World* stupefaction method, rather than the looming menace of brutality in Orwell's *Nineteen Eighty-Four*.

From the educational side, since the Ministry of Education was already ingrained in internal governmental secrecy, there was less need for covert oversight and management. Government officials either were intelligence operatives themselves, owned intelligence assets, or were subtly led by influential senior figures. Very commonplace. So, over a couple of generations, the premeditated and progressive dumbing-down of school curricula further incited the planned dereliction of British society. To be clear, the Ministry of Education (now rebranded as the Department for Education) in tandem with the mainstream media was never about education and enlightenment. They were about producing an apathetic, deferential and decadent population.

The earthly foe

It took a while for me to satisfy myself that the evidence for this damaging synthetic normality was consistent and solid. Years and years. But I wanted to be absolutely certain. And in time, I was. Once I knew this stuff was real, I then turned my attention to two questions I'd had all along: *Who?* and *Why?* Who had the method, motive and opportunity to herd society in such negative directions? And why is humankind being subjected to this cruel incursion? And we're not talking about the transitory flunkeys administering and maintaining things. They can be identified at any point in history without too much trouble. One need only glance at the present-day cast of unscrupulous rulers, politicians and industrialists to smell the familiar tang of treachery. My question went beyond that. Data pointed to coordinated orchestration from outside. From above. Meta-political, supranational, aloofly unprincipled. Traditional answers focused on formidable old aristocratic-style families preoccupied with power, control and greed. Whilst this was true in part, it was not a precise or adequate answer.

For me, a crucial clue regarding this riddle of *Who?* is given in the book of Daniel in Old Testament scripture. It is a complex book, authored in about 535 BC, and threaded with sophisticated encoded symbolism and real-world historical data. Daniel articulates several interlocking empires starting with Babylon, then Medo-Persia, then Greece, then Rome. They are presented in Daniel Chapter 2 as expressions of a single overarching entity. *The* empire. An unbroken corporate entity reaching through millennia from at least 600 BC to today. Significantly, in the latter days of the Roman phase of empire, there is a strong case to suggest that Daniel is telling us that the final form of this governing authority will be a kind of internationalist or globalist empire. Nonetheless, its malevolence, dominance and demon worship remain explicit, unmistakable, and constant in any rational scholarly study. Once again, I had to remind myself that this is not fanciful speculation – it is our history. The bad guys have routinely sacrificed human beings to demons – quite uninterrupted – for thousands of years. It used to be an open and public ritual; now it is simply hidden from view. It never stopped.

This kind of thinking took me out of the everyday socio-political world, and placed me squarely into the enigmatic spiritual world. More particularly, the realm of theology. Theology is the study of the nature of God, and rational inquiry into related spiritual questions and teachings. From the Greek *theos*, 'God', and *ology,* from *logia,* 'study of, branch of knowledge'. If physics, biology and chemistry are disciplines in observing the natural physical world, theology is the discipline of observing the supernatural non-physical world. Applied theology is the application of theological insights into our everyday life.

Nothing has been more valuable in my understanding of the problems of government, society and human nature than studying authentic mature spiritual life and the corresponding historical scriptural records within both the Bible and the surrounding body of intertestamental and mystical literature. It is starkly divergent from what is commonly and ignorantly parroted within institutionalised religion, I must say. Rather, true spiritual study is a deep and inherently countercultural work consisting of contemplation, scholarship, embodiment and inner renewal. Indeed, I can now appreciate that without a basic theological lens it is not possible to properly comprehend the root of the distortions in our reality, nor the identity of the real enemy. Like I did myself, one tends to go around in circles, pointing fingers at this man or that, this group or that nation, this social system or economic model, never really getting anywhere. Theology transcends all that and goes straight to the heart of the problem.

Allow me to present a speed-dial version of my understanding of the classical theological picture. God is real. He created everything. Humans are part of His emerging family. He made the earth to see which humans He could trust going forward. Will they exercise their sovereignly endowed faculty of free will to live honestly, lovingly, courageously, morally and humbly? Who loves what is true? Trustworthy humans are brought forward and given dominion over a new heavenly earth (where life really begins). Untrustworthy humans are annihilated. Harsh, but fair. Though God possesses the omniscience to see ahead and know who will do what, He does not make the decision for us. We do that all by ourselves. Our destiny is in our own hands.

Within this framework, the earth is best conceived of as a classroom, rather than as a resort. It is a top-notch academy of living spiritual principles, designed to educate, purify and uplift us. We're not here for a laugh or by accident. As part of the training, God also created another spirit being, 'the Satan' (*hasatan*). The Hebrew word *satan* simply means 'adversary'. It may also be considered a title or office, rather than just a proper name, like the office of the prime minister, the president or the chairman. The Satan's job is to test, watch and prosecute. He entices us to yield, to give in, to resign our goodness and just become part of the falsehood and immorality that surrounds us. Satan is not God's cosmic adversary – he is our earthly foe.

Over and over again in my studies, whenever I examined history, from 2000 BC to AD 2000, it is inescapable that empire unswervingly venerates Satan. It has willingly allied itself with this adversarial force. From Egypt to Babylon, from the horrors of Rome to the grotesque globalist deep-state skulduggery of our time, the bad guys always go against God. Some of them are intimately acquainted with the theology and its fundamental reality, whilst a great many of them have no idea whatsoever. They just think it's about power and money. But that doesn't change the facts of their disastrous allegiance and who is ultimately commanding them.

The biblical writer Paul, a supremely well-educated and erudite man, wrote a letter in around AD 62 to the growing spiritual community in Ephesus, reminding them of the same problem we are examining here. Basically, that it's not just about evil people – it's about evil spiritual beings too. He wrote, 'For our struggle is not against flesh and blood, but against the rulers, against the powers, against the world forces of this darkness, against the spiritual forces of wickedness in the heavenly places [spirit realms].' Ephesians 6:12.

If you ever wondered why mainstream culture is so coarse, so dysfunctional, so corrosive, it's because it is designed to conform to satanic principles. Slowly but surely, over time, it persuades people to reject divinity. Specifically, it is a lifestyle devoted to self, comfort, entitlement, diversion, prestige, relativism, unaccountability. Nothing higher than oneself except remote abstract notions of environmental and social factors on earth. Everyone with their own truth and no external absolute truth of any kind. Essentially, no discernment of good and evil. It's all about oneself. That's what satanism really is. The enthronement of self over God. The enthronement of *anything* over God. Every time a human just goes along with the mainstream programme, the Satan has done his job. Another poor soul bites the dust, consigning themselves to oblivion because they couldn't be bothered to genuinely embody what is good, right and true. Even though they were built to do so. Not because they didn't know, or because they were incapable, but because they didn't want to. Free-will self-destruction.

So, I propose that the *Who?* is the office of the satan. The *Why?* is to fulfil God's instructions to test us. In a sense, the bad guy is just doing his job. All part of the grand scholastic tapestry. A key element of our spiritual assessment. The intrinsically corrupt fallen state of the world is a calculated distortion that compels human students to distinguish between good and evil, right and wrong, true and false. Because it's all around us. You either face it and refute it, or you become part of it through passive consent.

This world is basically a study in evil. Good is here too, along with beauty, grace, mercy and absolution, but the overwhelming characteristic of the fallen earth is evil. Ice-cold, ugly, vicious evil. By design. What can we do to combat evil, wrongness and falsehood? Identify and understand them. Repudiate them. Don't become part of the problem. Don't roll over and think someone else will deal with it. Don't be timid in the face of an evil consensus. Embody goodness and speak the truth whenever you can. Sometimes with tact, diplomacy and understanding. Sometimes like a sledgehammer. We can't really complain. After all, back in the very beginning, God recommended we don't eat from the tree of the knowledge of good and evil. And you know how that went. Nevertheless, though we certainly chose the hard path, we already know the ending. Evil is defeated, punished and eradicated. Good shines forth, is distinguished, elevated, and goes on in a new world. Which was God's objective all along. To bring His family home.

SPIRITUALITY AND TRUTH

My Ongoing Journey to Awareness

MARKUS OLOFFSON

Markus Oloffson is a former counsellor/therapist at hospitals, clinics and rehab centres.

My life

I'm a fifty-nine-year-old Swedish man who mainly has worked as a counsellor/therapist at hospitals, clinics, and rehab centres for brain-damaged people. I've had plenty of other short-term jobs in various industries, such as driving a forklift truck; my first job was as an auto mechanic at the age of sixteen. When I was growing up, I also took part in a lot of sports, including rowing, football, tennis, weightlifting, boxing and ice hockey. Keeping fit has always been a huge interest of mine. Music has also always had a huge impact on my life – both listening to it and playing it myself.

I undertook seven years of study at university and have a Bachelor of Social Work degree, which in my country takes almost four years to finish. I also studied sociology at universities both in Sweden and England. In the course of my professional life, I worked closely with my father (a psychologist) for many years. Together we ran 'The Swedish Max Lüscher-Institute' (with Max Lüscher's blessing) for eight years, and there we trained therapists in Max Lüscher's colour test.

When I think back on my life and on the many experiences I've had, be it in an awake state of mind or during sleep, I realise that developing awareness is a gradual thing – an ongoing journey. As we move through life, we gather knowledge and therefore also some kind of understanding of what's happening, learning from our experiences.

I remember that as I child I was driven by emotions, but I also tried hard to understand other people's motives and underlying meanings. Whether this behaviour is genetic and/or socially conditioned is another question, but it is probably both. I liked to ponder things I had seen, heard or did not understand. I liked to be alone, playing alone, walking/bicycling aimlessly alone. I did not have the social skills other children automatically seemed to have. I lacked the feeling of borders. At least, that's the reflection I have now, as an adult.

When I grew a little older, in my late teens, I started to have this strange feeling that something was really wrong with the world I lived in. This observation was local at the beginning, concerning my home town, my country. I could never put my finger on exactly what it was that was so wrong, and that made me frustrated.

As I went through various forms of the school system, and ended up at university, I got the opportunity to put my observations on paper. The thing I mostly reacted to was the wage work system. To me, that was an obvious form of slavery, albeit wrapped in glossy paper. I gathered material on wage work for a few years, and I conducted interviews, telephoning people who had criticised the wage work system and writing to people. Finally I put it all down in an essay that formed part of my final exam at university.

It was a very good essay, and when I read it now, some thirty-plus years later, I am still rather impressed. Doing this work gave me the inspiration to continue to study sociology, and to delve into the machinery behind the controlling mechanisms of society. I wrote two more essays – in the second essay I explored the connection between our judicial/penal system and religion/capitalism, and in the third essay I presented the solution to end all this corruption: a spiritual awakening.

The time span between these three essays, from the first to the last, was fifteen years. The first two were taking an intellectual look at the mechanisms in society, and the third presented a spiritual solution. This fifteen-year time span goes hand in hand with my own spiritual journey.

At the age of twenty-five to thirty, I had the first spiritual experience that really shook me. It was when I took a nap on my old bed in my parents' house during a visit there, and drifted out of my own body. I separated from my physical body, and drifted through the roof. The strange thing was that all the time I had a 360-degree field of vision. I saw my own body in my bed, while my consciousness was hovering some thirty metres above the roof. Suddenly, out of nowhere, I became aware of a strong white light. I could look right into it without being blinded. Out of this light came gliding towards me a male (as I perceived it) figure, dressed in a monk's cape. I only saw the dark silhouette of this person.

As this person came closer to me, I was struck by a warm wind – but it wasn't a wind. It was pure love. I was in a blissful state, surrounded by pure love, and I didn't want to go down to my physical body again; I wanted to stay where I was . . . forever.

Suddenly I felt I was being drawn down to my physical body in my bed. I fought to not unite with my body, and I managed to get out of my physical body again and rise a couple of metres. Again I was drawn back into my body, and again I desperately fought back and managed to rise around ten centimetres above my body . . . and then I finally was sucked into my body, and woke up with a jerk.

The next thing that was rather pivotal occurred following really vivid and strong dreams about an old friend, four nights in a row. After these dreams, It was as if some kind of portal had opened during the night. It started with an enormous amount of information coming to me during a dream state. Every night I was visited by many people, dead, alive, known, unknown, animals, groups, individuals . . .

I started to write down the names of those I recognised in my dreams and compiled some statistics. During a period of almost four months I dreamt of 531 different persons and animals 1713 times. Some of these persons visited me more often than others. For example, my father visited me ninety times during these four months.

I also started to experience sound and colour explosions in my head. I've been taught how to leave my body, to fly and to pass through solid objects. In this awake state, I started to experience synchronicity and be subjected to gang stalking (which I believe is related to my spiritual awakening). So, here we have two parallel developments, one intellectual (and physical) and one spiritual (which also could be physical, albeit in the fourth dimension). This is important, I think.

Sometimes I meet people who seem to be totally aware of the corruption and the foul play in society; the moment I mention dimensions or synchronicity their eyes go blank, and they stare at me as if I was crazy. On the other hand, I have friends who are very much in tune with their own spirituality; they speak with animals and deceased friends, but are totally clueless when I talk about the JFK conspiracy or the transhumanist agenda. To me this is a strange and fascinating contradiction (or not).

So, there seem to be two strands of the awareness process, one intellectual and one spiritual, and I rarely see them go hand in hand. Since I believe that more people than myself have become aware of this difference between people, the questions must be 'Why are we so different?' and 'Does it matter?' Is it true that all of us sooner or later will be both intellectually and spiritually aware anyway?

The problem for me is that I have difficulties talking to people who are only spiritually aware or only intellectually aware (after all, we are talking about the left contra the right brain hemispheres here) because I believe that these two (seemingly) opposed stances belong together. I have only come across a few people who seem to be deeply aware both spiritually and intellectually.

Now, I do not claim to be one of those who have the complete picture, because I don't (and probably never will have). This is a gradual process (at least for me); and when I look back five years, I can't believe how unaware I was then. And in five years' time (if we still coexist on this planet in this form then) I will look back and think, 'Gosh, I really didn't know anything five years ago!' But since we all are different, I believe we all have different developments, for different reasons. One is not better than the other – it's just different.

Strategies to bypass existing non-beneficial structures in society

I strongly believe that one of the best ways to create a new and better society for all humans, animals and plant life is to bypass the old system. I do not think that a confronting stance is helpful; I believe we need to make the change ourselves by setting a good example, and letting others come to us. We need to go back to basics in all areas, be it the school system, the judicial system or the medical system.

I believe that everything comes from within, and that the basic building blocks are love and respect. I also think that there is no single solution that will fit everyone, but rather there are many solutions. For a new school system I would like to see much more home-schooling and some kind of mentorship. One child could have many mentors in various fields. Even another child could be a mentor. The important thing is that we respect that we are different, with different goals, ambitions, capabilities and development needs.

I also see us working more in teams. That way we could gather huge knowledge spread over a vast field. Where my knowledge ends, another person's might begin. For example, in my line of work I could say, 'I don't think I'm the right person to help you with this specific problem, but I know someone who can.'

A new and better world would emerge if these principles were followed.

PART III

Light Bulb Moments and Critical Thinking: Powerful Discoveries

Drawing the strands together

We have reached the end of an extraordinary journey that has taken us into the minds of twenty-four people across three continents. For the reader who has not read all of the first-hand accounts of our inquiring minds in Part II, we warmly commend them to you since each account distils a person's life's experience and the complex processes that ignited their questioning journeys. You may notice threads that bind the first-hand accounts together – threads that explain the questing process that each of our voices has been engaged on.

It is vital that we understand whether there is a pattern behind the triggers that prompt profound, life-changing questions. As you will have seen, the variety of subject matter in these accounts is extraordinary, each offering a dramatically distinct set of questions. This is an extremely diverse group of people, from a variety of backgrounds. The common feature is a propensity to pose questions and to have Light Bulb Moments.

So, we will begin with an understanding of what exactly triggered the journeys of our twenty-four inquiring minds. Was there a single set of factors? Then, we will move on to first ever findings of a survey to establish the triggers to Critical Thinking and look at the exciting responses to that. Following this, we will gather the responses of seventy-four survey respondents, in a first of its kind survey, and apply the attributes and triggers revealed in their responses to the narratives of our twenty-four inquiring minds. Not only that, but we will break completely new ground by revealing the extent to which the attributes and triggers also apply to our courageous literary heroes. Finally, to really get inside the minds of critical thinkers, we will do what has never been done before. This is to put the personalities of critical thinkers to the test and see if they share common features.

Now, one of our main aims in collecting these first-hand accounts is to make it possible to identify the triggers to Critical Thinking and the impact that follows on from this. Two other pieces of research help us with this investigation, the first being an online survey conducted amongst critical thinkers and the second being a survey of the personality types of such a group of people. Our aim through all of this is to discern whether there are patterns to the triggers that ignite the fuse of Critical Thinking.

It is vital that we do this, and discover exactly what prompts Critical Thinking, a skill that remarkable people through the ages have identified as essential to a civilised society. And the drive to develop these skills is still with us. Indeed, powerful establishment organisations such as the BBC and the World Economic Forum (WEF – a private organisation with a global reach that trains up world leaders today) speak of the importance of Critical Thinking, so we need to know how to bring this to the fore of people's thinking skills. We also need to understand the personality types most likely to have the heroic qualities of our three literary heroes. We say this since, in Part I we saw Jung's view that 'The ability to ask questions is the greatest resource in learning the truth'. And if your objective is a more practical one of survival and organisational efficiency, then these words quoted earlier from the Harvard Business Review (Brooks and John, 2018) underscore the importance of identifying the triggers to vibrant inquiry:

> Questioning is a uniquely powerful tool for unlocking value....: It spurs learning and the exchange of ideas, it fuels innovation and performance improvement, it builds rapport and trust among team members. And it can mitigate business risk by uncovering unforeseen pitfalls and hazards.

So, we will begin with an understanding of the factors that triggered the journeys of our twenty-four inquiring minds. After that, we will move on to the online survey, and responses to that, before finally looking at a study concerning the personality types of those with a strong questioning disposition.

A. Light Bulb Moments in the lives of twenty-four critical thinkers

In Part I we explained how the authors selected a group of people that they considered to be especially practised at Critical Thinking. This method of gathering a sample – identifying those able to offer rich data on the research topic in question (Palinkas et al., 2015) and available, willing and able to communicate their experiences and opinions in an articulate, expressive, and reflective manner (Spradley, 1979; Bernard, 2002) – is known as purposive and non-probability sampling (Palinkas et al., 2015). It sounds quite technical, but it's simply a way of gathering data.

The brief that we gave to the twenty-four critical thinkers was to produce a first-person account of the issues that caused them to question what they were observing and experiencing in life. All followed this brief with only one person deviating slightly by writing a third-person account, due we were told by time constraints. As you will have seen from reading the first-person stories, the brief prompted a wide variety of responses on an extraordinarily broad range of topics. For the questions that contributors posed of themselves took them – without exception – beyond the normal bounds of what we could call everyday reality. This shows us just how powerful Critical Thinking can be. No wonder that the Big Brother society of Oceania viewed Winston Smith, with his capacity for Critical Thinking, as such a threat. He had a powerful intellect and was able to apply this to his knowledge of earlier history and to the society in which he lived.

At one level it is fascinating to see the Critical Thinking of the twenty-four authors, who, Winston-like, leave the shores of received knowledge to embark on a journey of discovery to other ways of thinking. You may find their ideas appealing - or it is possible that you may not - but reading them will give you a sense of the triggers and personal attributes that prompt the questioning processes that Einstein identified as so critical to problem-solving. Indeed, as you may recall from Part I, Einstein advised people to 'Question everything', adding that 'The important thing is not to stop questioning. Never lose a holy curiosity'. He described the identification of the questions as the key step in solving a problem and you will see that the Light Bulb Moments that our contributors experience follow periods of intense questioning, leading them to rethink the nature of the reality presented to them. This process of questioning leads them to question and rethink:

- Official history (whether prehistory, biblical history, or more recent history, such as the Great Fire of London narrative, the sinking of the Titanic and contemporary events)

- Financial and legal systems

- Current geopolitical events, such as 9/11 and the pandemic of 2020–2022
- The current school and university systems
- The extent to which the woke agenda is influenced by Chinese Marxism
- The allopathic health system
- Child abuse and how this can be spotted
- The telecommunications system and the extent to which 5G and smartphones are serving humanity's interests
- The very purpose of life, and whether humans are purely physical or perhaps more spiritual beings; whether life is perhaps a test of how we respond to the information that comes our way.

In reading these rich accounts, you can share some of the Light Bulb Moments that critical thinkers, from a diverse range of backgrounds, countries and occupations, have experienced. If you do not have the time to read all the accounts, then we would encourage you to find some space, since the author of each account is following in the footsteps of literary heroes of iconic novels – *Nineteen Eighty-Four, Brave New World* and *Fahrenheit 451* did – by applying Critical Thinking skills to the worlds around them. So, if you enjoyed those novels, or the film versions of them, you will enjoy these stories too (even if you take issue with some of the views expressed), especially since they have the piquancy of being recounted by real-life people.

Of course, if you are someone who likes to read the conclusion of a book before the rest, then you may like to turn to the summaries of the critical thinkers' personal stories in Appendix A, with their r suggested solutions found in Appendix B. You will see that they have allowed their Critical Thinking to take them on a journey; and such is the transformational power of asking questions, this can take them to places that are far beyond the reach of received wisdom.

Almost as interesting as exploring these new vistas with our contributors, is understanding the triggers that give rise to profound questioning. What sets these twenty-four critical thinkers apart from those who like to hug the shores of received wisdom? We were able to follow the triggers for people's Critical Thinking through a process known as 'inductive coding' – a data-driven approach in which 'the research begins with an area of study and allows the theory to emerge from the data' (Strauss and Corbin 1998, p.12). Or, to put it another way, it is a method that allows a picture to emerge of the phenomenon that is being studied (Lodico, et al., 2010, p.10). In this case the topic under investigation was Critical Thinking.

Results and discussion

What we found through the process of inductive coding was that the main trigger to Critical Thinking and Light Bulbs Moments was the perception of an anomaly. Usually this was between what people were told or what they had read and what they perceived to be true. The two topics that were most likely to ignite the perception of an anomaly were firstly corruption (and deception, a subset of that) and then issues concerning health and well-being.

An example? The piece by Professor Gloria Moss describes how the official story of the Great Fire of London of 1666 – that this was caused by negligence on the part of Thomas Farriner, the baker in Pudding Lane – did not align with the evidence, much of which pointed to collusion by the authorities in London in 1666. The implications are massive since the damage to buildings was equivalent to £1.5 billion in modern values, and the human costs were equally severe since 100,000 people were rendered homeless. Those who had been tenants found themselves legally and financially liable for the damage to the property that they had occupied since the law at the time, renewed at the start of 1667, placed the liability on the tenants and not on the landlords.

When Gloria started to read accounts of the fire, she could not help but notice anomalies. For example, contemporary narratives described the fire fanning out to the east, north and south of the site in Pudding Lane where it allegedly started. Yet some of these accounts referred to an 'easterly' wind that, on its own, could not have caused the fire to spread in these various directions. The only way in which this multidirectional spread of the fire could have happened was if the fire was spread deliberately through the use of incendiary devices.

This is perfectly plausible since pieces of pottery were found near Pudding Lane that, according to a report by scientists in 1979, had been subjected to temperatures as high as 1,700 degrees Celsius (The Secret Professor, 2022). To gain a sense of the magnitude of this heat, you need only realise that paper and wood burns at a temperature of 450 degrees Celsius (yes, as the commentator, Livos, has revealed, Ray Bradbury meant Celsius rather than Fahrenheit when he entitled his novel Fahrenheit 451), and so the temperature at which the pottery was burning cannot have come about through the action simply of wood catching fire.

This means that another explanation had to be found. Now, knowing that England, just two weeks before the Great Fire had burned West-Terschelling in Holland to the ground, and had used fireships to burn up to 170 Dutch merchant navy ships, tells us that Stuart England had advanced knowledge of incendiary technique. Clearly, there was knowledge at the time on how to manufacture high and sustained temperatures. And there is another angle to this as well since during the Great Fire of London, many people were observed throwing fireballs (The Secret Professor, 2022). So there may have been an organised effort to spread the fire. Indeed, the very fact that multiple measures were not used that could have stopped the fire backs a conspiracy rather than 'cock-up' understanding of what happened. By way of clarification, the measures that were not in use at the time of the fire included a ready water supply from a reservoir in Islington (this was mysteriously turned off the day before the fire) and gentlemen and constables who should have been at their posts were reported as absent or inactive (ibid).

Moreover, the fact that all unauthorised accounts of the Great Fire were suppressed, that people who published and sold unlicensed books and broadsheets were arrested, and that in 1667 the Privy Council ordered the public burning of any pamphlet providing evidence to the Commons' inquiry into the causes of the fire is also extremely suspicious. Why would the authorities not welcome accounts from the populace as to what had occurred? One way of explaining this anomaly is to suppose that the authorities wished to suppress witness evidence.

The trigger to this realisation was a mental one, but also an emotional one since around 100,000 people were rendered homeless and held liable for the cost of repairs. The added knowledge that the authorities may have been complicit provoked a sense of disquiet causing mind and emotion to come together in triggering questions about this event. In a similar way, one of our contributors, Shannon Rowan, writes of the devastating loss of a friend in the attacks of 9/11 in New York and shows how the emotional pain she suffered kick-started a period of intense and careful Critical Thinking.

There are other examples too. Anne Currie speaks of the effect of a childhood with a father prone to erratic changes of mood. This had an emotional impact on her, triggering a long-lasting tendency to look beneath the surface. As she writes:

> It taught me to keep a careful eye on the weather mood and to recognise that appearances can be deceptive. And thus, I've lived most of my life in two worlds: the seen and the unseen, the public and the private, the overt and the covert.

She describes receiving a grounding in:

> gauging minute signals of mood and fluctuations in atmosphere helped me to discover material which was hidden, through shame and fear, both within myself and others.

This questioning of the people around her became a factor in her decision to train as a psychotherapist and explore beneath the surface. As she writes:

> Psychotherapy requires an interest in the subterranean, and very soon, in the course of my experiences, I found that I had developed a nose for what I would vulgarly call 'bullshit'. Any display of the inauthentic would cause me to develop an uncomfortable feeling in the stomach, and this has become a useful facility for assessing everyday life – one that I trust and value.

When she worked at a childcare centre, she found the atmosphere there toxic. She also found that almost all the young people were described and treated as wilful troublemakers or downright evil, and this led her to write that 'No one seemed to be interested in what lay beneath their behaviour.' She was personally able to do this, in fact, and discover histories of abuse through her heightened skills of Critical Thinking.

So, it seems that emotional and mental processes can act together to trigger Critical Thinking, thereby showing that the effects of emotion are not entirely negative, as had been presupposed in the earlier thinking discussed in Part I (Matsumoto, 2021). What is more, it seems that profound triggers can cause Critical Thinking to take place in the long-term and not just in the moment. And moreover, the Critical Thinking can grow in intensity and increase with the passing of time.

Here, for example, are the thoughts of Eve Gilmore on how the life-enhancing effects of Critical Thinking:

> This awakening from the consensus world view to a wider reality set me on a journey in which limitation was replaced by possibility and conformity by freedom.

Wendy Wendorff, likewise, speaks of the transformative impact of Critical Thinking:

> Once awakened to the knowledge that things are in fact so significantly different from the way we were taught, told, and believed as to be almost the reverse [hence the 'through the looking glass' reference], it was not only impossible to go back to sleep, but it was also impossible to stop questioning. . . .So, it is a coming-of-age, a stepping into our own power, and I can say from personal experience that this is a wonderful feeling – self-governance, self-sufficiency and open-minded learning. What a gift!

This echoes the sentiments that she expresses at the beginning of her thought piece:

> Prior to 2010, my computer had been tethered to my office and used exclusively for work. Post 2010, the advent of a new laptop and being introduced to Facebook and other Social Media platforms provided opportunities to dip in and out of an unlimited field of information at any time of the day. What I discovered was a 'breadcrumb trail' of mysteries and questions about our true history and the nature of our reality which gradually became a living adventure and, before very long, my main motivation.

So the accounts of the twenty-four critical thinkers provide insights into the transformative effect that questioning can have in our lives.

We will now move on and see what we can learn through the thoughts of those contributing to an online survey on the factors that triggered their own Critical Thinking.

B. Findings of an online survey concerning the triggers to Critical Thinking

We have seen how extraordinarily little we know about the factors that prompt people to exercise Critical Thinking, and this is a very concerning gap given the vital part that inquiring minds play in a civilised society. An important step in filling the gap involved finding out directly from critical thinkers not only the factors that triggered their questions but also what it was about themselves that differentiated them from others.

So, Critical Thinkers were invited to participate in an online survey, hosted on the website of the Truth University (www.truthuniversity.co.uk). The first question concerned the extent to which they trusted the mainstream media – a question that would be a proxy measure of the extent to which they placed unquestioned trust in official sources of information. Of the seventy-four survey respondents in the sample, 100% admitted to being 'uncomfortable' or 'extremely uncomfortable' about the way that events were portrayed by the mainstream media and government. This is a strong indication that the sample consisted of critical thinkers, the very group that the survey aimed to attract.

Three questions were posed on which comments were invited. One concerned the question of whether there was a specific trigger that sparked off their Critical Thinking skills; another asked how similar or different they felt from other people; and a third asked whether they perceived their childhood to have been a happy one. This final question was posed in order to ascertain whether becoming a critical thinker could be a reaction against an unhappy childhood or not. A summary of the responses to these questions is shown below.

Question 1: Was there a specific trigger?

There were fifty-three responses to this question, and a number of factors were cited as triggers to the development of Critical Thinking. Of these, the largest single factor was covid, with 42% of the sample quoting this as the main element that triggered them to become more questioning. Here are some of the triggers mentioned by the survey respondents:

> 'I was a clinical nurse (with p/g specialisation) and unwilling to be part of a clinical trial, so I left my job.'
>
> 'Being unable to find the contents of the vaccines, and being told that I would have to take responsibility for the after-effects of the injection and that I would not be able to sue the pharmaceutical company concerned; understanding that the people who were injecting the public did not talk through the possible reactions and that some sites for injecting were 'pop-up' tents with no facilities for treating anaphylactic shock.'
>
> 'It felt very odd when the narrative of what we were being told kept changing – i.e. the vaccines were 100% effective, then 60%, then 20%, now you need a booster, etc. I think another was the mask wearing. By trade, I am a product designer and I work on all kinds of projects. One of my early projects revolved around ventilation, so I know about the sizes of fabric meshes and airborne materials. . . I knew it would be like trying to stop a mosquito from entering a fully open window since the sizes of the virus are so small in comparison with the mask.'

Another trigger, this time for 15% of the sample, was the 9/11 tragedy. One of the comments mentioned the fact that

> 'some of the terrorists were still alive was really strange. And then they completely failed to follow up the story. I had never even heard the phrase 'conspiracy theorist' at the time, but I was probably given this label for wanting to know the truth about the terrorists.'

Another referred to the 'inadequately explained collapse of Building 7 after it was announced on TV'.

A further trigger for respondents was Brexit, with 11% of respondents mentioning this. Here are some of the comments:

'The overwhelming pressure from politicians made me suspicious and my trust went inward: trust myself only and question more.'

'Manipulation on both sides.'

'Being a first-time voter in 2001, I wanted to look into the issue of the EU. I realised very quickly we were being lied to and the media was biased.'

Other topics were raised, but with lesser frequency. These concerned unexplained loose ends: the global financial crisis, climate change, 5G, the American election; failing the eleven-plus, the death of Princess Diana; Medicine – 'A serious accident in my teens opened my eyes to the limits of allopathic medicine'; Television – 'I've never had a TV since I left home in 1975, and consequently I live in pure beauty!'; Novichok and the Skripal story – 'Knowing about chemistry it was clear we were lied to. A Swiss lab proved that the agent was an atropine derivative, which fully explains Skripal's symptoms'; Noticing propaganda – 'I lived in South Africa as a teenager (1970s–1980s) and became sensitised to not-very-skilful lying as a way of propping up an evil system there'; History – 'Having travelled the length of the Nile, it was patently obvious that the culture that existed and built the Pyramids did not do so with slaves and rudimentary tools'; *Codex Alimentarius* – 'that recategorised many nutritional supplements in favour of pharmaceutical products'.

So it seems that perceiving anomalies was central to arousing people's Critical Thinking and Light Bulb Moments.

Question 2: Why might you be different?

Responses to this question were many and varied, with various factors dominating people's responses. The most common explanation, found amongst 13% of responses, was **being curious**. Here are some people's comments:

'When something interests me, I study and explore it deeply, thoroughly and relentlessly, to gain full facts.'

'I am a curious person. I wanna know the answer to everything!'

'I research a large scope of subjects, not just one field.'

Another factor cited by respondents was **high intelligence** – something mentioned by 10% of respondents. So comments from separate respondents in this domain were

> 'I am of above average IQ.'
>
> 'I am intelligent – a member of Mensa. I have a logical mind.'
>
> 'I have an ability to analyse – a scientific mind – and able to spot things that don't add up.'
>
> 'I apply logic to answer my own questions.'
>
> 'I pick up contradictions pretty well.'
>
> 'I am a critical thinker / pusher of boundaries.'

Another factor, cited by 9% of respondents, was **distrust of authorities.** Indicative responses in this area were

> 'I believe that in my case I was born with a certain distrust of authorities.'
>
> 'A stubborn unwillingness to take order from people who I don't respect.'
>
> 'I'm from Africa, where we have a healthy disregard for government and authority – and especially for the WHO – and where we know what slavery looks like.'
>
> 'I have always questioned authority.'

Other factors emerged. A total of 7% of responses, for example, referred to the **high importance placed on discovering the truth**. Here are indicative quotes:

> 'Truth is extremely important to me – I seek it, speak it, uphold it and defend it.'
>
> 'A sensitivity about being lied to.'
>
> 'I'm not scared to tell the truth.'
>
> 'I want to know the facts.'

Similar numbers valued highly the role played by **parental guidance**. Some of the rich quotes emerging in this area were

> 'Parental guidance, close friends and a few of life's early experiences taught me to distrust that which cannot openly be seen to be true.'

> 'I think I was always brought up to question. I remember telling my mum about a story we'd been told from the Bible about a miracle when I was very young, 5 or 6, and she told me they were like fairy stories and it wasn't altogether true ... which made me doubt what the teacher said. Also, I remember a policeman coming to the school to tell us how to cross the road safely, and said there was a dog who crossed at the zebra crossing each day outside the police station. Mum said it wasn't true and dogs didn't do that so I didn't trust policemen either! I somehow 'feel' when something is true. I just know this feeling. 'Knowing' has just increased more and more over the past few years – it's like a giant jigsaw all fitting into place.'

> '[My] father taught me the importance of listening to both sides, to conduct due diligence and be willing to question when I found information was wrong.'

> 'My mother used to question what organised religion tells us and did not completely trust the medical system although she believed some of the things that the media and government tell us. She had a big influence on me in terms of questioning the system.'

> 'My parents were demonstrators.'

A further category was **a sense of autonomy** – a category of comment mentioned by 6% of survey respondents. Here are some of the comments that fell under this category:

> 'A very strongly developed sense of my own personal liberty and autonomy.'

> 'As I grew older and stronger as a person physically, mentally, emotionally and spiritually I became less afraid of not fitting in. Instead of wanting to join the in crowd I became my own in crowd.'

> 'I am not afraid to consider ideas that some people think are far-fetched.'

> 'My nickname was 20 Questions.'

Other factors that emerged related to the following factor: **little exposure to the media**. Comments included

> 'I watch very little TV and rarely read any newspapers.'
>
> 'Once you've lost trust in the mainstream media, you question everything they disseminate.'
>
> 'I'm not big on watching news or reading newspapers.'

A further factor was a **high sense of morality**. One comment offered here was

> 'I am not afraid to do the right thing.'

Another was **seeing the big picture**, with one respondent's comment being

> 'I am good at seeing the whole picture.'

Further factors were **willingness to change their mind** and **seeing what was taught at school**. In the latter category (really this category belongs as a trigger in questions 2) came the view:

> 'Having time to really see what my daughter was learning, going through the google class room, shocking!'

Four further categories emerged which are shown below (in bold) with indicative quotes below them since they are self-explanatory:

Brought up in a communist country – 'Upbringing in a communist dictatorship'

Refusal to accept the absurd

Sense of Justice – indicative quotes were:

> 'An inbuilt sense of the rightness of natural justice in all situations in life.'
>
> 'I have always had a strong feeling about rights and freedoms, and got angry when I saw them being violated even when others thought it was no big deal. I'm a logical thinker and when it came to things like our EU membership I always felt national

sovereignty was something that must NEVER be surrendered and it felt absurd that politicians would want to trade sovereignty for economics and jobs.'

History / doing research

'I have read more widely and deeply about history than most of my peers.'

Finally, we reach the last question in the online survey.

Question 3: Was your childhood a happy one?

A large number of comments were received from respondents as to the nature of their childhood and whether it was a happy one or not. Of the responses received, the majority indicated that they had had happy childhoods as you can see in Table 1 (below).

	Happy childhood	**Neither happy nor unhappy**	**Not happy**
Number of responses	35 (56%)	14 (23%)	13 (21%)

Table 1: The number and percentage of survey respondents who indicate whether they had a happy or unhappy childhood.

These reports of largely happy childhoods show that, contrary to a 2018 study (Green et al.), the questioning of mainstream knowledge is not necessarily the product of unhappy and discontented childhoods that result in what the researchers involved in that study termed 'anxious attachment style'. For, according to the two researchers involved in that study, Ricky Green and Professor Karen Douglas of the University of Kent's School of Psychology, an anxious attachment style perseveres into adulthood where it can colour many aspects of people's lives, for example their friendships and their attitudes.

The two researchers went on to claim that participants with anxious attachment style may experience general feelings of mistrust and while this may be the case, it does not take account of the fact that feelings of mistrust can arise in people with no traces of anxious attachment style. On the contrary, the evidence of the online survey shows that distrust arises predominantly in those with happy childhoods.

Discussion

The seventy-four responses to the online survey take us take us a huge stop forward. For, they show us, for the first time, the triggers and personal characteristics that lead people to have inquiring minds, the skills on which a civilised society depends. Given the importance of these findings, it is reassuring to know that the survey respondents constituted a valid sample of critical thinkers – in other words, people we could rightly describe as inquiring minds. The initial survey question that probed people's attitudes to the media was designed to detect whether participants had a critical thinking predisposition or not and since 100% of the respondents declared themselves 'uncomfortable' or 'extremely uncomfortable' about the way that events were portrayed by the mainstream media and government, this showed (regardless of whether their reaction was reasonable or not) that the respondents were using a questioning approach in evaluating information. So, we can be reassured that the sample in this survey were indeed critical thinkers.

What of their responses to the three questions that followed? The first question dealt with trigger factors and survey respondents' answers identified a broad range from covid to 9/11, to Brexit, to climate change; the US election; failing the eleven-plus, the death of Princess Diana, medicine, noticing propaganda, history, Codex Alimentarius and the Skripal incident. The trigger in all cases was the perception of an anomaly between two pieces of information, just as had been the case with our twenty-four Critical Thinkers. One of the guiding hands mentioned as drawing their attention to anomalies were parents.

The next stage of our research involved ascertaining the extent to which there was an overlap between the triggers identified by the online respondents and those mentioned by the twenty-four critical thinkers whose contributions appear in Part II. The results can be seen in Table 2 (below) and you will see how extensive are the areas of overlap between the triggers for online survey respondents and the Critical Thinking contributors.

Trigger topic identified by online respondents	Critical Thinking contributor who mentions this as a trigger
The death of Princess Diana	John Hamer reports how friends who had been in Paris at the time of Diana's death saw 'on a late-night French news TV broadcast, [in]the aftermath of the crash.... film images of Princess Diana *walking* into an ambulance'.
Medicine	Eve Gilmore: 'Many medical protocols are founded on myth rather than science.' Katherine Armitage: 'My experiences in practice have led me to distrust the advice and treatment suggested by many of the health profession.' Wendy Wendorff: 'people are taking their healthcare into their own hands and researching natural methods to maintain optimum health; there is a renewed interest in plant and herbal medicines and an emphasis on prevention rather than cure.'
History	Professor Gloria Moss reveals serious anomalies between the official history of the Great Fire of London (1666) and the narrative revealed by the evidence; likewise in relation to findings concerning the Dead Sea Scrolls site of Qumran. John Hamer discusses anachronisms in official accounts of the *Titanic.* Matthew Ehret discusses how the British Empire continued to exercise vast influence over world affairs through a certain type of coup that took control of the USA after the murder of John F. Kennedy. Wendy Wendorff highlights anachronisms in the construction of ancient sites that make it hard to accept official accounts of their dating and those responsible for the buildings and artefacts remaining.

Codex Alimentarius	Katherine Armitage describes the *Codex Alimentarius* as prejudicing small herbal-remedy producers and restricting levels of vitamin C in supplements. Wendy Wendorff questions why the *Codex* does not insist on the labelling of glyphosate as an ingredient since it is sprayed on to grain.
Education	Dr Ursula Edgington describes multiple failures in the education system leading her to assert that: 'Our universities have lost all integrity and credibility as meaningful and ethical education institutions. This is not due to incompetence or laziness. Over several decades, the valid outcomes from numerous research projects have been systematically suppressed. Evidence-based discussions of climate change, toxicology, democratic rights, gendered roles, colonial history, Best Practice Leadership (Secret Professor, 2022) and many other topics are off-limits because arguments that differ from the political narrative have been conveniently labelled 'conspiracy theories' or 'misinformation'. Neil Kramer writes of the school system as 'a government facility for grooming teenagers into their impending life sentence of soul-crushing nine-to-five serfdom. He goes on to suggest that 'mainstream schools and universities exist to standardise and flatten minds. Rarely, if ever, do they expand and uplift them.' The reason? After the Second World War, the government decided that 'the principles of wartime psychological conditioning through film, TV and radio would be extended indefinitely across the population to ensure the ongoing pacification of British society.'
Parental guidance	Jeff Wyatt frequently and fondly referred to his late father as his inspiration. He spoke of how his Dad brought him up to speak his truth. Without fail, Jeff would get emotional sharing stories of their strong bond and recalling the sadness of his father's passing just four years ago. He

	would also honour the memory of his grandfather, who was 'dodging bullets on the beaches of Normandy in 1944, fighting for our freedoms'. Ray Savage: 'Being my father's son has had an amazing impact on me., Born in 1916, he grew up in the 1929 slump, which had a major impact in his life. He watched his parents lose businesses in this period, ending their lives in near poverty. He became a self-qualified engineer, entering the war as an officer. He was a Normandy veteran, part of the First Tactical Air Force, which provided cover to the bridgehead from Normandy to Berlin. Ray goes on to write that 'He became very jaded when he met servicemen from other countries in Berlin since they were all questioning the war. He had personally witnessed many deaths and he would visit Normandy every year to pay his respects at the gravesides of many who died there; and walking up the Normandy beaches with him, in his nineties, was a very humbling experience. In later years, he felt there was a hidden hand directing world events that he did not fully comprehend.'
Covid	Anne Currie, Wendy Wendorff, Matthew Ehret, Nicholas Martin, David Adelman, Jeff Wyatt.
9/11	John Hamer, Shannon Rowan, Wendy Wendorff.
Climate change	Justin Walker, Nicholas Martin and Katherine Armitage question whether there is in fact any scientific consensus on climate change. In the absence of a scientific consensus, they ask why climate-change policies are being imposed?
Failing the eleven-plus test	Dr Ursula Edgington writes about the negative effect on her education of failing the British eleven-plus test for entry into grammar school followed by the surprise and shock, twenty years later, of discovering that a higher pass mark was set for girls than for boys.

Table 2: Overlap between the trigger factors identified by online-survey respondents and those referred to by our twenty-four critical thinkers.

The critical-thinking survey respondents were also invited to identify ways in which they might differ from other people, and this question prompted them to highlight twelve attributes that differentiated them from others. If then we continue our mapping exercise we can map these twelve characteristics against those that we can perceive or discern from the accounts of our twenty-four critical thinkers. Once again, we find a high degree of overlap between the survey attributes and those presented by our contributors (see Table 3, below). This shows an extensive overlap in terms of the personal attributes self-identified by the two groups.

Personality characteristic	**Critical Thinking contributor who appears to have this characteristic**
Curiosity	Eve Gilmore writes about how, as a child, she failed 'to understand what I had done to make me a sinner. I concluded religion didn't have the answers either.' Niall McCrae's piece shows his curiosity in understanding the roots of the woke culture. This personal curiosity stands in contrast to that of his students, who not only accept events at face value but assume a woke perspective. This lack of curiosity on the part of his students leads him to say that 'Lecturing in mental health, I was disillusioned by my students' lack of scepticism about the system.'
Distrust of authorities	Mark Devlin writes that 'it was always on the cards for me to stray from the crowd and take an anti-establishment approach to life.' Ray Savage discusses how certain elements of society escape the heavy hand of the law. David Adelman: Being rebuked for being five minutes late

	while a trainee solicitor at a law firm, leads him to move away from the authority system that he is part of. Markus Olofsson: regards the Wage Work system as a form of slavery: 'a huge brilliant set-up by those in power to feed off others' dire situations. To me that is slavery.' Jeff Wyatt: As Boris Johnson was giving the nation instructions to stay at home, Jeff instantly felt something was amiss. In his mind, the lockdown instructions were connected to the removal of civil liberties. This is the point at which his activism began in earnest.
Place a premium on the truth	Darren Smith writes eloquently about the way Critical Thinking can drive us towards the truth (see the After-word). Justin Walker has coined the word 'veritocracry' to implement Václav Havel's vision of the way in which a society rooted in truth can vanquish the lies on which a post-totalitarian regime is founded. Professor Gloria Moss believes in finding the truth through the rigorous application of evidence-based Critical Thinking. Darren Smith: 'Those who seek truth must be prepared to confront the bodyguard of lies.' Jeff Wyatt believed that good men and women have to stand up for the truth – 'and that if that's anarchy, then it's anarchy'.
Autonomy	Julian Rose, as a young boy, refused to repeat the priest's words 'Forgive me Lord, for I am a poor and miserable sinner' since he found it unreasonable to have the label of sinner imposed upon him. Eve Gilmore reports on having a very similar experience as a young girl and subsequently writes about the way in

	which her 'questioning led me to shun what was regarded as normal behaviour. For I had always been the only person in the cinema who never stood for the national anthem, despite my mother's embarrassment, and this questioning of the role of monarchy in our lives meant that I strongly resisted accompanying her to wave at the Queen Mother when visiting a nearby town.' Eve also writes that: 'It is true that acceptance by the tribe is hardwired into our psyche, and so questioning the way the tribe operates has at times been an isolating experience. However, I have found that, if balanced by a spiritual philosophy, breaking free from the trance in which most of humanity is enthralled can bring enormous rewards.' James Hunt provides a strong critique to the notion of deference, which he describes as underpinning much of people's lives.
Little exposure to the media	Nicholas Martin and Neil Kramer speak of the involvement of the intelligence services in the *Guardian*, BBC, ITV and Channel 4.
High sense of morality	Neil Kramer conceives of life as an elaborate test in which people's response to evil is continually challenged. Mark Devlin asks as to the morality of people allowing this system of human subjugation to continue through their tacit cooperation. Matthew Ehret conceives of a profound relationship between mind and matter that hinges upon truth and morality, and this, he believes, is at the heart of the meaning of humanity. Chad Manian perceived what he construed as police brutality and then devotes substantial amounts of his time to helping people in the courts.

Seeing the Big Picture	Julian Rose, as a young man, perceived the interconnected passage of time and place. From studying various books, such as the *I Ching*, those from Eric Fromm and Schumacher's *Small Is Beautiful*, he sees the relationship between the soil and the nature of man. Niall McCrae: 'The woke phenomenon was a progression from the cultural Marxism of past decades, but [it was] an uncompromising form of Marxism practised by Chairman Mao and his henchmen in the People's Republic of China [that] was exported successfully to the liberal West. . . . The reality is that Western society is being forced into undergoing its own version of Mao's Cultural Revolution, but is hardly fighting back.' Shannon Rowan experiences 'cracks in the façade', and describes feeling like a newborn baby emerging, Eve Gilmore writes, 'I believe in a greater intelligence and in a grand plan that is first going to expose and then – through our empowerment – lead to the disintegration of the control systems that have dominated this planet for millennia.'
Willingness to change their mind	Justin Walker learned, through a series of chance encounters and conversations, that the money system and climate change may not be quite as people imagine. He is able to shift his thinking in accordance with the new information he receives, and then to campaign on these two topics.
Refusal to accept the absurd	Matthew Ehret – refused to accept his lecturer's belief that 'the purpose of Art was to render an audience uncomfortable' or that 'it is only when an artist causes an audience to squirm uncomfortably in the face of the ugliness and irrationalism of existence that true art can said to have been attained.'
A sense of Justice	Chad Manian gives his time freely to help people navigate their way through the court system.

	David Adelman detected the erosion and neglect in modern society of the foundational principles of contract law. Restoring contract law so that people offer their consent to services would go far in restoring a sense of justice in society. This initiative extends to freeing families from the threat of criminalising home education. Jeff Wyatt never stopped resisting, defying tyranny and fighting for a stop to the erosion of human rights that he perceived.
High intelligence	Neil Kramer speaks of the agenda by the authorities of 'lowering IQ, seeding narratives and breeding indifference'. The measures taken by the authorities provide obstacles to the emergence of high intelligence in society.
A strong interest in History	John Hamer's insatiable interest in history led him to write books on the *Titanic* and to write the compendious *Falsification of History.* Professor Gloria Moss is interested in uncovering the truth about events and sites through a close look at the evidence, discerning anomalies in official accounts. Wendy Wendorff has a strong interest in what is known as prehistory and anachronisms that call traditional interpretations into question.

Table 3: Overlap between the attributes that online-survey respondents identify as differentiating them and those present in our twenty-four critical thinkers.

The strong overlap between the self-reported characteristics of the survey respondents and those of the twenty-four critical thinkers is striking. This leads us to sense that we have an answer as to those elements that prompt and facilitate the exercise of Critical Thinking and Light Bulb Moments. The prompts would appear to be a mixture of factors including the perception of an anomaly (whether from independent thinking or possibly parental guidance) coupled with a series of twelve personal attributes.

This an exciting conclusion since we have found that the triggers and attributes that drive the survey respondents also drive our twenty-four inquiring minds. This takes us several steps forward in understanding the unique factors that can create the questioning cast of mind that Descartes described so eloquently in his advice that 'Every part of thinking, should be questioned, doubted, or that Einstein summarised so brilliantly in the pithy phrase 'Question everything'. Our travels have not yet ended however since there is one thing more for us to do before we turn to the personalities of Critical Thinkers and whether they share unifying characteristics.

The triggers and attributes of literary heroes: a comparison with our two samples

The important task ahead involved mapping the triggers and attributes of our survey respondents against those that inspired our heroes in *Brave New World, Nineteen Eighty Four* and *Fahrenheit 451.* Will this, finally, give us clues as to whether there were common features leading them to abandon a life of acquiescence for one of relentless inquiry? Could this explain the source of their inner strength in standing up against repressive social systems? And finally, could it be that the characteristics of these literary heroes overlap with those of our twenty-four contributors and seventy-four online-survey respondents? This would be extraordinary indeed and we were just one step away from finding out.

With the novels in hand and our trigger and personal attributes clearly marked down in the first column of a new table, we started to see whether these factors were also mirrored in the lives of our three literary heroes, Bernard Marx, Winston Smith and Guy Montag. We had no idea how this final mapping exercise would work out, but we approached each trigger and attribute one by one and looked to see if there was a match in the lives of our three literary heroes.

For the first time, we have the opportunity to discover whether our 24 contributors and 74 survey respondents share attributes and thinking processes with iconic literary heroes. You can find the answers in Table 4, below.

Triggers and attributes (from online-survey respondents)	Literary heroes: Bernard Marx, Winston Smith and Guy Montag	Incidence in the literary hero of the trigger factors and attributes identified by the online critical-thinker respondents
Noticing propaganda	Winston Smith	He recognises that claims made by the Party are incorrect. So when hearing that the chocolate ration is reduced to twenty grams, everyone with the exception of Winston accepts this announcement without any suspicion. Winston, on the other hand, knows that this has been a reduction from the day before. Similarly, he recognises that the statement that 'The party has invented aeroplanes' is propaganda, not truth. Finally, the Party claims to have created a better life for everyone by reducing the infant mortality rate, increasing the literacy rate, and improving the cities. Winston believes this is untrue but he has no proof since the past has been changed. As the novel states: 'In the end the Party would announce that two and two made five, and you would have to believe it. It was inevitable that they should make that claim sooner or later: the logic of their position demanded it. Not merely the validity of experience, but the very existence of external reality was tacitly denied by their philosophy.' Winston

		understands this which is why he writes in his notepad that 'Two plus two equals four.
	Bernard Marx	He flirts with the notion of dissention by questioning the propaganda and turning down the promoted mind-altering drug, soma.
Interest in history	Winston Smith	Works in the records office of the Ministry of Truth, where his job involves revising newspaper articles and doctoring the truth – often censoring out 'unpersons'. This makes him nurse doubts about the Party and its monopoly on truth. Moreover, at a personal level, his decision to purchase a diary and begin recording his thoughts is an attempt to create memory and, through that, history.
	Guy Montag	Montag wishes to meet Professor Faber, in spite of risk to himself, in order to learn about history.
Curiosity	Bernard Marx	Is determined to visit the Savage Reservation against the wishes and advice of the Director in order to discover the nature of life away from the World State.
	Winston Smith	When he enters a pub and talks to the Proles he tries to speak to an old man and get to know some facts about the past. The fact that doing this puts him in danger shows the lengths he will go to in order to satisfy his curiosity about the past.
	Guy Montag	Montag visits English Professor Faber to gain more understanding about books and his recurrent thoughts.
High intelli-gence	Bernard Marx	As an Alpha Plus, he is in the category of people with high intelligence

	Winston Smith	He has the intellectual ability to reason about his resistance and also to hold a responsible job in the records office of the Ministry of Truth at the relatively young age of 39
	Guy Montag	His intelligence is revealed in his increasing dissatisfaction with the reality that has been carefully crafted by the system in which he lives. By contrast, most of the other characters in the book, such as his wife, Mildred, Captain Beatty, Mrs Phelps and Bowles, remain satisfied with the system and do not ask questions of it.
Distrust of authority	Guy Montag	His distrust of authority is shown by his act of keeping books due to be destroyed (an act in defiance of the authorities) in order to find out about the past
Sense of autonomy	Bernard Marx	Is pushed out of society so often (his small size is unusual for an Alpha Plus male in the World State where he lives) that he is often alone. While being alone, he is able to think for himself. He decides not to take the happiness drug Soma since he wants to be himself.
	Winston Smith	Many of Winston's significant decisions can be interpreted as attempts to build a sense of autonomy from the system. His decision to purchase the paperweight is driven by a desire to have something of his own that represents a time before the Party. Winston's relationship with Julia is also an assertion of his independence, free of Party control. His determination to keep out of the view of the telescreen in his home so that it cannot see him is also an act of defiance since it allows him to note down thoughts (for example, 'Down with Big Brother' and

		'Freedom is the freedom to say that two plus two equals four. If that is granted, all else follows') that are in opposition to the Party and Party policy since the Party demands uncritical acceptance of Big Brother and their belief that two plus two equals five.
High sense of morality	Bernard Marx	Feels disgusted by the World State's positive attitude to promiscuity.
Seeing the big picture	Guy Montag	After escaping from the City where he worked as a fireman, burning books, he joins a group that includes a man, Granger, who tells him the story of the phoenix that rises from its ashes to start a new life. This is the symbol for Guy to perceive a new life ahead of him.
Refusal to accept the absurd	Guy Montag	Refuses to accept a society in which books are banned and escapes to establish a new society.
Parental guidance	Bernard Marx Winston Smith	He, like others in the World State where he lives, were born in Hatching Centres, with babies produced in bottles so no one has experienced the influence of parents. He dreams of his mother and realises that she had 'sacrificed herself to a conception of loyalty that was private and unalterable. Such things, he saw, could not happen today. Today, there were fear, hatred and pain. But no dignity of emotion, no deep or complex sorrows.'

Table 4: The extent to which a proportion of the triggers and attributes identified by the online-survey respondents as triggering their journeys in Critical Thinking are present also in the trigger factors and attributes of the heroes of *Brave New World, Nineteen Eighty-Four* and *Fahrenheit 451.*

The finding from this mapping exercise? It is an extraordinary one, namely that the self-same triggers and attributes identified by the online survey respondents, that find a match in our twenty-four critical thinkers, also inspire the acts of courage that mark our three literary figures out as heroes. And while those characters cannot be said to be flesh-and-blood people, their characters are so convincingly portrayed that they are etched into our collective psyche. Now at last we can understand the attributes and trigger factors that give them the courage to stand up against the oppressive regimes that dominate their worlds.

The correlations between the trigger factors and personal attributes that act on all three groups of people – literary heroes, twenty-four contributors and survey respondents – are unmistakable. So, the final question in this part of the research concerns whether, like the characters from *Brave New World, Nineteen Eighty-Four* and *Fahrenheit 451,* our twenty-four contributors and seventy-four survey respondents can be considered heroes. Are these also courageous individuals fighting against repressive social systems?

It is not the authors' place to comment, but readers can seek objective evidence from the twenty-four contributions. So we leave it to you, dear reader, to determine whether what we are dealing with is societal repression or not. With this in mind, here are some excerpts to consider from the contributions of our twenty-four critical thinkers:

From psychiatric nurse and educator Dr Niall MacCrae, we have the following opinion:

> Through reflections such as this, and observing the tactics of those bearing Antifa flags, waving fists for Black Lives Matter or insisting on transgender pronouns, it appeared that we were not observing groups that were upholding liberal values. On the contrary, they appeared to be engaged in a mindless onslaught, the effects of which would be to tear society apart.
>
> At the time that I was mulling this over, I had a vague appreciation that the woke phenomenon was a progression from the cultural Marxism of past decades, but reading *The Strategy of Maoism in the West* by professors David Martin Jones and M. L. R. Smith (2022) showed very clearly how an uncompromising form of Marxism practised by Chairman Mao and his henchmen in the People's

> Republic of China was exported successfully to the liberal West. Suddenly a light bulb was switched on in my mind.

From academic Dr Ursula Edgington we have the following perspective on education:

> Far from being a 'critical conscience of society', then, our universities have lost all integrity and credibility as meaningful and ethical education institutions. This is not owing to incompetence or laziness. Over several decades, the valid outcomes from numerous research projects have been systematically suppressed. Evidence-based discussions of climate change, toxicology, democratic rights, gender roles, colonial history, best-practice leadership (The Secret Professor, 2022) and many other topics are off-limits because arguments that differ from the political narrative have been conveniently labelled 'conspiracy theories' or 'misinformation'. Researchers who have dared to question their censorship, have been faced with the overwhelming corporate power that is now being exposed to Joe Public (The Secret Professor, 2022; Shir-Raz et al., 2022).

From former school teacher, Jane Sherrard-Smith, we learn that her attempt to raise concerns about the electro-smog in the school and its possible effects on the children in children, with particularly harsh effects on those with electro-hypersensitivity, resulted in a disciplinary action against her. This fractured her relationship with senior management and led to her leaving the school after fourteen years there with an unblemished reputation.

Moving away from education to the world of journalism, the newspaper editor Darren Smith, in his Afterword, speaks of his fears that in attempting to put forth truthful journalism his paper could be shut down even though he maintains an editorial policy of objective evidence-based inquiry.

From Wendy Wendorff, a successful businesswoman, we learn that a court case was held to investigate why the Smithsonian Museum in the US was concealing the finds of giant bones. She also asks questions concerning the *Codex Alimentarius* (Food Law or Code), a massive multinational agreement concerning food and ingredient labelling. This agreement sits under the auspices of the United Nations and is the central part of a programme by the Food and Agriculture Organisation (FAO) and the

World Health Organisation (WHO). Since the protection of human health is part of the brief of *Codex Alimentarius*, and since it is an acknowledged fact that glyphosate is sprayed on to the grain just before the harvest and will remain there, why does the *Codex* not require glyphosate to be listed as an ingredient?

From David Adelman, a Cambridge-educated lawyer, we read of his view that the latest emergency is the 'threat of criminalising home education'.

Are these six cases instances of a repressive system that is not acting in the interests of people? If you think that what you have read is just a normal part of what any liberal and free society is engaged in, then these critical thinkers can be applauded simply for expressing their views. If, on the other hand, you think that what you have read is characteristic of a repressive society that does not respect people's liberties, then all of our critical thinkers must be viewed as heroes – like Bernard Marx, Winston Smith and Guy Montag – in speaking out. We leave it to you to decide.

Moving away now from the heroes of our three novels, and the possibility that our twenty-four contributors are in the same bracket, let us progress now to our third and final study. This concerns the personality features of critical thinkers.

C. The missing link: Personality

Divergent thinking and personality

We saw in Part I how thinking could be made more narrow by encouraging *convergent* thinking; but until we initiated the work presented in the earlier parts of this book, there had been no research identifying the elements that bring about *divergent* thinking – the kind of thinking that we find in critical thinkers. Now, as we saw in the last two sections, we have been able to identify trigger factors and also the attributes that will encourage Critical Thinking. Is there a broad-brush approach to personality that could help as well?

The world's most widely used personality test is the Myers-Briggs Type Indicator® (MBTI®) test, whose measures are based on Jung's four dichotomous personality types. These dichotomous forms yield sixteen different types, and data across large samples is available given that the test is so widely used. In terms of whether the test measures what it claims to measure (the 'validity'), there is strong support that it does measure Jung's types (Chen & Miao, 2007). Where reliability is concerned, studies have shown that, on average, 92% of adults who retook the test received the same four Jungian classifications (ibid). The MBTI® is a forced-choice test, and people who have completed it are recommended to read descriptions of the type closest to the four-letter description arrived at by the test and decide whether that type feels like a better fit. If it does, that will be the type to go with.

If you would like to undertake the test before reading on, please contact the Truth University (infotruthuniversity@protonmail.com) and we can advise you on the best and most cost-effective ways of doing this. If you have already completed the test, then please just read on!

As mentioned, the test measures four dichotomous pairs. The first of these measure introversion and extroversion, given the letters E and I respectively, and this pair refers to whether you take your energy from within (Introvert) or without (**E**xtrovert). The second letter refers to how you perceive the world. Is the world that you inhabit extensively that of the five senses? Do you relish activity, eye-catching visuals, concrete facts, culinary delights and detail (this would make you a Sensing type-**S**), or are you excited more by the world of possibilities, by the big picture, abstract patterns, theoretical ideas, depth of thinking, underlying concepts and putting things to the test (this would make you an i**N**tuitive type-**N)**. So, **S** or **N**.

This brings us to the third set of letters describing whether your decision-making is made principally through the use of logic (the custom of the **T**hinking, or **T**, type), or whether your decisions are driven by the use of logic and feelings (the trait of the **F**eeling, or **F**, type). The final pair of traits also refers to aspects of decision-making – in this case, whether you collect a great deal of information before making a decision (the hallmark of the **P**erception, or **P**, type), or whether you satisfy yourself with a minimum amount of data (the norm of the **J**udgement, or **J,** type)? Also, do you complete tasks ahead of deadline (the tendency of the **J** type), or leave things to the last minute, catching trains by a whisper (the habit of the **P** type)?

No type is inferior or superior to any other type, but distinct groupings of the four letters can be found in certain industries, occupations and countries. You will tend to find that the types most commonly employed in industry are the ISTJ and ENTJ types.

Back to critical thinkers. Gloria Moss, one of the co-authors of this book, had the opportunity to ask three sets of critical thinkers to undertake an MBTI test (one of the groups were those completing the online survey discussed in Section B), and the results are shown in Table 5, below.

Sample sizes		**Intuitive (N)**	**Intuitive + Feeling (NF)**
Sample I	**42**	**41**	**32**
Sample 2	**19**	**17**	**15**
Online survey	**24**	**21**	**11**
Total	**85**	**79 (93%)**	**58 (68%)**

Table 5: The most prevalent MBTI across three samples of people.

As you can see, the single most common personality type amongst the three samples of critical thinkers was the Intuitive type, with 93% of critical thinkers having this personality attribute. In terms of combinations of letters, the Intuitive-Feeling (NF) type was the most common, with 68% of the sample having this combination.

These results are extraordinarily exciting since they reveal the near-ubiquitous presence of the Intuitive type in populations of critical thinkers. On the other hand, the findings give cause for concern since the Intuitive type is a minority in most populations in the world, as is also the case for the Intuitive Feeling (NF) type. You can see this from the table below, Table 6, which presents the proportion of Intuitive and Intuitive-Feeling types in countries across the world. Note that this data has been abstracted from data published on Typology Triad: (https://typologytriad.wordpress.com/mbti-population-by-country/), where the source is given as the official MBTI manual supplements.

Country	N	NF
Australia	35.7	21
Brazil	33.2	11
Canada	38.8	23
Canada fr	26.7	18
China (SC)	30.1	13
China (TC)	27.2	13.6
Denmark	34.3	20
France	23.5	17
Germany	26	15
Greece	39	25
Ireland	42	28
Italy	23.7	14
Japan	58.8	34
Netherlands	23.3	14
New Zealand	44	17
Spain	24	14
UK	37.2	23
US	31.5	19
India	24.7	8
Israel	41.9	17
Russia	45	12
Poland	46.5	18

Table 6: Percentage of Intuitive and Intuitive-Feeling types in global populations.

One cause for hope is that the Intuitive and Intuitive-Feeling personality types – those associated with critical thinkers – are present in a higher proportion of the populations of some countries than others. In Russia and Poland, for example, the percentage of those with an Intuitive predisposition is approaching a little under 50% and in New Zealand it is 44%, Ireland 42%, Israel 41.9% and Britain, 37%. It is true that a significantly lower proportion of the populations in certain western countries – for example, France, Italy and Spain – have these predispositions; but knowledge is now global, and what is known in one country can – if Internet freedom exists – spread to another.

So the fact that only a small proportion of people in some populations have Intuitive and Intuitive-Feeling predispositions is not to condemn these parts of the world to a way of thinking that is devoid of criticality.

Much depends on whether Critical Thinking is encouraged within a population or whether controls are placed on the exercise and teaching of this skill. While Critical Thinking may come easily to an Intuitive (N) and Intuitive-Feeling type (NF), it is possible for its opposite type, the so-called Sensing type, to adopt a Critical Thinking style if material is presented in a way that makes it attractive to the senses of this part of the population. As a consequence, eye-catching graphics and well-turned-out TV presenters will help, but of course only if the message being conveyed is strictly evidence-based.

It is true that some mental adjustment would be needed on the part of the Sensing type to allow them to move beyond the limitations of five-sense reality and embrace a way of thinking that is more abstract and less concrete. Before then, the drive to build a new society rooted in Critical Thinking is likely to rest with the minority of **Intuitive** types, who may very possibly find it easier to see beyond the possibilities presented by the mainstream.

Interestingly, a professor of clinical psychology, Mattias Desmet (2022), has presented a different explanation for the absence of Critical Thinking on the part of two-thirds of the world's population. In his view, this is caused by a form of mass psychosis that only one -third of the population is easily able to resist. In actual fact, the personality predisposition data presented for the first in this book suggests that the obstacle to Critical Thinking is not so much a form of mass psychosis, but rather the absence in around two-thirds of the population of a personality predisposition that facilitates 'seeing through' complex narratives. This personality predisposition is 'Intuition' (as defined by Jung and by the MBTI, and not in the sense commonly used and understood), and the absence of this personality predisposition in at least two-thirds of most of the world's populations makes it hard for those two thirds (it is a lower proportion in Russia Poland, Ireland an Israel) to see beyond the five-sense reality presented by the mainstream.

If this analysis is correct – and new and compelling data is presented here – then strategies for increasing people's Critical Thinking will need to take account of their personality types. By way of example, if the aim is to target Sensing people within a population, then information will need to be presented in ways that are concrete and have appeal to the five senses. If the aim is to target information at the Intuitive types, then the information needs to be more conceptual in nature. All of this is do-able, but, as with all problem solving, the origin of the problem needs to be well understood before effort is devoted to producing solutions.

D. Conclusions

Our twenty-four critical thinkers have carefully set down the Light Bulb Moments that occurred in the course of their lives. These Light Bulb Moments followed periods of intense reflection and led them to rethink the nature of reality presented to them. As we saw earlier, that reality could have concerned official history (whether prehistory, biblical history or more recent history, such as the Great Fire of London narrative, the sinking of the *Titanic* or most recent events), or the financial and legal systems; recent geopolitical events such as 9/11 and the pandemic of 2020–2022, the current school and university systems, whether the woke agenda is influenced by Chinese Marxism, the allopathic health system, child abuse, the telecommunications system, including 5G and smartphones and, finally, the very purpose of life – whether humans are purely physical or more spiritual beings, and whether life is just a test of how we respond to the information that comes our way . If you have not had a chance to read all of the contributions, then you can find a summary of them in Appendix A, with the authors' suggested solutions presented in Appendix B.

We can see that the full-body exercise of Critical Thinking – something that we saw in the case of Winston Smith, a man of high intelligence coupled with physical problems and an acute moral sense of the importance of individual identity – produces an ability to look at information anew, with a fresh pair of eyes. This profound full-body exercise of Critical Thinking can lead people to have Light Bulb Moments.

What are the effects of such a profound engagement in Critical Thinking? It allows our three literary heroes, our twenty-four contributors and our 74 survey respondents to resist the pressures of conformity and propaganda that might otherwise weigh on them. In doing this, it brings them a sense of autonomy and freedom that had previously been beyond their grasp. Given the correlation of triggers and attributes between critical thinkers and the main characters in the three novels that have accompanied us on our investigation into Critical Thinking (see Appendix C) it is not surprising to find that it brings them to the questioning state of awareness of the towering heroes of *Brave New World, Nineteen Eighty-Four* and *Fahrenheit 451.*

What can we conclude? Profound Critical Thinking can lead to Light Bulb Moments that fully liberate people to think for themselves. One might cynically ask, as Mark Devlin has done in his contribution, whether a society would willingly encourage this free exercise of thinking or whether rather it would take every measure possible to constrain people's thinking and control activities such as the popular-music industry. Paranoid thinking? In fact, this idea is by no means extraordinary since Critical Thinking and Light Bulb Moments have the potential to revolutionise official thinking and, with that, society. So, they also have the potential to move us in directions far from that of the controlling hand of Big Brother. In fact, all of the contributors have put forward concrete suggestions for doing this (you can find summaries of these in Appendix B).

Some might regard this movement away from control as something to be valued and may start to regard the erosion of Critical Thinking training in our social systems (whether in education or in the media) as something to be deplored. If that is the case, then the first step in reinstating it is to construct alternative education systems with Critical Thinking at their core, both at school and further (higher?) education level. In actual fact, increasing proportions of parents are home-schooling their children but while the public examination system remains unaltered it is questionable how much change can be effected in that way. Perhaps therefore it is time to focus on creating a new public school exam system that puts Critical Thinking at its heart.

As for the higher levels of education, there is increasing realisation that universities are moving away from ideals of a liberal education to one of indoctrination (The Secret Professor, 2022). One of the results is the realisation by employers that they can no longer resource the personnel with Critical Thinking skills that are amongst their highest priorities. In this way, society is reaching a crisis point.

The question facing us then is a simple one. Do we continue with the erosion of Critical Thinking skills and Light Bulb Moments, or do we start on the challenging but exciting task of developing Critical Thinking throughout society?

References

Bernard H. R. (2002), Research methods in anthropology: Qualitative and Quantitative Approaches, 3rd edition. Walnut Creek, California: AltaMira Press.

Bradbury, R. (1953), Fahrenheit 451. New York: Ballantine Books.

Brooks, A. and John, L. (2018). The Surprising Power of Questions, Harvard Business Review, May-June, https://hbr.org/2018/05/the-surprising-power-of-questions

Chen, J., and Miao, D. (2007), Introduction to the Myers-Briggs Type Indicator. US-China Education Review, 4 (3), 44–53.

Desmet, M. (2022), The Psychology of Totalitarianism. White River Junction: Chelsea Green Publishing.

Green, R., and Douglas, K. (2018), Anxious attachment and Belief in Conspiracy Theories, Personality and Individual Differences, I25, 30, DOI:10.1016/j.paid.2017.12.023.

Huxley, A. (1953), Brave New World. London: Chatto and Windus

Livos. https://stefanoslivos.com/fahrenheit-451/

Matsumoto, D. (2021), Emotions and Critical Thinking, Humintell, January. https://www.humintell.com/2021/01/emotions-and-critical-thinking-update-2021/

Orwell, G. (1949), Nineteen Eighty-Four. London: Secker and Warburg.

Palinkas, L.; Horwitz, S.; Green, C.; Wisdom, J.; Duan, N.; and Hoagwood, K. (2015), Purposeful Sampling for Qualitative Data Collection and Analysis in Mixed Methods Implementation Research, Administration and Policy in Mental Health and Mental Health Service, 42(5), 433–455. https://www.ncbi.nlm.nih.gov/pmc/articles/PMC4012002/

Spradley J.P. (1979), The Ethnographic Interview. New York: Holt, Rine-hart & Winston.

Strauss, A.L., and Corbin, J. M. (1998), Basics of Qualitative Research: Techniques and Procedures for developing grounded theory, second edition. Thousand Oaks, CA: Sage

AFTERWORD

DARREN SMITH

The rulers have built a world of fiction and fantasy, and want to make anyone pointing this out a criminal.

No one is allowed to pierce the narrative of the show, even such an often badly made one, because pointing it out ends the façade, like the classic story of 'The Emperor's New Clothes'.

This is the ultimate expression of totalitarian control – over people's thoughts, ideas, concepts and in the end, our minds.

In Orwell's *Nineteen Eighty-Four*, the Party wanted to eliminate any potential for rebellion by making it literally unthinkable. Not only are those who really rule via the criminal banking system actually attempting this, with laws which will outlaw speech critical of government and corporate policy, but they use as many divide-and-rule topics as possible to drive a wedge between people on their emotive subjects, while we all should be punching upwards at the real causes of division, injustice and vast inequality across the world.

On our two-year birthday, we are proud that *The Light* paper is still a shining beacon of truth in this empire of darkness, deception and division, and that we poke holes in the fabricated stories and distorted versions of reality presented to the general public en masse through what is now a unified media propaganda machine. Not a single one of the newspapers or broadcast news outlets have questioned in any depth what the government, and those giving them their orders, are doing to the population. All dissenting voices are censored regardless of qualification (*The Light* 17, front page).

Today, this has accelerated to a point where people's minds have been taken and they have been all but turned into nodding robot dogs. It is almost as if politicians have never lied; media have never covered up the truth; and corporations have never polluted, harmed or defrauded anybody before.

How the population willingly accepts a trial injection of an unknown substance by a corporation that received the biggest fine for negligence in US history, $2.3 billion, is a thing of psychologically controlling awe. People are goldfished into trusting what comes out of the screen as authoritative information, even though it constantly contradicts previous advice, and is provably nothing but behavioural psychological manipulation, in order to get people to think and behave exactly as they want.

It should not be hard to imagine the end result of this lemming-like, collectivist herd mentality, if people continue to give their rights and thoughts over to a clearly criminal ruling cabal. Nietzsche's famous quote is apt here: 'Madness is rare in individuals – but in groups, parties, nations, and ages, it is the rule.'

For those in power, it is crucial to maintain the façade at all costs, and to this end, vast armies of online and offline agents are employed by both the state using your taxes, and corporations using your spending, with instructions to attack and smear everyone and anything daring to go against the prevailing narrative; who ask questions; and who refuse to comply.

This is usually by gross exaggeration, misrepresentation and false association – painting us as being on the 'wrong' side of as many 'debates' as possible – the black or white logical fallacy that George Bush Jr used so well: 'You're either with us, or you're with the terrorists' – as they bombed countries to smithereens.

Therefore, despite all being ordinary people of diverse backgrounds, different ages and of different geography, *The Light* will often be tainted as right-wing Nazi extremist, homophobic, antisemitic, Islamophobic, misogynistic climate deniers – the same names called to most who try to expose some or other aspect of the fantasy world created through the ubiquitous and incessant information and nudges transmitted through screens of various sizes directly into people's minds.

The strength of the grip they have over people's psyches is evidenced by people taking the politicians' and media's word over their own close friends' and family's, and even their own research and thoughts.

Those in power have everything to gain by maintaining their positions and lying through their teeth to people. However, the people who create and distribute *The Light* have nothing to gain, except the satisfaction of sharing truth.

Almost everyone involved is voluntary, and our only aim is to alert enough people as to what the rulers' plans are, and therefore stop them: once enough people know, the game is over. How long would all those CCTV surveillance cameras, smart street lights, and other digital prison infra-structure last once the football fans figure it out?

Of course, we can be bundled up and dismissed in one fell swoop as a 'conspiracy theory' paper, the ultimate easy trope of those who actually conspire to defraud and control the world. The point about most 'theo-ries' on what the government and corporations are doing is that they are more often than not correct, so as a news organisation it is a badge of honour to be called correct on our reporting and opinions.

The truth is elusive, and seemingly quite dangerous these days. We have no doubts that malicious and fallacious attacks on this paper and others shining light will continue, by those whose job it is to protect the rulers and help them achieve their ultimate aims of total control of mankind. We stand firm in the truth we print.

Darren is the editor of the people funded independent newspaper The Light.

Appendix A

SUMMARIES

Name	**Indicative content**
HOW WE ACQUIRE KNOWLEDGE	
Gloria Moss PhD	Over the course of three large research projects, she discovered that the mainstream truths about the topics explored in these projects was at odds with what she actually discovered herself. She also found that academic institutions and /or certain peer review journals were unwilling to accept her own findings. This led her to question everything in our society that passed as 'knowledge'.
Sir Julian Rose	His early life taught him to question religion and to keep his emotions hidden as a survival tool. Later, after an acting career in the US, he runs the Hardwick Estate according to Soil Association organic stand-ards.

MONEY	
Justin Walker	At the age of sixteen, a conversation with a well-connected relative introduced him to the notion that nothing in the press was to be believed nor anything promised by a politician since they can't act without the sanction of those in high places. Ten years later, a conversation with the co-founder of the Club of Rome revealed that they were creating a huge environmental problem that would frighten people into accepting a world government .... Further revelations, for example on the way that governments can print debt-free money set him on a journey that continues up to the present time.
LAW & ORDER	
D Adelman	During a challenging period in his life, he uncovers the legal freedoms that have been papered over by the system, including the fact that paying tax is voluntary and that domestic users cannot be disconnected for not paying their bills. Shock at the events of 9/11 was the trigger for rethinking our position in law and developing courses on this topic.
Chad Manian	The spectacle of seeing medical experts arrested at Speaker's corner kick-started a journey in understanding Common Law and defending people in court. This in turn led to the realisation that British courts operate as money-making machines.

James Hunt	When a mental health team is sent to his home after he requests a course of Ivermectin from his GP, the author awakens to the deference on which British society is founded. This leads him to ask whether *Magna Carta* can help restore the freedoms of the common man.
Ray Savage	Writes about his growing awareness of problems within the Police system, noticing the presence within the force of people affiliated to secret societies, and the immunity that often went with that affiliation for those facing prosecution. He also discusses the way that increasing centralisation removed power from the local police, with one of the side-effects being an increase in crime levels.
HEALTH	
Katherine Armitage	Seeing the suffering that her mother experienced in the face of so-called cancer treatments leaves the young author traumatised and determined to fight for a better approach to maintaining health. She discovers the cures that homeopathy can deliver and dedicates her life to fighting societal systems that cause harm to health and wellbeing.
Eve Gilmore	Training as a nurse opened her eyes to the hierarchical nature of medicine and the extent to which cancer therapies caused suffering. On leaving the world of conventional medicine, she moved into the media and this revealed the controlling hand of censorship. A chance viewing of an actor, shook her

	world through a powerful sense of fore-knowledge and this opened up a spiritual understanding of reincarnation from previous lives into this one. This then prompted a move into Natural Therapies and a strong sense that the control that she had witnessed earlier was lifted. The solution lies in empowering people with the knowledge and tools with which to maintain their own health.
EDUCATION	
Dr Ursula Edging-ton	She discovers how emotional labour – the need to display emotions in the workplace that may not be genuine expressions of the feelings of those express-ing those emotions. In universities, those who want to remain in employment often need to adopt a new set of emotions, set aside notions of ethics and integrity and suppress the valid outcomes of their research. This view is rooted in the fact that over several decades, critiques of climate change, toxicology, democratic rights, gendered roles, colonial history and many other topics are off-limits. Counter-arguments to the political narrative have been conveniently labelled 'conspiracy theories' and researchers who have dared to question their censorship, have been faced with the overwhelming

	corporate power that is only now coming to light. The solutions lies in more home schooling and a new University (Truth University).
Jane Sharrard Smith	Her experience in school education opened her eyes to the removal of childhood spontaneity and autonomy caused by covid restrictions. At the other end of the age spectrum, she reflects on the replacement of human service personnel by automation and the way that this leaves the elderly isolated and with ever reducing human contact.
HISTORY	
John Hamer	His light bulb moment came in 1997 when he met friends who, in Paris at the time of Princess Diana's death, described late night footage in which they had both witnessed Diana *walking* into an ambulance after the car crash. At the time they assumed that she was shaken up and just being taken to hospital as a precaution. They were shocked the next day to find that she had died. This story shook him to the core and after a chance encounter with books of a conspiratorial nature, he started writing articles and then books on the truth behind history and geopolitical events.
Wendy Wendorff	An avid traveller, the moment of questioning came when she read about Puma Punku in Bolivia, a site containing structures of such size and accuracy that it

	would be impossible to recreate them with the technology available today. Modern academia shied away from answers as to its construction, location and placement and her quest to find answers led her down a rabbit hole that caused to question ancient structures as well as recent events.
POLITICS AND CONTEMPORARY AFFAIRS	
Shannon Rowan	After training in a liberal arts degree that included photography, the author worked as a commercial photographer in advertising. She learned firsthand the lengths that advertising art directors and their hired studio photographers would go to in order to manipulate and deceive audiences into buying (often cheaply made, sometimes dangerous) products. Disillusioned by the commercial advertising world, she moved onto journalism but her world splintered after losing a friend in 9/11 and questioning the official narrative of that. Also, her life-long electro-sensitivity brought her face-to-face with the inadequacies of the regulatory system. She now writes books exposing the deceits that she has encountered on her journey.
David Henry	As the author hears talk of the Kalergi plan to encourage mixed race coupling, he finds more and more anomalies in the accounts presented in school

	textbooks, on the airwaves and in government policies. His eye for anomalies makes it impossible for him to accept the mainstream narrative on so many topics.
Anne Currie	Little by little by little, the unquestioned world in which she lived fell apart. Her charming father has a different side, full of anger; in 1963, as a young mother expecting her second son, she heard rumours of babies born without limbs and with other deformities. Two of her friends, who had taken Thalidomide for nausea in the first trimester, produced babies who were so badly affected that they died at birth. Her faith in doctors and medicines began to falter, particularly when seeing the effectiveness of alternative systems such as homeopathy and osteopathy. She discovers that children labelled as trouble makers can conceal experiences of sexual abuse and abuse; then, shortly before the Covid Lockdown is declared, she learns that the gravity of the pandemic has been downgraded. These anomalies help her realise the way in which actions can carry out the will of the divine. One of the solutions is to maintain cash so that control is not exercised through a digital currency system.
Jeff Wyatt	This posthumous account from his friend Jill shows

	how Jeff's desire to stand up restrictions to freedom. He was arrested on 16 May 2020 for exercising his right to protest whilst being in a group of more than 2 people at Speakers Corner in Hyde Park. Jeff devoted himself to the cause of Free Speech. It was the quashing of what he perceived to be his fundamental rights that released a lion like instinct that translated into speeches of great courage at rallies.
CONTEMPORARY CULTURE	
Mark Devlin	Describes his growing awareness of the controlling hand in society, whether in the popular music industry or beyond. The solution lies in a major shift in the human mindset such that it is no longer held back by the opinions of others.
Niall MacCrae	His contribution, 'Waking up to Woke' charts the influence of the Frankfurt school and Chinese Marxism on the woke mentality and culture, aimed at subverting Western society.
Nicholas Martin	Reflects on the power of spirit and the truth to lead humanity into a better space. In the course of his piece, he discusses the thinking of Krishnamurti and also the nefarious effects of Wifi and 5G. He also discusses the hidden hand controlling the publication of the news, focusing on the *Guardian* and its links to intelligence.

CULTURE AND PHILOSOPHY	
Matthew Ehret	On the way that high culture (art for example) has been debased as a way of lowering human consciousness. He also writes about the hidden hand of Britain in Transatlantic assassinations.
Neil Kramer	How life on earth tests our reactions to evil and whether we coalesce with it and reap the benefits of a system mired in it, or whether we take up arms against it. Fighting the evil relies on a determined will to resist it.
SPIRITUALITY AND TRUTH	
Markus Olafsson	From an early age, he questioned the Wage Labour system and out-of-body experiences reinforced his sense that he was different from other people. He suggests that major changes need to be made to the education system.
Darren Smith	The importance of exposing the truth.
Total contributors	
24	

APPENDIX B

SOLUTIONS

Name	Solutions
HOW WE ACQUIRE KNOWLEDGE	
Gloria Moss PhD	The process of questioning followed from noticing anomalies between official accounts of events and phenomena and underlying facts. It continued in the face of evidence of the determination of vested interests to keep a lid on certain truths. Ultimately, we are led to the realisation that the mainstream system cannot be relied upon to present us with unvarnished truth and that this is best found away from mainstream systems, be they publishing houses, academic journals or universities.
Sir Julian Rose	Set your sights on realising your innate potential 'To Be As Gods' – and open yourself to being an emissary of higher powers. Dedicate your actions to giving pleasure to the source from which you come. Similarly, use your talents to give service to humani-ty. Soon you will carry such a power of positivity and determination within you that no demon or demonic

	force can strike you down. Nothing or no one that you feel moved to take on or confront will present an impossible challenge. On the contrary, the more you challenge the source of evil, the stronger becomes your confidence and ability to win the battle which stands in front of you.
MONEY	
Justin Walker	A society based on the power and direction of the truth – what we might call a 'veritocracy' – can harness the collective wisdom and spirituality needed to generate real and lasting peace, happiness and prosperity for all. We stand on the shoulders of giants, so let us learn from their wisdom whilst living in a diverse, balanced and healthy natural world. In other words, Real Ecology!
LAW & ORDER	
Ray Savage	For positive, people centric, service policing; a per capita number of cops is necessary. The remit of the old-fashioned beat bobby was perfect to manifest the original oath of the bobby which was really based around prevention of crime, support and service. The reinstatement of the local bobby as the friend of the local community, a service backed by sufficient mobile units, detectives and collators of intelligence, forms the basis of that successful Unit Beat Policing system.

David Adelman	The matrix is imploding. The safest exit strategy is to turn blind, fearful and ignorant compliance into a knowing, peaceful and confident non-compliance. When we withdraw our time and energy from the narcissistic system, which has no life force of its own, it collapses, and we regain our beloved freedoms. The war on humanity continues with threats of catastrophic weather patterns, global power outages and mass food shortages. Information alone will not save us, but it is an essential starting point and helps bring us together with unity and a common purpose. This is what will save us from a 'smart' life in 'smart' cities with our young ones captured inside the metaverse.
Chad Manian	A more honourable legal system would return the duty of dispensing justice back to the public. Up-standing members of the community would take back this duty and hold public hearings which would be convened to determine the truth rather than a system in which verdicts are swayed by the most persuasive performer. A functioning equitable justice system would be built on trial by jury, where twelve men/women of reasonable mind, drawn from the community, would decide a matter upon considering all sides. In closing, it is worth considering the words of Lord Denning, who once said, 'The law is a shield, not a sword.' The great tragedy of our present legal system lies in it being used as a weapon of oppression rather than as a protection against injustice. Perhaps the

	time has come to restore our rights and rebuild the system from the ground up.
James Hunt	We must become more personally resilient, prepared to take moral personal stands and be loving in all that we do. The starting place for this must be a profound reconnection with nature and a love of Mother Earth. At the core of this New World must be communities of sovereign men and women who have the self-confidence to do what they feel is right. By accepting the unfathomable mysteries of nature, we connect with the deepest sense of ourselves. Food, farming and education must be re-imagined on a small local scale. 'Small is beautiful' needs to be our mantra at the same time as we embrace collaboration with others on a regional, national and international basis. *Growing sovereign* is the answer for each of us as we chuckle and giggle at the current silly world of kings and queens, princes and princesses beloved of Republicans and Democrats. The 'powers that be' must be each of us. It is up to us, not *them*, to take responsibility for all the important decision-making.
HEALTH	
Katherine Armitage	If we love and care for each other, we can ask the unpalatable questions and share the answers to help shine a light where there is confusion and darkness. If

	we keep our minds open and explore the road less travelled we may find all sorts of solutions to our health problems that are not on offer from our doctor's surgery. We can become self-reliant and self-responsible. This can build a community of healthy and resilient men, women and children who are equipped to create a better future.
Eve Gilmore	With knowledge comes choice. Sovereignty becomes possible when you understand how to protect your health or how the financial system works, for example. By embracing a new value system in which simple pleasures replace gratification, I have been able to reconnect with who I really am. I try not to betray my sense of self to societal norms, such as valuing intellectual prowess over intuition or practical skills, and I try to live an authentic life. I am not pessimistic since I believe in a greater intelligence and in a grand plan that is going to first expose and then – through our empowerment – lead to the disintegration of the control systems that have dominated this planet for millennia. I like to think I have a role to play in bringing in a better world and am grateful for the experiences outlined above that have prepared me for this moment.
EDUCATION	
Dr Ursula Edging-ton	Now it is time for universities to rise to the post-covid challenge to provide authentic student-centred learning. Communities which value democratic rights demand higher-level learning organisations that are

	without the boredom and restrictions of academic bureaucracies and government qualification frameworks I describe above. As the Truth University[18] sets out, students can be equipped with genuine critical-thinking skills, through high standards of intellectual engagement and innovative curricula free from outside influence or agendas. Re-envisaging and recreating authentic university education for lifelong learning is an historic and well-overdue paradigm shift, and humanity needs this change urgently.
Jane-Sherrard Smith	I feel blessed to have the curiosity to learn from a wide range of sources, together with the courage to debate and question. Every day is a learning day. It is within each of us to seek and preserve our real connections, to our inner self, to our intuition, to our fellow earthlings, to the beauty and wonderment of Mother Nature, to our joy of family and friends. I trust in God and pray for a bright future for mankind.
HISTORY	
John Hamer	If the spiritual awakening of the whole world is to take place, as I believe it will, as 'good' is a far more powerful force than 'evil', then this will surely facilitate a much fairer and more equitable world for our descendants. I envisage a world where reality will no longer consist of satanic inversion. Health care will not destroy health for the benefit of a small clique, and politics will facilitate a much more benevolent society, where everyone will be assured of sharing all

[18] See www.truthuniversity.co.uk including https://truthuniversitycouk.uk/truth-university-interviews/; see also *The Secret Professor* (2022), pp.192–95.

	aspects of the fruits of human endeavours.
Wendy Wendorff	There is a saying that 'with knowledge comes power' and I like to think that having looked at things differently I have a better understanding of what I am up against and therefore am much better able to prepare and protect myself against the various top-down control systems imposed at ever increasing speed. Using critical thinking allows the individual to take full responsibility for him or herself. There is no longer the need to rely on the protection or support of Governments because they do not have our interests at heart. So, it is a coming-of-age, a stepping into our own power and I can say from personal experience that this is a wonderful feeling - self-governance, self-sufficiency, and open-minded learning - what a gift!
POLITICS AND CONTEMPORARY AFFAIRS	
Shannon Rowan	...to continue to work on forthcoming books on a variety of important topics related to health, liberty and corruption within politics and industry. In addition to my own rejection of 'SMART' surveillance technology and my decision to opt out of tyrannical pandemic policies and never to 'accept cookies' or access the Internet wirelessly, I hope to keep freedoms alive through my writings and through the exercise of critical thinking.

David Henry	As we talked to more and more like-minded people and read more and more evidence-based books, like *The Real Anthony Fauci*, we were more and more convinced that we would never change our minds; we would never surrender our freedoms!
Anne Currie	What can we do? As a child, I was told that our hands on earth are God's hands. He can turn evil into good when we act. Since a digital currency is fast approaching on the horizon, I suggest there is one small positive action in which we can join, all pulling together, whatever our views: pay for as much as we can in cash. In this way, we will retain some of our freedoms, privacy and individuality. God bless us all.
Jeff Wyatt	'When the law becomes tyranny, rebellion becomes duty'
CONTEMPORARY CULTURE	
Mark Devlin	And so, it becomes clear that a major change in the human mindset — brought about by a radical shift in consciousness — is vital if this world is to ever come close to being a just and moral place to live. Losing the fear of what others might think is

	the first change that has to happen on a major scale. But an understanding of the moral laws of the Universe — on a scale that rivals the knowledge that's been hoarded by the dark occultists who have held humankind in slavery for so long — is also essential. [p.487] *Musical Truth,* volume 1 (2016):
Niall McCrae	We should develop and maintain a parallel society, living alongside the majority, but disengaging from systems that deny our fundamental freedoms and rights. Unlike the woke, our cause may be summarised by a chant at the huge anti-lockdown protest in Berlin in summer 2020: *'Frieden! Freiheit! Keine Diktator!'*
Nicholas Martin	That unfettered flowering out of public awareness is something which might create, naturally, a rightful societal environment – a healthy soil, so to speak, for all the roots of all the organs of our society. A soil in which just organs of society can develop sui generis and operate in a way that is utterly coherent with compassion – and coherent too with the innate decency of being which characterises the noble values common to all of us as free and equal humanity.

CULTURE AND PHILOSOPHY	
Matthew Ehret	Any value that I find in the research that I've done and small discoveries I've made in the field of history is entirely due to my traumatic experiences post-2001. These experiences were accompanied by the impetus to heal the sick intimidation of the postmodernist academic ethic – an impetus that led me to discover Lyndon LaRouche's writings and their special emphasis on the mind of Plato.
Neil Kramer	This world is basically a study in evil. Good is here too, along with beauty, grace, mercy and absolution, but the overwhelming characteristic of the fallen earth is evil. Ice-cold, ugly, vicious evil. By design. What can we do to combat evil, wrongness and falsehood? Identify and understand them. Repudiate them. Don't become part of the problem. Don't roll over and think someone else will deal with it. Don't be timid in the face of an evil consensus. Embody goodness and speak the truth whenever you can. Sometimes with tact, diplomacy and understanding. Sometimes like a sledgehammer. We can't really complain. After all, back in the very beginning, God recommended we don't eat from the tree of the knowledge of good and evil. And you know how that went. Nevertheless, though we certainly chose the hard path, we already know the ending. Evil is defeated, punished and eradicated. Good shines forth, is distinguished, elevated, and goes on in a new world. Which was God's objective all along. To bring

	His family home.
SPIRITUALITY AND TRUTH	
Markus Olofsson	I strongly believe that one of the best ways to create a new and better society for all humans, animals and plant life is to bypass the old system. I do not think that a confronting stance is helpful; I believe we need to make the change ourselves by setting a good example, and letting others come to us. We need to go back to basics in all areas, be it the school system, the judicial system or the medical system. I believe that everything comes from within, and that the basic building blocks are love and respect. I also think that there is no single solution that will fit everyone, but rather there are many solutions. For a new school system I would like to see much more home-schooling and some kind of mentorship. One child could have many mentors in various fields. Even another child could be a mentor. The important thing is that we respect that we are different, with different goals, ambitions, capabilities and development needs. I also see us working more in teams. That way we could gather huge knowledge spread over a vast field. Where my knowledge ends, another person's might begin. For example, in my line of work I could say, 'I don't think I'm the right person to help you with this specific problem, but I know someone who can.'
Darren Smith	The truth is elusive and seemingly quite dangerous these days. We have no doubts that malicious and

	fallacious attacks on this paper and others shining light will continue, by those whose job it is to protect the rulers and help them achieve their ultimate aims of total control of mankind. We stand firm in the truth we print.
Total contributors	
24	

APPENDIX C

HEROIC CRITICAL THINKERS IN LITERATURE

Three novels featuring heroic Critical Thinkers

1.*Brave New World*

This novel by Aldous Huxley was published in 1932. Set in 2540 CE, the book presents a nightmarish vision of a future society. According to the novel, the year is set in 632 AF, with 'AF' standing for 'after Ford' since Henry Ford's assembly line is revered as godlike, with the era beginning when Ford introduced his Model T car. The novel examines a futuristic society known as World State which revolves around science and efficiency. In this society, emotions and individuality are conditioned out of children at a young age, and there are no lasting relationships because 'Everyone belongs to everyone else' – a common World State dictum.

There is one character that does not fit in – Bernard Marx. He feels an outsider because of his short stature, and this feature, unusual for an Alpha Plus, leaves him with a strong sense of being different. This leads him to be a critic rather than a proponent of the World State in which he finds himself. He eventually goes to the Savage Reservation, against the wishes and advice of the Director, in order to discover the nature of life away from the World State.

2. *Nineteen Eighty-Four*

This novel by George Orwell, published in 1949, is set in Airstrip One, formerly Great Britain, a province of the superstate Oceania, whose residents are victims of perpetual war, omnipresent government surveillance and public manipulation. The book follows Winston Smith, a thirty-nine-year-old Outer Party functionary as he seeks to fight back, through knowledge and free thought, against the totalitarian party that is in power. Winston is portrayed as having a bent back and health issues, including a varicose ulcer above his right ankle. He works at the Records Department at the Ministry of Truth, where his work involves changing past records of events and his intellectual capabilities are recognised in the responsibilities entrusted to him at a relatively young age.

3.*Fahrenheit 451*

Written in 1953, this is a dystopian novel by American writer Ray Bradbury. It presents an American society where books have been outlawed and 'firemen' burn any that are found. The focus is on Guy Montag, a third-generation fireman whose job is to burn books and the homes of those in whom illegal books – the seeds of free thought – are found.

Montag gradually becomes a critic of the system and the spur and trigger to this is presented as being the teenage Clarisse McLellan, whose love of nature, conversation and observing other people changes him. Montag's contact with Clarisse makes a lasting impact on Guy who seeks learning and knowledge from Professor Faber. Eventually, he escapes the City and enjoys a small group of refugees who, between them, remember the content of books. One of them, Granger, describes the symbol of the phoenix that can rise from its ashes to create something new and this prompts Guy to return to the City and offer his help.

Printed in Great Britain
by Amazon

14457281R00203